"With the luminous prose we have come to expect from one of our finest novelists, in *My Life as a Prayer*, Cunningham brings her thoughtful sensibility to bear on her own life. Cunningham's honest and often deeply philosophical struggles, her exquisite poetry and descriptions of nature, her timely reminders and probing questions, her words of both comfort and heartbreak, make this a gift to the world. Vivid, at times wildly funny, often deeply moving, and always impossible to put down, *My Life as a Prayer* offers valuable insights to anyone, no matter how they define their spirit path."

—Cait Johnson, author of *Witch Wisdom for Magical Aging: Finding Your Power through the Changing Seasons*

"In *My Life as a Prayer*, Elizabeth Cunningham writes with remarkable candor, humor, and beauty about her constant wrestling with the mysteries of life. She shows us how to examine our own experience through many different lenses, including the stories we love, the stories we create for ourselves, and the stories we wind up living."

—Jack Maguire, author of *The Power of Personal Storytelling* and *Essential Buddhism*

"Elizabeth Cunningham's lifelong aspiration to be a writer and to develop an understanding about the purpose and practice of prayer informs this thoughtful memoir. Readers will find inspiration here from a seasoned writer who successfully challenges the structures of religion in both her life and writings in order to express her authentic self in poetry and fiction."

—Tom Cowan, author of *Fire in the Head: Shamanism and the Celtic Spirit* and *Yearning for the Wind: Celtic Refle⸱⸱⸱ ⸱⸱ Nature and the Soul*

"The book is crafted with a unique, beautifully thorough touch. Exploring our most profound questions with a brilliant combination of gravitas and humor, and moving from deeply touching personal experiences to philosophical, theological, and ultimate questions of human character and meaning, *My Life as a Prayer* breaks through conventional questioning to reveal sparkling curiosity, capture the experiences of being the child of a minister, and sorting out a religious upbringing to discover a resonant relationship with Jesus, Goddess, and ultimately the author's acceptance of herself."

—Rebecca Singer, author of *Singing into Bone* and
Earth Practices

"Elizabeth Cunningham's fiction has always indicated that her personal experience with the Divine is complex, sometimes comical and not at all conventional. In *My Life as a Prayer,* she reveals the journey of the seeker: her youthful inclinations to resist submission, her lifelong relationships with divergent faith communities, and the details of internal ruminations that have enabled her to both respect and revolt from tradition. While her path is indeed *hers, My Life as a Prayer* creates a blueprint for us all to pave our own spiritual road."

—Tim Dillinger, Author of *Express Yourself In Me:*
Black Power, Gay Pride and Disco Heat
with a Holy Ghost Touch

"One of the most engaging memoirs I've read in ages. The wise and feisty voice I've come to know and love in Elizabeth Cunningham's Maeve Chronicles fills these pages, and carried me away. Anyone who has forged an independent path through the luminous moments and deepest shadows of a soul-filled life will recognize their own spiritual adventures reflected here."

—Mirabai Starr, author of *God of Love* and *Wild Mercy*

"Full of poetry, wisdom, and a remarkable generosity of spirit, *My Life as a Prayer* is the kind of memoir that takes the reader on a life-changing journey and becomes a constant companion, a guide on the spiritual path for years to come. Highly recommended for just about everyone!"

—Barbara McHugh, author of *Bride of the Buddha*

"Elizabeth Cunningham has written a tour de force, a book that follows the trajectory of her path from an Anglican minister's daughter, through Paganism and Quakerism, to assume her adult vocations: novelist, interfaith minister and counselor. This fascinating, beautifully-crafted, engaging memoir is the portrait of a highly-spirited, intelligent, and creative woman discovering her whole life as prayer, a meditation that finds a resting place in silence and gratitude."

—Mary Swander, author of *The Desert Pilgrim: En Route to Miracles and Mysticism*

"I have been a long-time admirer of Elizabeth's fiction and poetry. There is almost no one who can take a word and have it dance in all its variations within a single sentence the way she can. There is absolutely no one who can weave the devastatingly tragic with the transformative touch of the hilarious within a single scenario the way she can. It has made reading her fiction a joy. And it makes reading her memoir an absolute delight.

As Elizabeth illustrates so gracefully, prayer can take many forms and she has gifted us with a precious sharing of how to engage in meaningful, responsive, dynamic relationship with Spirit. *My Life as a Prayer* is a beacon of encouragement for anyone who has taken—or pondered—the maverick road and a precious, validating narrative for all women who have felt the yearning for a reflection of Spirit that mirrors their own soul. *My Life as a Prayer* is how you want life itself to be: full of vibrant characters; moments of curiosity and elation; and wisdom won through both courage and grace."

—Tiffany Lazic, author of *The Noble Art: From Shadow to Essence Through the Wheel of the Year*

MY
LIFE AS
A PRAYER

A MULTIFAITH MEMOIR

ELIZABETH
CUNNINGHAM

Monkfish Book Publishing Company
Rhinebeck, New York

Paperback ISBN 978-1-958972-10-6
eBook ISBN 978-1-958972-11-3

Library of Congress Cataloging-in-Publication Data

Names: Cunningham, Elizabeth, 1953- author.
Title: My life as a prayer : a multifaith memoir / Elizabeth Cunningham.
Description: Rhinebeck, New York : Monkfish Book Publishing Company, [2023]
Identifiers: LCCN 2023021689 (print) | LCCN 2023021690 (ebook) | ISBN
    9781958972106 (paperback) | ISBN 9781958972113 (ebook)
Subjects: LCSH: Cunningham, Elizabeth, 1953---Religion. | Novelists,
    American--20th century--Biography. | Prayer. | Spiritual life. | Women
    priests--United States--Biography.
Classification: LCC PS3553.U473 A3 2023 (print) | LCC PS3553.U473
(ebook)
    | DDC 813/.06--dc23/eng/20230602
LC record available at https://lccn.loc.gov/2023021689
LC ebook record available at https://lccn.loc.gov/2023021690

Book and cover design by Colin Rolfe
Cover photo by Natalie Parham

Monkfish Book Publishing Company
22 East Market Street, Suite 304
Rhinebeck, New York 12572
(845) 876-4861
monkfishpublishing.com

For my brother and sister, Harry and Ruth,
the best childhood and lifelong companions anyone could have

CONTENTS

OPENING

I don't know what prayer is. I don't know what it isn't. I don't know how prayer works, or if it works. I don't know who receives prayers or who answers them. Or if not who, then what. I know only one thing for sure. If a singer is one who sings, and a writer is one who writes, then it follows that a prayer is one who prays, which means...

I am a prayer.

I have never written anything but fiction and poems, apart from an essay now and then. I never intended to write a memoir, and I am not sure that I have written one in any conventional sense. Prayer is the filter for selecting what to include and what not to include. And my life is a lens for looking at prayer, one of the great mysteries and consistencies of human existence. And why just human? Who is to say that trees don't pray—or rivers, or rocks, or all of the life (the one life) that is this earth?

I remember the exact moment when most of my novels came to me, where I was, the time of day, the cast of light. I don't remember how this idea arrived. Subtle, insistent, a wind, a whisper, between sleeping and waking or on a walk in the woods or in my uncertain daily attempts at prayer, the still, small, nagging voice: *Write about prayer, write about prayer, write about being a prayer, a book about being a prayer.*

The book came to me in two parts. The first is chronological, the stories of the people, communities, and experiences that have shaped my life as a prayer from early childhood to the edge of old age.

The second part is topical, reflective, more than my own story, touching on mysteries I continue to ponder. I would be honored to have you join me.

PART ONE

BELOVED COMMUNITIES

CHAPTER ONE

CHILDHOOD

CHURCH, WOODS, AND BEYOND

OUR FATHER WHO ART...

Grace Church, in Millbrook, New York is the first home I remember. My family gathers for bedtime prayers in my little sister's room. Her room is the largest of the three children's separate bedrooms. The rambling Edwardian rectory (yes, built by Anglophiles circa 1903) has five bedrooms altogether, including one where bishops and grandmothers sleep, though of course not concurrently. I have the smallest room, because I was the baby when my parents moved in. There is a bathroom between my room and the master bedroom, but I mostly use the one at the top of the stairs. Better than falling into the toilet when my father leaves the seat up or happening upon one of his unflushed cigars, floating there and turning the water brown.

When I was maybe six or seven, I begged to share my sister's room, which had an extra twin bed available. In my nightmares a devil behind the shade of a wall lamp whispered the words "potato chips." Across Franklin Avenue herds of black bears ambled across the lawn of the high school. A robot would stand in the open doorway and lurch towards me. When I tried to scream no sound would come out.

At an even earlier age, two or three, I would sneak out of my bed at night, make the long journey down the hall, and climb into bed with my big brother, where we were both protected by dozens of his toy animals. These nighttime excursions were firmly discouraged, and I never moved into my sister's room. I am not sure why my parents were so insistent that we sleep alone. Eventually I managed to invoke angels, inspired by the verse of a favorite hymn that assured me they were watching round my bed. I pictured an impenetrable wall of white wings.

(Note: Angels were not part of my family's cosmology. They didn't even show up at the Christmas pageant. I understood at an early age that little girls with spray-painted haloes and gauzy wings were in poor taste, as were party dresses with crinolines. There is a photograph of me at my sixth birthday party surrounded by girls in poufy pastel confections while I wore a dark blue cotton dress edged with white embroidery.)

At bedtime prayers, all five of us sit on my sister's bed, the one in the corner under the sloping ceiling. My parents are on either side of my sister, who is already tucked in. My brother and I perch halfway toward the foot. It is not necessarily comfortable. The word "snuggle" does not come to mind. We sing two songs: "Jesus, Tender Shepherd Hear Me" followed by a sung version of the Lord's Prayer.

In my memory I can hear my mother's soprano voice clearly, and less distinctly my father's rumbling bass an octave, maybe two, below her. Probably my sister and I sing along. We were both in the children's choir before we could read. I don't remember more than the title words of the first song. I remember disliking the tune of "Our Father Who Art in Heaven" even then. It was bouncy, up and down, like a merry-go-round jingle. Of course I did not know the word "incongruous" then, but that's what comes to me now. The songs were followed by "God blesses" of grandmothers and other relatives, anyone we could think of to extend the time before we had to go to our solitary beds.

This memory might be one of my first of prayer. It is not happy or unhappy. I did not feel close to Our Father or the Tender Shepherd, nor, in that moment, to either of my parents. It interests me that I did not like the songs, because music was hugely important in my childhood. A vague sense of awkwardness persists, maybe because that picture of the family gathered for prayers just doesn't ring true to me now and didn't even at that time. As children we rarely saw our father. The three of us ate supper in the kitchen: hamburgers and french-fries or (demonic whisper) potato chips. When my father came home, he drank gin martinis and read the paper. My mother cooked a second dinner and ate with him later, before or after these prayers, I am not sure. We weren't there.

When I probe the memory, I wonder if the prayers also felt awkward because we never otherwise talked to or about God. I suspect that would have been in poor taste. I have a vague memory of my father trying to reassure me that there was no literal devil. "Just take away the 'd' and what do you have?" he asked. *Evil*, which was not reassuring. There was evil, but no devil, just people like Hitler. We also did not talk about sin. We didn't have to. The other s-word sufficed. *Selfish*, it was the worst thing you could be. And as far as I could tell, there was no salvation from it. You just had to do your hypervigilant best to appear to be unselfish. It was hard to believe I could be forgiven for anything at all. It still is.

Our father who art in heaven. To many, the words "our father" are comforting. Perhaps they were to Jesus of Nazareth, who is supposed to have taught this prayer to his followers. Our Father is a formal English translation of a more intimate term for father, *Abba*. Aramaic scholar Neil Douglas-Klotz believes Jesus would have said "*Abwoon*," a word that combines *father* and *womb*. But the words that permeated my childhood were the ones we recited every week from the 1928 Book of Common Prayer, the Anglican words. Anglicans did not sin or have debts. We trespassed, perhaps because Anglicans came from a landowning class. The signs posted at the border of the woods next door reinforced the gravity of this offense.

Long before I became a literal trespasser, the words "our father" held no comfort for me. When I close my eyes even today, I see my father in the pulpit of the church, dark, cavernous emptiness above him. I don't know why it is dark, because, except for magical candlelit Christmas Eve, we would have been in church in the morning. But that's what I see: a father I could not reach and an invisible God surrounding him. There were dead grandfathers, too, although not in this image. My paternal grandmother told me that if ever I needed to know right from wrong, I should picture my grandfathers in heaven, nodding or shaking their heads. They were, apparently, always watching me. I remember worrying that they could see me in the bathroom.

All these fathers, dead, alive, or divine, were judging me (that is, when they were paying attention at all, which my father did only rarely and unpredictably). Moreover, God the Father had sacrificed his only son in order to reconcile us to him, which made me feel sick at my stomach and still makes no sense to me. Jesus, Tender Shepherd, this is who you pray to?

If that is the first prayer I remember praying, then you could say my life as a prayer got off to a rocky start. Yet this prayer, and all the liturgical prayers, still ring in my bones, sing in my blood—the rhythms, the cadences. They repeat and repeat in my mind in times of extremis, even though I no longer believe in them, in fact repudiate them. Words like *"dear Lord and Savior Jesus Christ, only begotten Son of the Father."* No, no, no, no, no. But the words, the prayers are still there.

More than once I have written my own version of the Lord's Prayer. This is the only one I can still find:

Heart: After the Lord's Prayer

O broken heart
here in this broken world
your truth be told
your healing be one
with the healing of this earth
that is our heaven.
In you we have everything we need.
We forgive ourselves and everyone else.
In your daring we are safe.
For you are our strength and our grace and our home
now and beyond time.

—from my *journal*

LAMB(S) OF GOD

When I was two years old, lambs were my favorite animal. Lambie, a small toy lamb with its fur loved off, went with me everywhere. Lambie was small enough for me to hold by the neck. I also had lots of other lambs of various shapes and sizes, including a black one with a thick curly pelt. I do not remember why I favored lambs so much, but apparently I did.

The Christmas Eve pageant was a magical event, the whole church transformed into a fragrant candlelit evergreen forest. As mentioned, there were no little girl angels in the tableau. According to the Gospel accounts of the Nativity, there should have been. Who else was talking to those shepherds—the ones who stole my lambs?

At age two, I am sitting in a pew with my mother. When I see the shepherds processing down the aisle, shepherds' crooks in one hand, my lambs in the other, I start to howl for my lost sheep. I have a vague memory of my mother explaining that my father had only borrowed the lambs and I would have them back after the pageant.

Had I been asked and said yes, without understanding that my lambs would be in the possession of strange, older boys? I only know that in that moment I am outraged and bereft. I do not want to share my lambs. I want them back. Now.

TIGGER, TIGGER BURNING BRIGHT (DID HE WHO MADE THE LAMB MAKE THEE?)

No doubt my lambs were returned to me after the pageant. But by the time I was three years old, I had transferred my devotion from lambs to lions. Instead of clutching Lambie in one hand, I used both arms to haul around a large lion named Glumph, for the effort it took to heft him. The Christmas I was four years old, my grandmother gave both my brother and me Steiff-made tigers with eyes that glowed in the dark (painted with the same radioactive material used to paint the faces of wristwatches). Soon my little sister had her own tiger to prevent her from trying to take ours.

All three tigers were named Tigger, though each one had a distinctive face and personality. My Tigger was boastful (something I was not allowed to be). He also tended to be critical of me. I don't remember what faults he found, but I do remember the lore I created about him. Tigger had done something bad in his earlier immortal life (perhaps in the Garden of Eden). He'd had a falling out with God on a par with Satan's or the serpent's. Tigger's punishment was to take care of me for life. He was impatient, long-suffering, and fiercely loyal. He could disparage me, but no one else could or they'd have to reckon with him. Tigger used the pronouns he/him (in today's parlance), but he was also a mother (not a father) to Baby Tigger, a smaller Steiff tiger with movable arms and legs. Gender fluidity ran in the family, at least on the maternal side. My mother had a rabbit named Rumbo who also used masculine pronouns and wore a dainty cotton dress. Rumbo is still in my care.

Tigger was my first BIFF (Best Imaginary Friend Forever). Although I didn't write novels about him, he was the first character I imagined so fully that he took on his own autonomous life. Some thirty-four years later, along came Maeve Rhuad, the Celtic Magdalen, narrator of The Maeve Chronicles. It struck me early on that she had the same coloring as Tigger (orange hair that convention calls red) and green eyes. Though we completed our work on The Maeve Chronicles in 2011, she is still my BIFF. She is kinder to me than Tigger was, but quite willing to call me on my crap. Though I would not describe her as boastful, she has a healthy self-regard that I only aspire to.

Tigger is with me still, sitting behind me on the top of the couch as I write. Remembering Lambie prompted me to search for him or her (Lambie is nonbinary) in a big basket where Rumbo rests along with some of my children's favorites (bears and a monkey). I excavated poor floppy-necked, hairless Lambie. They (to use the gender-neutral pronoun) are now lying next to Tigger, who also had the fur loved off him, much of his faded orange covered in green corduroy patches.

The tiger lies down with the lamb. A little child loved them both. An aged child is reuniting them on the couch and perhaps within her psyche.

SACRIFICIAL LAMBS

Tigers and lions remained my favorite animals for the rest of my childhood. I don't really know why I made this abrupt switch from lambs to lions, but I would like to indulge in some theological speculation.

At age two, all I knew was that lambs could be stolen and made into accessories for shepherds. I was already getting a bad impression of God the Father (and my father, who represented him) that was only reinforced as time went on. As noted, lambs could be ... borrowed. Lambs were also prime sacrificial material. That's why Jesus was called the Lamb of God. His father and/or bad people (i.e., Jews or sinners, or you and me) had sacrificed Jesus so his father would not be mad at us anymore. Lambs were sacrificed to mark the houses of the Hebrews in Egypt so that the angel of death would pass over them. Some lamb or another was always getting sacrificed.

(Confusingly, Jesus was also the Good Shepherd, who carried the lost sheep in the crook of his arm, as depicted in one of the stained-glass windows in the church. Jesus also judged between the goats and the sheep on Judgment Day, and only the sheep got to go to heaven.)

At that early age, I probably didn't yet know the story of Abraham and Isaac. If I had, it would have confirmed my worst suspicions about God and fathers, as later it did. God tells Abraham to sacrifice his only son ("*whom thou lovesest*") and without a murmur or a peep of protest, Abraham sets out to do just that. (Even as a child, I noticed that Abraham didn't say anything to Sarah about God's command to kill their son. I like to think she would have pitched a fit.) At the last possible minute, the angel of the Lord stops Abraham ("*lay not thine hand upon the lad*") and provides a ram (aka a large boy sheep) to sacrifice instead.

I have heard sermons about Abraham's obedience to God, how God came first before any other human loyalty or love. If you put anything or anyone before God, it's called idolatry. I have also heard preachers make the case that the story of Abraham and Isaac is about God putting an end to the practice of human sacrifice (at least until God killed his own son or had us do it). There is always some excuse for God's bad behavior. They don't call it Christian apologetics for nothing.

Yet people still sacrifice their children to what they perceive as

God's command. Maybe not on some stone altar in the wilderness. But some parents strive to kill their children's sexuality if it does not conform to the heterosexuality they believe is ordained by God. Or they might try, as my father did, and likely his father before him, to destroy their children's gifts. If there is such a thing as grace and mercy, the parents do not bestow it.

An angel intervenes—or a tiger.

As for the lamb or ram, he probably gets roasted and eaten. Or perhaps resurrected?

Theology is confusing at any age.

DEICIDE

I was a very theologically-minded child. At age three, I had it in for God and Jesus. (The third member of the trinity appeared in my imagination as Caspar the Friendly Ghost, who flitted about the church and did not appear to pose much threat.) Until I remembered that the sheep rustling must have taken place when I was two years old, I thought the plot to kill God was one of my two earliest dated memories.

I know I was three when I became deicidal, because that was our first summer at Kittyhawk, North Carolina, and the first time I saw the ocean.

I don't just see the sea, I rush into it, arms wide. The water churns around my legs, the wet sand slides under my feet, the surf roars in my ear, and I sing as loud as I can, "Ducky, ducky, ducky, duck!"—an ecstatic hymn of joy and praise. I fall into deep, idolatrous love at first sight, scent, and sound of the sea.

That sense memory of meeting the sea has always been linked with a memory that took place in my imagination.

At that age, I have never seen a desert, but I know the desert is where God and Jesus live. And somehow I know what the desert looks like, from illustrated Bible stories or Roadrunner cartoons. It is vast, dry, and empty. God is a black thundercloud floating over the desert floor. Jesus in a white robe floats beside God. Though, unlike his father, he has feet, he does not need them to walk. I am looking down at them from the top of a high pinnacle. I have a huge boulder ready. When they pass below me, I will push the boulder over the edge and crush them.

I don't know how often I played this scene in my mind, but it remains vivid. Maybe I would have forgotten it, if I had not confessed it.

It's dark. I'm sharing a room with my eleven-year-old cousin.

"I am going to kill God and Jesus," I tell her.

"You better say the Lord's Prayer, quick!" she says.

I don't remember saying the Lord's Prayer. Maybe we recite it together. I do remember feeling scared. Wanting to kill God and Jesus is bad, very bad. I am bad. Now my cousin knows how bad I am. And so do God and Jesus.

*

Why did I want kill God at such a young age? I don't know. I can only speculate. God and my father were all mixed up in my mind. Did I think God had taken my father away from me? He was always working. In his office, at a meeting, at a conference. He had begun to withdraw from us by then, my mother says, because some female psychiatrist told him "to stay away from his daughters." The marriage was unhappy. He drank a lot. His temper was unpredictable. Maybe it was better to blame God than my father. And who was Jesus in all this? The thundercloud's sidekick. Where were his sheep? Lost, all of them, lost.

*

In September, I turned four years old. That Christmas Tigger arrived. The following spring, I got pneumonia as a complication of measles and almost died. My fever was 106 when I was rushed to the hospital in the night. I remember being stripped down and given an alcohol rub. I remember screaming and reaching for my mother as they wheeled me into X-Ray, where they diagnosed the pneumonia. They had missed it before, because I had no cough. I was put on an IV drip of penicillin. Or maybe they gave me shots and the IV was to feed and hydrate me. I know I fell out of bed once, and the IV was ripped out of my arm. After that they kept the bars up on the bed. I remember how strange it was to see my mother sleeping in the armchair with her coat on. (Strange to see a mother sleep.) I have memories of my recovery, including my little sister banging on the hospital door. I also took pleasure in throwing my animals out of the bed—until the nurses refused to pick them up.

But even more vividly, I remember my delirium.

I am in that desert again, the same desert, wandering there, amid what I called hard numbers and soft numbers. I do not see the numbers. They have textures. One hundred is a hard number with the texture of a thunderclap. Soft numbers are ones and twos with a texture like applesauce. (I still don't like to eat foods with that texture.) I am alone in this desert where I plotted murder, and there is no help for me.

GRACE

Except for the sung bedtime prayers, there was only one other prayer I heard at home, which was grace before family dinners, spoken by my father and probably his father before him, and his before him, all of them Episcopal priests. I know the Grace by heart, although it occurs to me that I have never spoken this Grace in my own adult life:

Bless, O Lord, this food to our use and us to thy service. Make us always mindful of the needs of others. Through Jesus Christ Our Lord. Amen. [We all repeated *Amen.*]

Food was not for pleasure but for use and God's service. Being mindful of the needs of others was at the heart of my paternal lineage. My father's mother (Nana) used to say: Stop woolgathering, do something for others. Stop moping. *Do something for others.*

Nana could also be a lot of fun. She taught us to play cards, and she would cry out in fury, "You skunk!" when we were beating her. She also played several forms of solitaire (at which she cheated). If we spilled milk she called us "Cow!" And if we dropped a morsel of food on the floor, she allowed us/told us to pick it up and eat it. "You're made from dirt, and a little more won't hurt you!" In lieu of cursing, she said, "Thunder and botheration!" I still find it a satisfying expression. She was not a baking cookies sort of grandmother, but she took us for walks, went skating with us, slipped and broke her crown. I remember her being tucked up in the four-poster grandmother-bishop bed with her head bandaged.

She lived in Hartford, Connecticut, in an apartment complex for clergy widows. She had her own bit of garden where she grew roses and other flowers. More than once, she took us to visit a vast rose garden nearby. I still love roses. Unlike my maternal grandmother who never learned to drive and hired a chauffeur named Elmer, Nana got her license as soon as the first automobiles hit the road. She kept butterscotch Lifesavers in her car, and whenever we went anywhere, she would say, "I wonder where this road goes?" And she would set off to explore with no fear of getting lost, something I still love to do.

She was outgoing and a great favorite among my father's parishioners. I don't think she was remotely interested in theology. She was not introspective or intellectual. She was not a reader. She was a doer. When she visited, she needed to clean and organize. My mother, in a brilliant, deflective move, would say to her mother-in-law, "I've saved this closet for you to sort."

My mother was fond of Nana, who was so much easier for her than her own mother upon whom she waited hand and foot, bringing her breakfast in bed, fetching and carrying as my grandmother sat enthroned all day draped in shawls, fanning herself, and criticizing everything my mother did—and everything her grandchildren did.

Alas, over the years I heard many criticisms of my mother from Nana and my aunts. They claimed my mother was cold, "frigid." They accused her of shutting my father out, of having spoiled us children. (*Spoiled*, another S word, more or less a synonym for selfish.)

As noted, I was a woolgatherer. I was moody. My mother, I realize, was chronically depressed. I suppose her children were, too, to varying degrees. I can remember being six years old and feeling heavy, weighed down. I knelt by my mother's bed and said, "I wish I could start my life over."

What had I done? What hadn't I done?

> *Bless O Lord this food to our use and us to thy service. Make us always mindful of the needs of others.*

My mother was constantly serving. Well into our adulthood, if anyone at the dinner table so much as glanced around, looking for something, she sprang to her feet.

"What do you need?"

She took no joy in cooking, but until we were teenagers, she cooked two evening meals. (I believe the hamburgers at the kitchen table of our earlier childhood went unblessed.) Every Sunday morning she hurried back and forth from church to the rectory to check on the roast. I wonder if anyone noticed her service or did it not count because it was simply her unquestioned, invisible duty. Others, as in "the needs of others," probably meant the less fortunate, not her husband and children.

> *O God, who art the author of peace and lover of concord, in knowledge of whom standeth our eternal life, whose service is perfect freedom....*

That phrase *"whose service is perfect freedom"* has always stayed in my mind. I don't think my mother found that freedom, though she was a suffering servant to all of us. She confessed to me that though she wanted to, she could not manage to believe in God. An architect who never practiced, a sculptress who hid the white plaster bust of her father in the linen closet, a passionate lover of music, she encouraged her children to pursue (indulge?) our talents. She is the first person to whom I confided, "I want to write a novel." She answered, "I believe you will."

I have written novels, choosing my mother's belief over my father's declaration: "You can't write novels, because you know nothing." He wanted me to be a social worker and then, perhaps, when I was forty I might have something worthwhile to say.

*

(Note: My paternal grandfather was a chaplain in World War I, stationed in France. He also presided over an urban church during the Depression. My paternal grandmother fed hungry people from her own kitchen. My father was a private in World War II, also serving in France, though he was an engineer and did not see combat. From letters I now cannot find, I know that my father hated the army. He was demoted for disciplinary reasons back to private of the lowest rank. He signed up only reluctantly or perhaps he was drafted. His father told him, "You must face the challenges of your generation." My father's original intention was to pursue graduate studies in English literature. He may have wanted to write?! Only after the war did he follow his father's footsteps into the ministry. When I consider what my father and his parents must have witnessed in wars and the Depression, I understand better their emphasis on self-sacrifice, and how self-indulgent some of my generation must have seemed to them.)

*

To this day, I struggle to see writing as service. I still feel that I have not done enough, not been mindful enough of the needs of others—or maybe sometimes I am too mindful but not effective.

Have I spent my life woolgathering?

As a child I didn't know what woolgathering was, only that it was bad. I looked up the definition. It dates to the 1500s, "indulging in wandering fancies and purposeless thinking," from the literal meaning "gathering fragments of wool torn from sheep by bushes, etc." according to the online source "English Language and Usage."

I wonder, were those fragments of wool left there by lost sheep? And why would it be purposeless to gather this wool?

THE BOOK OF COMMON PRAYER

> *ALMIGHTY and most merciful Father; We have erred, and strayed from thy ways like lost sheep. We have followed too much the devices and desires of our own hearts. We have offended against thy holy laws. We have left undone those things which we ought to have done; And we have done those things which we ought not to have done; And there is no health in us. But thou, O Lord, have mercy upon us, miserable offenders. Spare thou those, O God, who confess their faults. Restore thou those who are penitent; According to thy*

*promises declared unto mankind In Christ Jesus our Lord.
And grant, O most merciful Father, for his sake; That we may
hereafter live a godly, righteous, and sober life, To the glory of
thy holy Name. Amen.*

Until I looked it up again, I had forgotten the general confession from the 1928 United States edition of Book of Common Prayer began with lost sheep. The Book of Common Prayer has a long history, dating back to Cranmer in 1564. The date of the first enclosure act in Britain is 1604; sheep being enclosed enabled Britain to become a center of the wool industry. The rural poor lost their rights to the use of common lands. Dispossessed, they became the urban workers in the industrial revolution. They were, you could argue, sacrificed to the interests of the wealthy. Concurrent with this huge change in the economic life of Britain, the King James Version (UC) of the Bible was published in 1611.

I think of the Lamb of God, aka Jesus, aka the Good Shepherd, who told Peter to "feed my sheep." From what little we know, Jesus was not a shepherd or a fisherman like some of his disciples but a carpenter, who grew up in Nazareth and possibly worked in the Greco-Roman city of Sepphoris. But the scriptures and stories he knew by heart came from a once-nomadic, pastoral people. And of course in his time, animal sacrifice was still practiced in the Temple of Jerusalem.

I was much further removed from nomadic or sheep herding people, though dairy farms were plentiful in our region. (Calves will come into the story later.) My father grew up in Hartford, Connecticut, but that did not stop him from going on a rant about the Good Shepherd. The Good Shepherd didn't walk around cuddling cute little lambs (like Lambie or the sheep my father borrowed for the pageant). No, the Good Shepherd took the shitty-ass sheep and dipped them in sheep dip to rid them of parasites. Tough love for those sheep! He probably didn't say "shit" or "ass" when he used the rant as a sermon, but he loved to jolt his parishioners awake. He began a Christmas morning sermon with "Jesus Christ had diaper rash!" And an Easter sermon with "Christ is risen. So what!"

*

In my childhood, we had morning prayer three Sundays out of four, with Communion, as we called it then, being offered only once a month. Children were dismissed for Sunday school before the sermon, as an act of mercy or to insure that they did not distract or disrupt. But we were present—and kneeling—for the general confession.

As I read it again, I remember that we pronounced "erred" as *erd* (rhymes with herd), not as you might think, like *err* as in "error." No, we *erd* and strayed like lost sheep. I liked saying *erd*. I liked words, their sounds, their rhythms. I heard liturgical language before I could read, and no doubt the sonorous words affected me in ways they might not have if I hadn't heard and spoken them aloud, over and over. This tongue-twister has stayed with me for life: "*We have left undone those things which we ought to have done; And we have done those things which we ought not to have done*" and the devastating conclusion "*and there is no health in us.*" It didn't say we had done those things "sometimes or by mistake." It was a blanket statement. No exceptions, no excuses. No health in us. At all.

Then came the big but: *But thou, O Lord, have mercy upon us, miserable offenders.*

Apparently no one told Cranmer, or whoever else wrote and revised the Book of Common Prayer, that most people don't hear, or believe, anything that comes after the word "but." I believed in my miserableness but not in God's mercy.

Still I enjoyed rhythm of these lines: "*Spare thou those, O God, who confess their faults. Restore thou those who are penitent.*" The phrase "*a godly, righteous, and sober life*" also made an indelible, but depressing, impression.

It is probably a good thing I did not recite the confession used during Communion services until after confirmation at age twelve. At that age I did not take the words so much to heart. But I did (and still do) enjoy saying, *"We acknowledge and bewail our manifold sins and wickedness, which we from time to time most grievously have committed provoking most justly thy wrath and indignation against us."* I am especially fond of the word "bewail," though I never heard anyone in church do any actual bewailing.

Yet I never liked saying the prayer of humble access, also recited at Communion.

> *We do not presume to come to this thy Table, O merciful Lord, trusting in our own righteousness, but in thy manifold and great mercies. We are not worthy so much as to gather up the crumbs under thy Table. But thou art the same Lord, whose property is always to have mercy: Grant us therefore, gracious Lord, so to eat the Flesh of thy dear Son Jesus Christ, and to drink his Blood, in these holy Mysteries, that we may continually dwell in him, and he in us, that our sinful bodies may be made clean by his Body, and our souls washed through his most precious Blood. Amen.*

The prayer conjured up such a vivid image of crawling under a giant-sized table among huge masculine legs where God, apparently a messy eater like my father, had dropped crumbs (and maybe other things, ugh!).

These prayers of my childhood and adolescence confirmed my initial impressions of God. He was dangerous and thunderous. He didn't like me. And I didn't like him.

Yet I loved words and music. We also sang at morning prayer, not just hymns but canticles, adapted from the Psalms. I can still sing these verses from the Jubilate.

O be joyful in the Lord all ye lands;
serve the Lord with gladness
and come before his presence with a song

Be ye sure that the Lord he is God
it is he that hath made us and not we ourselves
we are his people and the sheep of his pasture....

No getting away from being sheep, erring, straying, no escaping the Good Shepherd and his sheep dip.

RELIGIOUS EDUCATION

When my son was young and receiving minimal religious instruction at our Quaker Meeting First Day School, I read aloud to him from a children's Bible. He was riveted until we got to the New Testament. He took the book from me and firmly closed it. Stories of Jesus healing and preaching did not stack up against tales like the plagues of Egypt. When I did a stint as a teacher at Quaker meeting and had the children dramatize some of the stories from the Old Testament, some adult Friends objected that the stories were too violent.

My approach to religious education was based on my childhood experience. In our Sunday school, dramatic renditions of Bible stories were standard fare. We had a machine (who knows where it came from) that simulated the sound of the storm wind that howled when rebellious Jonah got tossed overboard for his sins. I don't recall exactly how we enacted the whale swallowing and then disgorging him. It might have involved painted bedsheets. In one class we staged the story of Esther and her life-and-death beauty pageant as a puppet show. The performance concluded with the Haman puppet hanging from the gallows.

Sunday school classes were taught by women, usually someone's mother, with the exception of Mr. McCanlis's class on the prophets for fifth graders. It was not a participatory class. He talked, and we listened, or rather sat and fidgeted. The only story I remember is this one.

"I was walking down the street one day, minding my own business, smoking a cigar, when this preacher-fella made a point of crossing the street to stand right in my way. He yelled at me: 'Jesus Christ didn't smoke cigars!' And you know what I said him? I said, 'Well, Jesus Christ didn't wear pants, either!' And that was the end of that."

My cigar-smoking father no doubt approved of that story. He also relished liturgical drama and brought it inside the church on occasion. My sister recalls being terrified when Mr. Fettes (aka King Balthazar) burst into the church as John the Baptist wearing a facsimile of camel skins and menacing the congregation with a staff as he shouted in his formidable bass voice: "*Repent ye: for the kingdom of heaven is at hand!*"

My mother did not teach Sunday school, because she sang in the choir. But she had her chance to volunteer at "released time," a short-lived violation of the separation of church and state. On Monday afternoons, we were "released" early from public school and escorted to one of the three village churches. (I don't know what happened to the Jews and the atheists.) My father marched us along, brandishing a rolled-up newspaper. If any child misbehaved, he roared "Bend over!" and whacked the offender's behind. I kept as far away from him as I could.

I liked having my mother for a teacher. She let her repressed artistic talents have free reign. That year in her class we constructed a large cardboard cutout of a calf and mounted it on a pedestal. My mother was an Egyptophile. In her youth she had visited Egypt, where she rode on a camel and climbed a pyramid. She no doubt researched the calf in her art books. It looked as much like an Egyptian idol as an arts-and-crafts project could—especially when we spray-painted it gold.

Our calf was a prop for the climactic event. One afternoon we all left our separate classrooms to wander in the wilderness (top to bottom of the parish house) searching for manna (marshmallows) that the Lord had graciously provided. But were we grateful? No, we were backsliders, longing for the fleshpots of Egypt. After gorging ourselves on marshmallows, we took our golden calf outside to the lower part of the driveway and worshipped our idol, circling and bowing, and carrying on in a joyful, heathenish manner.

Until Moses, black-robed, bearded, bewigged and bellowing, came down from Mount Sinai brandishing not a rolled-up newspaper but the tablets (papier-*mâché*?) inscribed with the ten commandments. Hurling them away, Moses whipped out his cigarette lighter and set fire to our beautiful golden calf right there in the driveway. When it had burned to the ground, Moses scooped up the ashes, stirred them into a pitcher of water, and poured the mixture into dixie cups. We drank the ashes of our idolatry. Gold spray paint and all.

*

Formal religious education culminated in Saturday morning confirmation class—taught by my father, but without any biblical theatrics.

"And what is the eleventh commandment?" he asked with his signature smirk.

No one answered.

"Thou shalt learn the other ten!"

I don't remember anything else my father said in that class, though I can still picture the morning light coming into the room where coffee hour would be held on Sunday. Saturday was the holiest day of the week: no school, no church. I am sure none of us wanted to be where we were, listening to Mr. Cunningham drill us on an "An Outline of the Faith, commonly called the catechism." If we had a quiz, I must have passed it, but of those pages and pages at the end of the Prayer Book, only this question and answer remains with me:

Q: What are the sacraments?

A: The sacraments are an outward and visible sign of inward and spiritual grace...

*

Maybe I liked the idea of outward and inward, visible and by implication invisible. Maybe I hoped that the onerous Saturday morning classes were preparing me for something magical and out of the ordinary.

Unlike many Protestants, Episcopalians practice infant baptism. Unlike the Roman Catholic church, where six-year-olds dress like miniature brides and grooms for their First Communion, we had to wait until we were twelve to receive the sacrament. Far from adulthood, barely adolescent, we were nonetheless presumed to be old enough to confirm for ourselves the vows our parents and godparents had made for us at baptism.

> *Do you reaffirm your renunciation of evil?*
> *I do.*
> *Do you renew your commitment to Jesus Christ?*
> *I do, and with God's grace I will follow him as my Savior and Lord.*

I don't actually remember reaffirming my vows. It was just as well I had not yet grown into a rebellious teen when I likely would have taken pleasure in saying I do not! At twelve I was still capable of (at least outward) conformity.

I do remember my dress, which, though white, was not at all bridal. It was a plain A-line with short sleeves and embossed with white embroidery. I also remember the weight of the bishop's hands on my head and the words "Defend, O Lord, this thy servant...." Though they were not the exact words he spoke, the rhythm of the phrase lodged in my mind as "*Defend, O Lord, this thy Child, from all the perils of this night.*" (The last six words became the title of what I call a numinous thriller.)

No doubt we had been taught that unlike the (primitive, lower-class) Roman Catholics, we did not believe in literal transubstantiation. Our practice of Communion was a memorial of the Last Supper. But it seems a fine distinction. As the priest dispensed the host, he murmured:

> *The Body of our Lord Jesus Christ, which was given for thee, preserve thy body and soul unto everlasting life. Take and eat this in remembrance that Christ died for thee, and feed on him in thy heart by faith, with thanksgiving.*

Then came the wine. Wiping the chalice with a cloth after each pair of lips touched it, the priest intoned:

> *The Blood of our Lord Jesus Christ, which was shed for thee, preserve thy body and soul unto everlasting life. Drink this in remembrance that Christ's blood was shed for thee, and be thankful.*

The communion wafer looked like a full moon. (It had been made by mysterious, seldom-seen Episcopal nuns who wore white habits, unlike the black-clad Roman Catholic nuns who taught at St. Joseph's School.) It was probably my father who placed the wafer in my left hand, which I cupped in my right to guide it to my mouth, as we had been instructed to do. As I recall, we weren't supposed to chew Christ's body, so it stuck to the roof of my mouth. The barest sip of watered wine from the chalice did not dislodge it, but eventually it dissolved enough to swallow. Nothing fleshy or bloody about it.

Was I disappointed in this initiation into full, adult Christianity? Probably. I did not feel any mystical union with Christ or with my fellow communicants or with the Church, which to me meant the literal building across the driveway from the rectory.

I suspect Jesus still floated in the desert realm of nightmare and delirium, his feet not yet touching the earth, his story not yet gripping my imagination.

NARNIA

I was seven years old when I first laid eyes on a hardcover set of C. S. Lewis's The Chronicles of Narnia in the parish house library. I can picture the sunlight falling on their smooth covers with Pauline Bayne's delicate, unequaled illustrations beckoning. Is there something significant in the fact that I discovered them before they were given to me? As sure as the titular wardrobe, where fur coats gave way to the branches of a snowy wood, the books became my portal to another life, as real or more real than the life of family, church, and school.

My mother read the books aloud to us, probably more than once. And then I read them to myself over and over again, year after year, until well into my teens. The stories did not stay between the covers of the books. They suffused my whole life with expectation. When I explored a hidden space at the back of the hall closet, I willed to find myself in Narnia. In school, I would gaze across the playing fields to the woods. If Jill and Eustace could run away from school and find themselves in Aslan's country, maybe I could, too.

The great golden lion paced through my dreams at night. As a minister's daughter, I could not avoid knowing that grownups regarded The Lion, the Witch, and the Wardrobe in particular as Christian allegory. Aslan to them was Jesus, and his death on the stone table was parallel to the crucifixion. Resurrection followed, and I suppose weeping Susan and Lucy stood in for the faithful women at the tomb. The grownups knew all about C. S. Lewis's conversion to Christianity. They read *The Screwtape Letters* as avidly as we read the Narnia books. C. S. Lewis was all the rage.

I didn't care about any of that. Narnia and Aslan were real. In Narnia there was no church, no Sunday school. There were adventures and battles, peril and courage. The Emperor Beyond the Sea (a nod to God the Father) stayed put. He didn't come into the story demanding to be worshipped or placated. I suppose he was the author of the Deep Magic from before the Dawn of Time, the magic the White Witch reckoned without, the magic Aslan willingly invoked when he offered himself as a sacrifice in place of Edmund. What a wild rendition of resurrection! Lucy and Susan clinging to Aslan's fragrant mane as he bounds across Narnia, leaping the wall of the witch's castle, breathing life into the creatures she turned to stone. No doubt C. S. Lewis had some allegorical intent, but just as Aslan was "not a tame lion" nor was Lewis's imagination.

What mattered to a child like me was that everything in Narnia was alive. Animals could speak. Trees and waters were dryads and naiads. There were centaurs, dwarves, giants, and horses that could fly. Children faced real dangers and were capable of redeeming their cruel or cowardly acts through their bravery.

When I cast my mind back over the stories, the scenes that have stayed with me, I often return to Lucy's quandary in *Prince Caspian*. The four Pevensie children have returned to Narnia (hundreds, maybe thousands of years after their idyllic reign as kings and queens; I confess it always troubled me a bit that they grew to adulthood in Narnia, then had to go back to being school children in England). They have gotten hopelessly lost trying to find their way to the camp of the beleaguered prince. Aslan appears to guide them, but at first only Lucy can see him. The others don't believe her. Tired and cross, they refuse to follow her in a direction that would require backtracking. Heartbroken and bitter, Lucy gives in, and they become even more lost. That night Aslan comes to Lucy. In his stern, golden, lovingly relentless presence, Lucy sees that she did have a choice. She still has a choice. The next day she tells the others that she is following Aslan, no matter what they decide. Reluctantly, they go with Lucy. At last they are all able to see Aslan.

As I recap this scene, I wonder why it moved me and does still. Why did Aslan test Lucy and the others in this way? Why didn't he just show himself plainly and say, "Hey, you're lost, let me show you the way." Why am I not angry with C. S. Lewis, the allegorist, with Aslan, with Jesus? I don't think I have ever asked myself that question before. I am not sure of the answer. Maybe it is that this story, so deeply embedded in my imagination, has given me courage to trust my own glimpses of the divine mystery in the midst of loss and confusion. Maybe it is Lewis's depiction of a presence that makes it bearable and imperative to face myself.

*

I wonder if the Christian allegorist in C. S. Lewis had children like me in mind when, at the end of *The Dawn Treader*, Aslan tells Lucy and Edmund that they will not be returning to Narnia again, that they must come to know him in their own world. In *The Last Battle*, Lewis makes it clear that Narnia has ended as all worlds must. They are only shadows of the real and eternal world. I was never persuaded, even as a child, by Lewis's Platonic vision of what he didn't quite call heaven (where everything good in England and Narnia still exists), though the journey there is exhilarating with its rallying cry "further up and further in." I didn't want Narnia to end, and I pretty much ignored Lewis's insistence that it had. He was just the author, not as real to me as the world he had invoked. I forgave him that treachery then, and I forgive him now, because his heartbreaking vision of a last and losing battle, valiantly faced and fought, spoke and still speaks to my condition, as the Quakers would say, or to our condition.

When I was sixteen, rereading the Narnia books for who knows how many times, I was dismayed to realize that Lewis's depiction of the nefarious southern Calormenes was racist. The appearance, style of dress, and speech patterns of these foes of Narnia, even their architecture and landscape, strongly resemble the Middle East in our world. Of course in Islam there is no equivalent to the evil god Tash. I was nevertheless disillusioned. I stopped rereading the books for a time. When I read them to my children, I remained conscious of Lewis as a man of a particular class and generation.

(Note: I later came to appreciate his prescience. In *The Last Battle*, the beginning of the end is heralded by a dryad dying at the king's feet as her tree is felled by greedy men clearcutting the forests.)

Although Tolkien's Middle Earth never captivated me as it did so many others, I recognized that the world Tolkien created was much more complete than Lewis's. The two men were members of an informal group of writers that met at an Oxford pub called the Eagle and Child. As I recall, Tolkien criticized his fellow Inkling for his implausibility. In Narnia a cheerful dwarf can fry up a breakfast of sausages and eggs, and you never wonder (or Lewis never seems to) who keeps the chickens and where did that sausage come from. Surely not a *talking* pig! The quality that makes Narnia more compelling to me than any other imagined world, even one as complete and magical as Middle Earth, is this one: you can get to Narnia from here, from your own ordinary life.

To this day, when I am exploring a new trail in unknown terrain, I am filled with a sense of joyous excitement. I am on an adventure. It is possible to walk from one world into another world. At any moment.

TRESPASSING

When you look out the windows of the rectory across the driveway, you see the church, cloaked in green ivy, with arcing red doors that open out. A pretty little church. Beyond the church, as high as the steeple, the trees of what we called Wings Woods, pines, hemlock, hardwoods. If you walk down the driveway and across the lawn between the church and the parish house, you will see a stone wall and posted on a tree a sign that reads:

"No Trespassing."

Here is the way between the worlds. The other side of the wall may not be Narnia (or maybe it almost is), but it is another world, the Other World. And stepping through the gap in the stone wall from one world to another is the story at the heart of my stories, of my life and work and play. For the purposes of this work, it is perhaps at the heart of how I pray.

Wings Woods was an old, abandoned estate, complete with a stone bridge over a stream, a pond, an empty icehouse, a haunted falling-down mansion, overgrown gardens and orchards, and trees, trees that, if only I knew how, I could awaken to their dryad forms.

It is possible that my father took us for a walk there when we were very young. I do remember that at some point he secured permission for us to go into the wood, permission to trespass without fear of divine or human retribution. I have no further memories of my father in the wood. I know I went to the wood with my brother to find trees to climb—we were always on that quest. Once my brother Harry and his friend, Jon, who had no little sister of his own to tease and terrorize, threw a paper bag over my head and dragged me over the gap in the wall (well, probably not dragged; I must have put up a little resistance for form's sake, but I was thoroughly enjoying the attention). They took me, bag over my head, up the hill and around the pond. I couldn't see, but I knew every step of the way. Then they opened the door to the icehouse, whose scent and dank temperature I recognized, and tossed me in, slamming the door behind them.

Ha! I remember thinking, pulling the bag off my head. They think I'm scared of the *icehouse*?! Ha! Stupid boys.

I suppose I might have been more scared if they'd been able to lock me in, but there was no lock. It was easy to push open the door and hoist myself up and out. Much worse was an earlier prank when they had stolen all my stuffed animals and arranged them on top of the stone pillars by the gate house, far beyond my reach. I must have been younger then and had not yet become proficient at climbing stone walls. (I soon learned in order to be able to scale the wall of the parish house porch from whence it was possible to open an unlocked window, climb through and have the run of the huge building when no one else was around.)

My most vivid memories are of going to the wood by myself, passing the No Trespassing sign, and entering the world of leaf-shaped light and shadow, banks of vinca, hanging vines, the stream roaring or trickling by. I recall looking for fairies and seeing signs of them in thick moss and dewy cobwebs. I loved the moment of coming out of the wood and looking across the pond at an old orchard. If you walked around the pond, you crossed a dam and then a series of stepping stones, separating the main pond from a little inlet of water lilies where you could see frogs, turtles, and jewel-like dragonflies, rich habitat for fairies.

Further up the hill lay the remains of terraced gardens, old stables, with the huge empty mansion above all. In my memory the mansion is open to the air and the sky, yet somehow still standing. Eventually it was torn down, but not before I'd had the chance to brave it alone and prove to myself that it was haunted. Why else would a shingle fall to the ground in the midst of such emptiness and stillness. What heart-racing excitement to run all the way back down the hill and through the woods, afraid only to a pleasurable degree, satisfied that ghosts, fairies, and magic were real. The fact that the public school and athletic field bordered the upper part of the wood, and the church and rectory the lower, only made the Otherness of the wood more distinct, confirming my belief that the world of school and church was not the only world. I had only to step through the gap in the wall.

I would not have used these words then, but I knew: the wood was a holy place, one where God had no jurisdiction and neither did Jesus. The wood did not belong to people, though I would not have been surprised to glimpse a flash of tawny gold between the trees. The wood was also a refuge from the desolate desert where I was still a fugitive wanted for deicide. In the wood I was as an outlaw, free as Robin Hood, freer. No Sheriff of Nottingham menaced.

Until one day the worlds collided.

At the edge of the wood, next door to the church was the gatehouse to the abandoned estate, the gate being between the two stone pillars where my stuffed animals had been held hostage by Harry and Jon. The little house, tiny and cozy enough for a Beatrix Potter figure to inhabit, had pink gingerbread shingles and a round turret. It looked like a candy house. And in lieu of Mrs. Tiggy Winkle, a witch could easily have taken up residence and enticed little children to come inside.

In fact the last resident of the house had been a tiny old woman, a former maidservant, who had survived the wreck of the Titanic. When my sister and I were quite small, I believe we went there to tea with our mother. The old lady gave my sister and me toy mice, just the size of real mice (and I fear their fur may have been real!) in Victorian dresses complete with bonnets.

Years later, when I was maybe in middle school, the gatehouse stood empty. I decided to break in. I am not sure how I did it, whether I found an open or broken window, a door I could kick in? There must have been some kind of breaking involved in my illegal entry. All I remember of the inside is that it was empty, except for cobwebs and mouse droppings. No furniture, no rugs, all the coziness and magic gone.

Did I flee the scene of what I suddenly understood was a crime?

The next thing I remember is my mother tending me while I had one of the awful migraine headaches that plagued my childhood. My mother believed they were triggered by getting wound up. (No one talked about stress then.) I lay on my mother's bed, weeping and terrified. It was not quite a delirium hallucination but just as vivid. Mr. Cunningham (the town policeman who mysteriously and terrifyingly had the same name as my father) was going to arrest me for trespassing and put me in jail. I can still picture the jail cell I imagined. A dank underground chamber with high barred windows.

The migraine ran its course, pain that made me wish I could die, relieved only by repeated vomiting. Usually when the pain passed, I found myself in a fragile, transcendent state. The peace that passeth all understanding comes close to describing it. This time the fear lingered, with the knowledge that I had done something I could never confess to my mother or to anyone, certainly not my father let alone God the Father. I never even told my brother.

The phrase in the Lord's Prayer "*forgive us our trespasses*" still calls up the No Trespassing sign. I don't believe I ever prayed, at least not sincerely, for forgiveness. Fear of being found out is not the same thing as repentance. I like to trespass. To this day, I will walk past most private property signs to explore a trail or a field. Whether it is reasonable or not, I feel safe outdoors, protected by the woods' legendary alliance with the outlaw. But I've never broken into a building again, never even felt tempted. Is it because the one time I did, the magic was gone? Or am I still afraid that somehow God or Mr. Cunningham will find out and throw me in jail?

SING CHOIRS OF ANGELS

There was yet another world in my childhood. God and my father could stand back, appreciate, support that world, but all the authority belonged to Miss Schultze, the brilliant, eccentric, exacting musician, organist and director of the adult and children's choirs.

She was small, with short gray hair; she dressed in pants before any other women did. Strict, fierce, and funny, she could throw a fit, all the more impressive for her German accent. She was a World War II refugee, though I don't know the details of her story. My sister remembers her pacing the choir room slapping a rubber galosh in her hand, ear cocked for anyone singing offkey. She demanded as much perfection as she could from her amateur choirs. She taught us all to read music, but more than that, she taught us to love choral music, harmony, descant, counterpoint.

Miss Schultze was also a family friend who came to dinner with her awkward, beautiful, and perhaps mentally imbalanced partner Kit. We called her Kit instead of Miss Neilson. I'm not sure why. Kit was our piano teacher, and my impression is that giving lessons pained her. She did not relate easily to children or perhaps to anyone but Miss Schultze. They had us to dinner at their house, too, a dark little cottage on a back road. They had a pair Siamese cats with startling blue eyes. Miss Schultze loved cats and had a special affinity for our aloof black cat JoJo who would stroll across the driveway to greet her. My mother was her best soprano. "Your mother!" my sister recalls her exclaiming. "She could sing standing on her head. Your mother!" Miss Schultze was also particularly fond of my father, who respected her talent and supported her campaign to raise funds for a German built tracker-action organ. They also chose together (and probably argued over) the hymns for each Sunday, with an eye—and ear—to assuring that they were musically and theologically sound.

I don't know if anyone talked about lesbians then. My impression is that everyone knew that Miss Schultze and Kit were a couple, but no one mentioned it, not in so many words. They had a volatile relationship. They both drank, sometimes to excess, and would call my father late at night in the midst of their fights, or to pick a fight with him. I am not sure which. My father never discussed it, but my mother complained about it. She did not like living in the rectory, called it "like living in a fishbowl." I knew no other life. Though my father was an unpredictable and often frightening person at home, I believe he was an excellent parish priest. The congregation was lively, engaged, racially and economically diverse, and full of eccentrics. My father challenged his parishioners to be involved with the wider community as well as the parish.

No doubt my father was inspired by what Martin Luther King Jr. called the Beloved Community, a term coined by the theologian Josiah Royce. This small-town church, where all were welcome, became a lifelong template for me.

And we had excellent music thanks to Miss Schultze and her lasting legacy.

Miss Schultze died of cancer while still in her forties and did not live to see the organ built. Such a fine instrument attracted excellent organists. Father Beaven, one of my father's successors, was also a musician. I hope Miss Schultze's soul rejoiced in decades of choral and organ concerts and a faithful choir that maintained her high standards.

In my youth, the children's choir sang once a month. I remember two anthems, Brother James Air, J. L. Macbeth Bain's setting of the twenty-third psalm. I got to sing the descant that came in on the third verse with the words, *"Yea though I walk through shadowed vales yet will I fear no ill."* We also sang the hymn *"Ye Watchers and ye Holy Ones"* as a canon, a glorious invocation of all the angels, bright seraphs, cherubim, and thrones. *"Raise the glad strain, Alleluia. Cry out dominions, princedoms, powers, virtues, archangels, angel choirs."* All those mighty winged ones I had invoked to make a wall around my bed.

The highpoint of the year for children, and especially for the children's choir, was the Christmas Eve manger service, the one where shepherds watched by night with my pilfered lambs. Now, as a choir member, I was part of the pageant. Preparations for the event went on all day. The men in the congregation gathered masses of fresh greens and small trees, transforming the church into a forest. The women of the altar guild cleaned the sconces and fitted them with the candles that would provide the only light apart from the long-tailed star over the stable. Yes, a real wooden stable and a manger filled with straw.

In the parish house, the three kings donned their robes and took up their gifts of gold, frankincense, and myrrh, while they no doubt terrified the shepherds into their best behavior. Just before the service the kings and shepherds crowded into the choir room where we waited dressed in our red choir robes and white surplices (with their wide, winglike sleeves). The kings were wonderfully scary, especially King Balthazar (aka John the Baptist). He was tall, massive, black-browed, and glowering. Every year when he sang the line "*sorrowing, sighing, bleeding, dying,*" his voice broke on the word "*dying.*"

The children's choir was invisible in the choir stalls, behind the stable, behind the trees and a black cloth. The congregation could not see us. And we could not see Mary and Joseph or the stupid boy shepherds (against whom I still held a grudge). Did I mind not being able to see the pageant? Not at all. No one said it, but I knew. We *were* the angels; we did not need wings and halos.

There is a particular silence before everything begins, everyone in their places, everyone expectant, even the rustling in the pews ceases. Miss Schultze's hands are poised over the organ. She plays the introductory line of the opening hymn. Watching her in the mirror, we see her nod, and we begin.

The snow lay on the ground, the stars shone bright....

And now it is Christmas Eve. The magic is here. The angels sing.

PHOTOGRAPHIC EVIDENCE

I suppose my childhood ended at twelve. A few months after my confirmation, I got my first menstrual period. Just before my thirteenth birthday and the beginning of eighth grade, we moved from the rectory to a house five miles out of town, the first one my parents owned. My father was leaving the parish ministry to work for the Office of Economic Opportunity in Poughkeepsie, a program funded by President Johnson's short-lived War on Poverty, as short-lived as his presidency, which was hopelessly mired in the other war: Vietnam.

I wore my confirmation dress to the parish's farewell reception for our family, which was held on the lawn between the church and the parish house, next to the gap in the wall that marked the way between the worlds. An outspoken parishioner approached me to say, "I always thought you were the ugly duckling of the family, but you're actually turning out to be quite pretty. What a surprise!" I don't remember what I said to her. Maybe for once I didn't have a smart remark at the ready.

Today I might have been diagnosed with oppositional defiant disorder (ODD). Whatever I thought grownups wanted to hear, I generally said the opposite.

"Do you like school?"

"No, I hate it." (Which probably wasn't even true.)

I see myself at twelve standing awkwardly and maybe also gracefully on the lawn, not sure what to do with the information that I was no longer an ugly duckling. I don't know if I was sad to leave the rectory where I'd lived all my life next door to an enchanted wood. I was probably excited by the prospect of a new house, surrounded by fields and woods to explore. I did not yet know that I would come to feel trapped there, completely dependent on my mother to drive me if I wanted to go anywhere. I had no inkling that my parents would decide to send me away to boarding school, and that for years I would feel at home nowhere.

What did I know at age twelve about prayer? What would I have said if anyone asked? But of course no one did ask. There was only one parishioner in the church who pestered my father about her devotional life. Both my parents spoke of her with derision and called her "the God lady." As noted, Episcopalians had the Lord's Prayer, Grace before dinner, and prayers for almost every occasion in the Prayer Book. No one, not even my father, prayed extemporaneously.

On the brink of adolescence, I had not forgotten my plans to kill God and Jesus at age three, but maybe I had stopped being afraid of direct retribution. Our God was a very wordy God. You could not see him (except when he incarnated as the Son, but I never quite accepted that they were the same person). But in the Bible stories, at least, you could hear him. He talked a lot. And when we prayed to him we were equally if not more verbose. All talk, no action, on either side. Perhaps I was beginning to ignore religion.

I will close this section with a photo op. I was maybe nine years old, judging by the hairstyle, still in barrettes. (I had not yet won the battle with my mother over the bangs I've worn from age ten to present.) I still sucked my thumb in private, my first addiction, which prompted my first decision to stop cold turkey. I cannot imagine what possessed my parents to allow a reporter to take our picture for the local paper for a Thanksgiving piece. Surely the whole thing was in poor taste, in fact the very definition of the word smarmy. And where were my parents? Why were we alone in the church with the photographer?

"What are your names?" he asked.

Being nine to my sister's six, I answered for us both.

"Elizabeth and Ruth."

"What nice Biblical names," the reporter gushed.

"No," I contradicted him sharply. "We were named for our grandmothers."

"Oh, how nice. Now how about you both come over and kneel right here."

He led us to the small altar at the side of the church. A stained-glass window showing President Lincoln wearing a purple cape stood over the pews that were never filled except on Easter or Christmas. There was a rail in front of the altar with cushions for kneeling on the rare occasion Communion was administered there.

We knelt. In prayer. Two little girls giving thanks. My sister knelt upright, hands in classic prayer posture, eyes gazing upward toward the altar. I went for what I must have imagined was a more contemplative look (though I am sure I did not know the word "contemplative"). I sat back on my heels (there is a term for this posture, the Episcopalian slouch), eyes closed, head bowed, hands folded in my lap. It is possible that I actually attempted to pray. The picture made the front page of the local newspaper. My sister looked cute, alert, and devout. I looked ghastly. I had not reckoned on how the contemplative posture would affect my pudgy midriff, how my bowed head and closed eyes would come across as a gloomy pout.

I can see the photograph quite clearly in my memory, whether or not any copy exists. It brings to mind Jesus's excoriation of public displays of piety. Pray in a closet, he said. I am sure he did not make this pronouncement to save me from the humiliation of public exposure. But I still think it's excellent advice, especially for a contemplative prayer like me.

CHAPTER TWO

ADOLESCENCE

BETWEEN THE WORLDS

Adolescence is by definition a between-the-worlds time. Between childhood and adulthood, one body and another, sexual innocence and experience, terror and wonder, belonging and exile. Adolescence has been prolonged in modern Western culture. Even in times and places where adulthood begins not long after the onset of puberty, the passage between the worlds is often marked by initiation rites or ordeals, tests of courage and resourcefulness that the young person might or might not survive. No one set me such tasks, but I went willy-nilly on my own perilous journey and returned changed.

JESUS'S FEET TOUCH THE EARTH

Like my early childhood memories, my earliest memory of adolescence is theological. As a deicidal three-year old, I had envisioned Jesus floating beside his thundercloud father along the desert floor, his feet skimming the ground. As resistant as I continued to be to trading in Aslan for Jesus (as the Lion told the Pevensie children they must), the Gospel story began to take hold in my imagination. Jesus's feet touched down.

I don't remember my exact age, but I do know the time of year. I know what day it was. Or days. And it may have happened the first time before we left the rectory. It kept happening every year, its time not chronological but liturgical, cyclical—events that happened once in time and yet are always happening, unchanged and changing as we change.

Palm Sunday. The triumphant (seemingly interminable) hymn, "All Glory, Laud, and Honor." Palms waving. (I expect in first century Jerusalem, people had branches of palms rather than one palm leaf held by each member of the choir and congregation at Grace Church.) As I look up the Gospel for the day, I see that the reading ends with Jesus's entrance into Jerusalem. Palm Sunday is also called Passion Sunday, the beginning of Passion week. In Grace Church, my father adapted the story of Jesus's trial. We all took part. Mrs. Fettes (aka King Balthazar's wife, Miss Schultze's staunchest alto), was always Pilate's wife. I can still hear her voice ringing out. *"Have thou nothing to do with that just man: for I have suffered many things this day in a dream because of him."* Someone played Jesus (likely Mr. Fettes) and someone else played Pilate. The rest of us were the crowd. When Pilate asked us which man to release we cried, *"Barabbas!"* And we sealed Jesus's fate by shouting: *"Crucify him!"*

Making it our fault, every year. He died for us and/or we killed him. Seemingly, I had numberless co-defendants. We were all deicides.

It's fine for a bunch of Episcopalians to shoulder the blame for the crucifixion. To the lasting shame of Christianity, starting with the Gospel according to John, Christians have blamed the Jews, justifying centuries of persecution, oppressive restrictions, inquisitions, pogroms, holocausts. Historians have corrected this lethal error. Jesus's death sentence was passed by the Roman governor, crucifixion being the standard Roman method of torturing the seditious to death. Pilate did not need the urging of the crowd. He did not wash his hands of Jesus's blood (a Jewish custom, not a Roman one). As a novelist, I've made sure my account also makes explicit the nature and power of the Roman occupation of Judea that killed Jesus and countless others.

I had my own amends to make. I am remembering Michael, a childhood friend of my brother's, probably one of the only Jewish children in our small-town public school. Unlike Jon, Michael never teased or tortured me. He and I played the mice to my brother's cat. I recall him pacing around our mouse hole (a corner of the living room), plotting how we would foil our nemesis. I can also picture being with Michael in our kitchen one day. I cannot remember whether I asked him why *he* killed Jesus or why the Jews did. I can't have been more than six or seven years old, maybe younger. Surely my parents had never said the Jews killed Jesus. Yet somehow this question existed in my mind, so I asked the only Jewish person I knew.

"I didn't! They didn't!"

He was upset, angry, and hurt. He might have cried. I still feel badly about it.

Jesus was a Jew, calling for the reform and renewal of the Judaism of his time. The scholars I read when researching The Maeve Chronicles surmise that he probably had no interest in starting a new religion. (We have Paul of Tarsus to thank or blame for that.) But that is getting ahead of the story. Back to Jesus's feet. On this earth. And how his story took hold of my heart and imagination, how he became the good cop/god to his Father's bad.

As a teenager, I joined the adult choir, singing alto beside Pontius Pilate's wife, falling in love with the intricate harmonies of Bach's choral music, the excruciating beauty when two vocal lines meet in a moment's dissonance before resolving. I have heard Bach described as cold and mathematical. How does anyone fail to hear the heartbeat in the opening of his Saint Matthew's Passion or the love song in the aria, "*make thee clean my heart from sin, unto Jesu, welcome giving*"? How can you not love someone when you sing to him year after year, "*O sacred head sore wounded*" and "*O dearest Jesus, how hast thou offended?*"

At that one time of year, individually and collectively, we mourned; secretly or openly, we wept. Or I did. I must have needed to. And Jesus's death gave me the chance. I never believed that he died for our sins to reconcile us to the Father. I did not concern myself with his overcoming death so that we could share in his eternal life. I loved him because he had suffered, too. He had felt alone. Forsaken.

He was human. He had feet. He washed feet. His own feet had been bathed with a woman's tears.

I believe my first distinct theological difference with my father dates to that time, though I do not remember voicing it. Now that we were older, we ate with our parents. Meatloaf, beef stew, my favorite lamb curry (made with the leftovers from the Sunday roast). My father probably had two martinis in him on an empty stomach by the time we sat down to dinner, when he moved on to wine. At some point he crossed the threshold from mellow to mean. He liked to hold forth. I think my mother, brother, and sister did their best not to listen and to keep their heads down. I was the only one who was foolish enough to draw his attention.

(In addition to the well-known fight-or-flight response, I believe there are two more. One is freezing. Rabbits, my mother's favorite animal, freeze when they can't find cover. So do deer. Then there is crazily, almost suicidally, running out into the open and drawing the danger to you. That's what I did, over and over.)

During the long hot summer of 1967 when city after city erupted in riots, my father worked for the Office of Economic Opportunity in the ghetto of Poughkeepsie. He got me a volunteer job at a day-care center on lower Main Street. I remember visiting one child's newborn baby brother who'd just joined his ten siblings in a two-room apartment. I don't know why I argued with my father when he insisted that reality was grim; personal choice was a middle-class privilege—or illusion. All people were products and victims of circumstance. At age fourteen I insisted (until I ran from the kitchen table in tearful defeat) that life was also beautiful, and that I (at least) was responsible for my own choices.

My sister remembers these nightly arguments, my father stabbing the table with his finger as he made his point (whatever it was that night) over and over. "It's as if you were mashed under that finger," she said.

I don't know why I didn't challenge him when he held forth about the twenty-second psalm. According to my father, when Jesus cried out, "*My God, my God, why hast thou forsaken me,*" he was not expressing despair, he was quoting the psalm, which ends in triumphant affirmation of faith.

Could it be that, uncharacteristically, I kept my feelings to myself and pondered the mystery in my heart? I am still pondering the mystery of my father, who on the one hand declared reality grim, and then on the other hand insisted that Jesus did not despair. My theological dispute was not only with my father, but also with evangelists' insistence that Jesus knew he was going to rise again on the third day "*in accordance with the scriptures.*" As a novelist-to-be, I didn't like this certainty as a plot device. Foreshadowing is one thing, but the "*in accordance with the scriptures*" refrain struck me as cheating.

Maybe I began even then to retell the story to myself. I believed that Jesus cried out from the cross in despair, that he did feel forsaken by the God he called Abba. I did not believe he always knew what he was doing or that it would all turn out all right in the end. So what did I make of the Resurrection? The triumphant hymns, the lilies on the altar, the pots of geraniums we all got to take home were more or less on a par with all the chocolate and jellybeans that would give me a stomach ache at the end of the day.

It's not that I denied the Resurrection. I can still see, hear, and smell the Resurrection Garden, the intimate, mysterious moment when Jesus speaks Mary's name, and she recognizes him. That was and is enough. Salvation, eternal life are too abstract for me. And I always did wonder, and still do, what were we saved *from*? If our sins were redeemed, why do we go on hurting and killing each other?

Theological fine points aside, the Passion story, the yearly liturgical catharsis, got to me in my teens. I did not become more religious or observant. It's just that Jesus became real to me, distinct from his Father, distinct, in a sense, from the Christianity into which I had been baptized and confirmed. I did not consciously begin to pray to him. He was just there, with me, with us, his bare feet on the earth, walking with us in what I later called "the Country of Life."

> "The country of life makes me weep. The stones here are
> so hard. They cut my feet. It takes so much time to walk
> this road. Yet I know the other worlds are here, too, at the
> edges of my vision...."
>
> —from *The Passion of Mary Magdalen*

SENT AWAY

From kindergarten to eighth grade, I attended the local public school, where I was a stellar student with lots of friends. My mother, who was passionate about education, felt that public school was not sufficiently challenging for me. She decided—in consultation with my father?—that I should take the PSATs and apply to boarding schools. I don't recall being asked if I wanted to go away to school, but I did not resist the idea. I probably thought of it as an adventure, something I had told my sixth-grade teacher I wanted more than anything.

The summer before my freshman year, I fell thirty-three-and-a-half feet from a tree, cracked three vertebrae and an ankle. In September 1967, still in a leg cast, I went off to a small, progressive, coed school in Vermont. The founder had just retired, leaving an interim headmaster in place. Neither he nor the not-so-permanent headmaster who followed were remotely prepared for the upheavals of the late sixties and its effect on the student body. As a naïve girl from a small, rural town, neither was I. In answer to Jimi Hendrix's recently released song, "Are you experienced?" my answer would have had to be, "Um, no."

The year I arrived, the school had just adopted an innovative four-term plan. Faculty and students would be able to take off any term, not just the newly-instituted summer term. My happiest memories are of my first summer there, when I grew strong pitching hay bales onto the truck driven by the school farmer. Later I would accompany the farmer as he drove the back roads to remote farms where we delivered the hay. Even though I was a freshmen, I had been put in charge of the outdoor work crew. I was already smiled upon by adults for being a responsible community member and an excellent student. (Unlike what I called "the cool crowd," who smoked cigarettes and other illegal substances.) Though I had friends from various cliques, I did not fit in with any of them. I developed a wariness of peer groups that lasted for many years. I do remember chafing at so much adult approval and expectation. I decided it was high time to break some rules, but I didn't get up to much that first year apart from sneaking out of the dorm one night, with a couple of friends, to raid the kitchen.

*

I could have written a book—and did; it's in the attic somewhere—about friendships and betrayals, falling in and out of love. But here, the beginning—and end—of my time at boarding school must serve as a frame for another story.

WHAT I COULD NOT TELL THE GROWNUPS

Because I had attended summer term, I was eligible to take off winter term. My uncle, an executive with Mobile Oil, had been transferred to work in London for a year. My parents sent me off to visit my aunt (my father's sister) and uncle, who lived in a drab suburb outside the city. Though it was the winter of 1969, the height of the Vietnam war, they proudly displayed an American flag in their front window. On weekends, when we went on tourist expeditions, my uncle wore his bright red Boy Scoutmaster uniform, complete with hat. When they hosted dinner parties, they toasted President Nixon. My aunt, who I generally liked because she was the only adult in my father's family who would tell stories (dish dirt), had a very loud voice and embarrassed me by complaining about the inferiority of British Woolworths while we were shopping in one.

As noted, at school I had never been cool, but I was so much cooler than my aunt and uncle, it was excruciating. At some point during my visit, my aunt had to go the hospital for a sinus operation. I was left alone with my uncle the scoutmaster, who did nothing to hide his dislike and disapproval of me.

I feel sorry for him now. One day, during my aunt's hospital-ization, he took me into London. He went to the office while I was turned loose with a map to go sightseeing—in a long, faded skirt and a purple, flowered hat, vintage rummage sale. I had never been alone in a big city in my life. I began to wander, paying little attention to where I was going. When I sat down to rest on a park bench, a man came to join me.

"What's your name then, luv?"

"Eliza," I answered in my best approximation of Eliza Doolittle's cockney accent, determined to pass for English and disavow my nationality.

To me, the man looked old, as old as my father (who was in his forties). I figured there was no danger in talking to such an old per-son. At fifteen, though I'd kissed a couple of short-term boyfriends, I was staggeringly innocent. I carried on the conversation in character as surely as if I'd be cast for the part of the cockney flower girl I'd always wanted to play on stage. Once I'd started, I did not know how to break out of character.

The man told me his place was nearby. Was I hungry? He would fix me something to eat. I followed him to a tube station, from one train to another. As the train went underground and overground, I saw the splendor of central London give way to rundown outskirts. I began to feel scared, but I had no idea what to do. Then I found myself in the man's flat, one room, with a fake coal fire, and a detached, shared toilet. True to his offer, the man cooked up bangers and mash—while plying me with drink after strong drink.

Everything after that is a blur until I was on the bed. My skirt was pulled up, my underwear pulled down. The man was doing things to me that I did not know existed. I am not someone who easily slips the body, but I do remember a basement window above the bed. Then I was above the bed too, looking down at the man, his pants off, snapping on what I know now must have been a condom. I will never be sure whether or not partial penetration occurred.

Still drunk, I put up my first and only resistance, pushing him away, sobbing loudly and uncontrollably.

He stopped. I will never know why. He could have easily overpowered me.

Did he decide that he did not want to force someone so drunk and helpless?

Did he think I was crazy?

Did he figure out my story didn't add up, that I wasn't the cockney waif I pretended to be and he could get in trouble?

Did I babble on about my uncle expecting me back at Mobile Oil headquarters?

I must have. I remember being dropped off by a taxi, my uncle waiting for me grimly outside the office building.

I was drunk and disheveled and probably incoherent.

I don't remember my uncle asking me anything. Nor did my aunt ask what had happened while she was gone. No one asked, and I never told. Years later I did find a letter to my parents from my aunt. She wondered if I might be "fey."

*

Her word choice stayed with me. *Fey* as in crazy, touched. Away with the fairies. I was away, but not with the fairies. Just the opposite. I felt exiled from my childhood sense of magic, from Narnia. I had stumbled through my own folly into "grim reality." I remember writing in my journal, praying in some inchoate way to Aslan-Jesus.

I believe now that help came. I have few memories of my aunt and uncle after that near-abduction but many recollections of staying with their friends, who gathered me into their lives and families with extraordinary kindness. (I expect my aunt and uncle wisely gave us all some much-needed respite from each other.) I never told any of these adults what happened to me, but I remember them all. One man in particular changed my life.

The late Jay Williams was the first novelist I ever met. He had known my aunt and uncle when they all lived in a small town in Connecticut. He had since moved to London with his wife and a daughter who was just a little older than me—though a lot more sophisticated. They were all warm and welcoming. One day, when his daughter and wife were otherwise occupied, Jay took me to see the Tower of the London. But instead of wandering around reading historical plaques, Jay pretended we were Tower inmates, and he gossiped with me about our fellow prisoners. I had never known a grownup willing to engage in play, to take on the persona of a fictional character—just as I had with such disastrous consequences.

On another occasion, I confided in Jay that I wanted to be a writer.

"But I don't know anything yet." (My father had made this clear to me.) "Maybe when I'm forty, after I've been a social worker, I'll be able to write."

Jay listened, shrugged, and said:

"Jane Austen. What did she know?"

And from that moment on, I no longer needed my father's approval in order to write.

*

When I returned to school for spring term, most of my friends had left, for their own term off, for other schools, or because they'd been kicked out by the new broom of a headmaster. The banished included a boy I had been in love with. The faculty, too, had changed for the same reasons. The lack of community and continuity was a serious drawback to the four-term plan. I was far from the only one lost and in crisis. The whole school was in disarray.

I made a few new friends, and I may have confided in some of them about what had happened to me in London. I did not turn to any adults for the help I hardly knew I needed. My high-spirited intention to break rules had turned into a listless resistance. It dawned on me, for the first time in my life, that I did not have to do anything. No one could make me. I did not have to study or turn in homework. I don't think I shirked the rotating work jobs we all had, but I didn't volunteer for any responsibility. I was done with being good for the grownups. I would do only what I felt like doing.

In summer term I felt like going skinny-dipping in at a nearby mountain stream that had a series of pools. We were transported there most afternoons by one faculty member or another. I always wandered downstream to a secluded pool and occasionally shared the pleasure of this place with friends and even a couple of teachers. But it was my pool, and I liked to swim naked there. Alas, when it was time to go back to campus, whatever teacher was on duty had to walk downstream to find me. Apparently my nudity became a hot topic at faculty meetings. I had put the school's reputation at risk. I found out that the two teachers who had gone skinny dipping with me never admitted it and did not stand up for me. I (heroically, I thought) never gave their names.

Just before the end of the term, I was called in to see the headmaster, who told me I was either a psychopathic liar and/or mentally ill. In either case, he informed me, I would not be asked back to school. I believe now that my nudity was a pretext. I was expelled for failing to live up to my early promise, for having a bad attitude, for being, as one faculty member called me, "incorrigible." Not for lack of willingness, I had never broken the big rules against taking drugs or having sex. So public nudity had to suffice.

No adult ever asked me: What happened to you?

If they had, I would not have told.

*

I did not want to tell, even now, more than fifty years later. Not because what I did or what happened to me was so shameful or even so terrible. Much worse has happened to generations of runaway or cast-out teens who were not lucky enough to escape, as I did, who had no adults in their lives to pick up the pieces.

I believe now that the near-rape rose from some depths like a nightmare, an event that pointed to events more shadowy, impossible to remember coherently. A murderous God, with a texture like a thunderclap who would hunt me down in the desert. A father who changed unpredictably, who became as remote and terrible as God the Father after a psychiatrist warned him to "stay away from his daughters." These are the unremembered memories I could only heal through writing novels, surely a form of prayer for myself and for those others who did not make it back to safety.

PROBLEM CHILD

When I was kicked out of school, no one knew what to do with me, though there were various plans for reforming me under consideration. A second paternal aunt and uncle were sure they could undo the harm of my being hopelessly spoiled (by my mother, of course). My father decided I should be sent to a tiny remote boarding not-exactly school which, as it turned out, was run by a former colleague (and crony) of his.

My three-day trial visit to the school of maybe twenty students was as traumatic as anything else that happened during my adolescence. In my initial interview, the headmaster bullied me into telling him every bad thing I had ever done. Every drug I had taken (really, not too many). Every sexual act (I did not tell him about the near-rape, but confessed I was not a virgin, though I now suspect I was). Then, as I learned later, he reported everything to my parents.

After this third-degree grilling, I lived and worked with the other students, except that there was no school, just a little math on occasion and a smattering of Spanish. Everyone worked from dawn till dusk on the headmaster's subsistence farm. Which would not have bothered me in itself. As noted, my favorite aspect of my former school had been the farm. But at that school we *did* have classes and teachers. At the place my father wanted to send me, there was only this one man, no teachers.

Every evening after dinner, while we were all still seated at the table, the headmaster got up and began to pace. Then he chose a victim and verbally tore the unlucky person to shreds in front of everyone, exposing and humiliating him or her. I have a vivid memory of one boy choking back his tears.

Later I asked the students if they minded what the headmaster did to them. "Oh no," they said. "We know he knows what's best for us."

I must have had another private interview with this man in the course of my visit. Bits of this exchange remain indelible.

"Why do you think I started this school?" he demanded.

"I suppose because you want to help people?" I said dubiously, assuming this must be the answer.

"Wrong!" he said. "I run it because I want to keep my family away from the world. The world is an evil place. If you come here, you must leave it behind. There will be no drugs, no sex, and no particular friendships with other students. If you come here, you must give up everything and follow me."

Run, every fiber of my being screamed, *run!*

When my parents came to pick me up after my three-day trial, I told them I did not want to go to that school. I tried to tell them what had happened, how the headmaster publicly browbeat the kids, how he wanted them—and me—to give up their will to him.

My father did not believe me. I don't know if my mother did or not. She was fixated on the drugs and the unspecified sex. I don't know why they did not force me to go the school. Maybe the headmaster refused me admission, though that seems unlikely. He was a friend of my father's and probably would have taken pleasure in breaking my will.

Whatever the reason, they did not insist. I still feel lucky to have escaped. But for many years, these words haunted me: "Give up everything and follow me." Very likely he knew he was echoing Jesus's invitation/command to his disciples. And for years I feared that if Jesus had turned to me and said: follow me, I would have answered: No Fucking Way.

This resistance to following may have stood me in good stead. Unlike some of my generation, I was immune to gurus, religious or secular. Yet I remained troubled that I would have turned away from Jesus. As I wrestled with these questions, I made a distinction. What was the intent of the command "follow me"? To liberate or to enslave? It occurs to me now there is a world of difference between choosing to trust someone you love and submitting to someone you fear. I still ponder these questions.

There was a more immediate question at that time: what was to become of the adolescent conundrum that I was? I did not want to live with another aunt and uncle (and my mother who had antagonistic feelings toward her sister-in-law was glad to say no). I did not want to go back to public school (where I probably would have gotten expelled again). My brother finally came up with a solution that shaped the rest of my life:

"Send her to Olga. Olga will find something for her to do."

TWO WOMEN

During that critical juncture in my adolescence, two women came into my life. They could not have been more different from each other. Born in 1904 and 1913, respectively, one was an Anglican mystic and the other, though baptized Roman Catholic, was more ignorant of and indifferent to religion than any person I have ever met.

That would be Olga.

OLGA

Olga and her late husband Julian founded High Valley School, first as a boarding adjunct to Poughkeepsie Day School, where they taught for many years, and then as a school in its own right. The twenty or so students, some boarding, some day, might at a later date have been placed into classes for special education. Olga didn't go in for labeling people. "Education at own level" was the school's motto. If you didn't fit into a conventional classroom for whatever reason, you might thrive at High Valley. When the public school in our small town was about to place my brother in a class for the retarded because of his undiagnosed dyslexia, my parents sent him to Poughkeepsie Day School and then to High Valley when it became independent.

Unlike the equally small school I had escaped, High Valley had a proportionately large and diverse staff of gifted teachers who worked with the equally diverse students (ranging in age of from five to early teens). And if a child was having or creating difficulty in one of the two classrooms, he (they were mostly boys) could always be sent outside to Olga, who was usually working in her gardens. She would find him "something to do."

I vaguely remember my initial meeting with Olga outdoors under the huge old maple tree in the front yard. I have the impression that she was not particularly interested in whatever crises had brought me to her, but no doubt she could find something for me to do too. So without much discussion, it was settled that I would show up at High Valley on a daily basis.

I was not a student, though I did have an independent study with one of the teachers, the marvelous Marguerite Strehlau. She welcomed me each Tuesday after school hours to her apartment, where she served me cinnamon toast and we discussed the course of Irish literature she'd designed for me. She also taught me to play guitar and encouraged me to keep a journal. I was certainly not one of the adults. A sort of tweeny maid, I worked and ate in the kitchen, serving both the kids and, later in the evening, the adults, who ate together and drank wine. During school hours I helped out as a tutor. On my first day, I was assigned to read with a boy of about eleven years old. I anxiously asked Olga, "What do I do? I've never taught anyone before." I will never forget her answer.

"Just make it fun."

Making it fun was a succinct summary of Olga's approach to teaching. She would observe her students keenly, discover what interested them and encourage them to pursue it, whether it was airplanes, baseball, comic books, fishing. They all, as far as I can remember, learned to read. I also worked on math with anyone who needed help, not my best subject. I found that having to relearn fractions helped me teach them—if what I was doing could be called teaching. Sometimes my task for the day was to follow an adorable five-year-old around and make up poems and stories with him.

I don't remember exactly what hours we spent in the classroom, but there was plenty of outdoor time. My first year there, we thinned a pine grove that Olga and Julian had planted when they first arrived in 1945 to hold soil that had been depleted and eroded by poor farming practices. I have memories of jogging down the hill carrying one end of a tree while one of the boys held the other.

One day in early spring, I discovered a treehouse at the top of the hill beyond the woods we'd been thinning. It was a fully enclosed space with a trapdoor entrance accessible by a wooden ladder. It had a big glass window and was furnished with a couple of cots. It had been a getaway for Olga and her late husband, but no one had used it since Julian's death. I asked if I could live there. Olga, being Olga, said, "Sure, why not?"

After an evening of playing cards with the kids, Spit and Gin Rummy being the favorites, I set out in the gloaming to the treehouse. Probably I had a flashlight, but it was not always easy to find the treehouse, picking my way through the thickets to where it nestled in the tree branches. My first night there, I hadn't been settled long when I heard scuffling and voices, as several boys climbed the ladder and came through the trap door.

"We're running away from school!" they gleefully informed me.

I spent the night persuading them that they must not. Sure that I had averted a disaster, I triumphantly brought them all back with me next morning. I expected to be congratulated and praised. Olga was merely irritated and clearly unimpressed. She did not appear to have been concerned at all about her missing students. I was disappointed to have what I considered my heroic effort ignored. But I suspect her response was also a relief and a revelation to a person who had lived (and still lives) in such a fearsomely moral universe.

It soon became routine for boys to run away to the treehouse every night. We took some pleasure in frightening each other with tales of a deer-headed man we were sure we had seen lurking in the swamp. One night I heard the trapdoor creak open and, instead of a boy, antlers appeared. I had a moment of sheer terror before the antlers were followed by Chuck, one of the nightly runaways.

I have fond memories of those nights. I was sixteen, and most of the boys were twelve and thirteen, pubescent, surely, but our nights together were sweetly innocent. They slept on the floor and on the other cot, and one of them, usually Chuck, slept back-to-back with me. That cozy, animal closeness must have been a balm to my beleaguered adolescent spirit. I have never known anything like it before or since.

During my two years at High Valley (I shared a room with another tweeny girl the second year), I viewed Olga as someone to be avoided. She saw everything and could pounce fiercely without warning. Yet there was something not kindly exactly but benign about her. Or maybe I mean impersonal. She was a force of nature, not always pleasant, but bracing, enlivening, and unconventional. She was neither permissive nor punitive. Just five feet tall, she could pitch an impressive fit that would stop the biggest and most obstreperous boy in his tracks. She had not the least objection to being hated. If anything, it amused her. I don't believe people feared her in the ordinary sense. I would describe the general feeling as fond wariness, with some eye-rolling mixed in. For me, a former teachers' favorite turned bane, it was salutary not to crave an authority figure's attention.

Olga was also an entirely different kind of woman than I had ever known. She had been married (and apparently had a son somewhere; I saw his photograph in the music room and considered that he wasn't as handsome as his younger cousin who taught at the school and took care of the horses). She had a career, and not just any career but one where she reigned supreme. She had fun. My strongest memory of Olga is of her throwing back her head and laughing. Born in Venezuela, with her childhood spent on Trinidad, Olga was beautiful, sexy, swam naked into her old age. She liked to change for dinner. But most of the time she wore no makeup, had her black and gray hair in a wild pile on top of her head, and dressed in worn, torn clothes suitable for gardening. (I have inherited her signature straw hat.)

For most of my life I had been surrounded by women in shirt-waist dresses or neat blouses and skirts. They powdered their faces and tastefully applied lipstick. When it became common for women to wear pants, my mother never looked back, but her neatly pressed navy blue or tan slacks were a far cry from Olga's patched jeans.

I did not know a woman could be so free, so careless of appearances, so indifferent to the opinions of others, as well as serenely gorgeous and supremely confident. In my life as a prayer, I had met someone who was neither moral nor immoral. Good and bad, right and wrong were not her framework. She was delightfully, and sometimes appallingly, as I later learned, amoral. At a time when everyone was worried about me and wanted to save or reform me, she was just exactly what and who I needed.

MISS SANG

Eventually I called her Betty. But I invoke her memory with the name I first called her. When I think of Miss Sang I see her in a pew on the right-hand side of the church near the window of Jesus holding the retrieved lamb in his arms. The light shines through the lamb onto her white hair, soft and curled. Her face is in three quarters profile to where I am sitting in the first raised pew in the back of the church.

I don't know why this image is so strong. That spot is where she sat when she was part of the congregation, but she also sang in the choir, a soprano, like my mother, though her voice was not as strong. She and Miss Schultze were very good friends. Maybe I noticed Miss Sang before I knew her, distinguished her from other older parishioners, because of that stained-glass light and her hair, pure white, no gray, no tinge of blue, no sallow yellow.

I was sixteen (the same year I was dispatched to Olga) when Miss Sang invited my family to dinner at her old house (old enough to have been a stop on the Underground Railroad and probably older still with its low dormer windows under the eaves). Late afternoon light came into her old-fashioned living room and shone on her bro-cade-covered sofa and chairs with wooden arms, comfortable, but not soft, where we sat and visited before dinner with aperitifs, soft drinks for my mother and us, maybe sherry for Miss Sang, probably something stronger for my father. Miss Sang loved to cook, but I don't remember what she served us that night.

What I do remember is how she moved, the pleasure she took in creating comfort—and beauty. Nor do I recall anything she or anyone else said. I was in the midst of an epiphany. This is grace. Setting a table, cooking a meal, refilling a glass, clearing a table. This is beauty. This...sorry, no noun comes to mind...this, I somehow knew, is what I was trying to say to my father. Life is not just grim, it is...*this*.

Miss Sang was someone I knew I needed to know. She had nothing in common with Olga, except that she also was unlike any woman I had ever met. She had never married and had no children, but that is not what made her different. The child of an American mother and a British father—whose own father had run away to Paris to be a painter, for which he was disinherited—Miss Sang spent her early years in France and spoke French fluently. When the World War I broke out, she was sent to school in England. Her father died in combat when she was nine years old. After the war, she did a stint at a finishing school in Switzerland before eventually returning with her mother to the States. She trained to be a nurse and served as an army nurse in England in World War II, though she often told me she would have preferred to go into the arts. She described herself and her two brothers as "cosmopolitan kids." Of the three places that shaped her life she said, "I love the United States the best, it's my country. I feel most at home in England" —(and she never lost traces of British elocution)— "but I have the most fun in France!"

Miss Sang's mother, originally from Pittsburgh, chose, as her final home, a little hamlet in Dutchess County by closing her eyes and sticking a pin in a map. Mrs. Sang moved to the place she called Tippingrock Farm with her brother. They kept bees for a time and enjoyed watching the Perseid showers from a flat rock at the top of a hill. I don't know when Betty came to live with her mother and uncle, maybe after she returned from the war. My parents knew Betty's mother. But by the time Betty came into my life (or I into hers, for I believe it was my idea) her mother had died. Betty lived alone in the lovely old house, her bedroom the smallest one at the back, probably once a maid's.

Soon I was a regular guest in one of the other three bedrooms—a front room that had sloping eaves and windows at the floor level as well as a full-sized window on another wall that overlooked the garden. I slept in a sleigh bed under a satin coverlet. Sometimes Betty's best friend, a fellow former army nurse and her husband, stayed in the big bedroom across the hall. We were a jolly company, like guests at an English country house, but less formal, as we all helped with cooking and washing up.

I don't think Miss Sang chose a solitary life. She told me that she would have liked to have married and had children. Whatever regrets or mistakes were in her past, some of them tragic, by the time I knew her, she had made what seemed a kind of transcendent peace with herself and her life. She loved the prayers and rituals of the church. She was a sensitive. She believed certain places where people had worshipped for hundreds of years held the imprint of all the individual and communal faith. I sensed, though I might not have had the words, that her own faith was not bounded by church. She did not have to pray the words of a liturgy to be a prayer. I suspect she did not need words at all. It was all prayer, making coffee, sweeping the floor.

She must have been lonely sometimes or at some time in her life. Of course when I was her guest, she was not alone. And yet I sensed her solitude. When I attempt to say what I mean, I see that light again in the living room, or morning light coming into the kitchen. I see the rooms of her house filled with presence, her presence and the Presence that filled her.

She was, of course, a good person, who had surely done good works. But she did not define herself or justify herself by what she had done. For someone who felt—and still feels—that I have never done enough to serve others suffering this grim reality, Miss Sang's way of being, her being, was…I was going to say a revelation, but that seems too abstract. Maybe more like drinking water from a clear spring when you did not know how thirsty you had been.

Until I knew her, I knew nothing of the contemplative tradition in Christianity. No one, not my father, not my grandmother, both of whom respected Miss Sang, could say that she was selfish or self-indulgent. She did her part as a member of the parish community. I'm sure no one would have accused her of woolgathering or even daydreaming. But she had a luminous stillness and a silence at her core that give me hope and comfort to this day.

CODA: ON LOVE AND LOVERS

Both Olga and Miss Sang made a lasting impression on me as women who were whole-in-themselves, not defined by a relationship to a man at the time they came into my life. But of course they had led long (from my viewpoint) lives that had included fulfillment and heartbreak. I was just at the beginning of my own (mis)adventures in love.

I want to remember here the wisdom they shared with me.

When my first serious love affair broke up, Olga came to visit me to offer comfort and counsel. By then I was in college and had known her for four years. She confided that she'd had many lovers before, during, and after her marriage, but that her husband had been the only mature man she'd ever known, her partner in every sense. A bit of a female supremacist, she told me that most men were boys. She advised that I might find that some were not worth the trouble. (I never had the chance to dismiss that many men.) But these words of Olga's still touch me:

"All love affairs end, even if only in death."

Miss Sang witnessed with great kindness one particular love affair of mine that she could have considered immoral, and maybe she did. She had made her own mistakes and regarded mine with compassion. Gently, she told me:

"It is never wrong to love; it is only what you do with that love that can be mistaken."

From her own experience, she bore witness:

"God is our last, best love."

CHAPTER THREE

UNIVERSITIES

QUESTIONING, QUESTING

TWO MEN

I had been out of school for three years when I began college, two years at High Valley, one spent variously getting my GED, taking SATs, living for a time with a kindly cousin in Gloucester, Massachusetts, where I discovered that without a car or education, and with zero skills, I was highly unemployable. During my sojourn in Gloucester, I often visited friends in Boston who were already in college. A guidance counselor encouraged me to apply to the College of Basic Studies at Boston University, a two-year program tailored for people with less than stellar high school backgrounds.

So at the age of nineteen, a year older than most freshmen, I headed to Boston University, with a developing drinking problem, an incipient eating disorder, and as I soon discovered, gonorrhea picked up while hitchhiking through Quebec. I lived in a huge dorm in a box of a room with a roommate who slept round the clock, except when someone rang the fire alarm in the middle of most nights and the dorm had to be evacuated. I had literally unmemorable one-night stands, ate mostly chocolate chip cookies from vending machines, and wore loose denim overalls to school every day.

I also discovered I that loved being in school. It felt, for the first time, like a choice.

RW

CBS, as it was called then (all the schools at BU were known by acronyms), had a team-teaching system. The professors (humanities, social science, physical science, and rhetoric) shared a suite of offices and worked together with the same students. There was a lounge where we were always welcome to hang out with each other and any available professor. Amazingly, generously, our professors seemed to like engaging with us outside the classroom. And they clearly enjoyed their camaraderie with each other. We sometimes submitted cross-disciplinary papers to more than one teacher. To my shock, on my very first paper I received a "D," something that had never happened to me, not even in my rebellious phase just before being kicked out of high school. Turns out I did not include a thesis sentence—because I had no idea what a thesis was. I believe it was the rhetoric professor who gave my paper a "D." But I suspect it was the humanities professor, Wexelblatt (or Wex as we called him), who explained the lacunae and encouraged me to rewrite the paper. I will never forget finding my second attempt in my mailbox, the title page emblazoned with "Splendid! RW." For a time I wondered if RW was an acronym for rewrite. In fact, RW stood for Robert Wexelblatt. RW is how I still address him when I email him, fifty years later.

It is strange now to think that he is only nine years older than I am, not yet thirty when he was my teacher. If any man filled the (rather vacant) role of father in my life, he did. It was not that I thought of him as a father then. He had a slender build, thick black hair, startlingly pale blue eyes, and more often than not a look of amusement on his face. He was passionately engaged by what he taught, a rigorous mix of literature and philosophy. And he was available, above and beyond any call of duty, to his students.

(Note: Robert Wexelblatt is not only the beloved mentor and teacher of decades of students, but he is also a brilliant writer of fiction, both short stories and novels, as well as essays and poems. Look him up and start reading.)

I had little or no idea of what a father could or should be. It is still sometimes hard for me to grasp. Wex was to me—and no doubt to many others—someone who was keenly interested in who I was, in all my gifts and my foibles, without judgment or inappropriate attachment. He was also someone I could call on for help in life emergencies, not just academic ones. I do not remember the circumstances, but I do know that he rescued me one rainy night, putting me up as a guest in the home he shared with his wife and three-year-old daughter. One of the offices of a father is to help a young person make her way into the world, to reach out a hand if she stumbles, and then let go again, having faith that she will right herself. RW did all those things.

He also had a lasting influence my intellectual, literary, and theological development.

*

I did not have much of a social life in college. I avoided group activities. But Matthew 25, my grandfather and father's credo, was always with me. (*I was naked and ye clothed me, hungry and ye gave me to eat…in prison and ye came to me…*) So I joined a social action group and went once a week to visit prisoners in a correctional facility. There I was courted by an inmate. When he was released, we became lovers. I had left the dorm after my first term and lived in a boarding house full of misfits and eccentrics, most of them older than me, where I felt more sense of belonging than I did at school. I had a tiny room on the top floor where I was not supposed to entertain overnight guests, a rule the manager let me know he intended to enforce. His concern was about rent not morals. When a larger room became available in the basement, he offered it to my lover and me. We moved in together, sharing the kitchen with the other residents, who included a tortured gay Roman Catholic who could not stay away from trysts on the Esplanade.

I gave myself over to my first ecstatic sexual experience. For a while it did not matter that we had no conversation. At the end of the academic year, we left the boarding house and rented an apartment next to a bar frequented by bikers. We got jobs in local stores. By then, I was aware of a loss of what felt like sight, not in a literal sense. It felt as though the me who noticed things, the observer, the witness, the one who lived between the worlds, was no longer looking out through my own eyes. I was homesick for something. Not that any of that was my lover's fault. He was young, given to habitual, but not in the least malicious, lying and petty thievery. It is hard to explain, but there was something innocent about him, about us.

While he was incarcerated, my lover had applied to college and been accepted into the University of Wisconsin. At the end of the summer, he left for school. Shortly after winter vacation we broke up. Predictably, he had found a girlfriend in Wisconsin and lied about it. But this story is not about love affairs and loss. What matters here is that I remember little from my heartbroken, frequently drunken, sophomore year except for my independent study with RW. I don't know why I had an independent study with him. I had a full academic load with the second-year program at the College of Basic Studies. RW recently recalled that he designed that long-ago course with my theological development in mind. On our curriculum: Kierkegaard's *Fear and Trembling*, Shakespeare's *King Lear*, and *The Book of Job* from the Bible.

ABRAHAM AND ISAAC

In reading *Fear and Trembling*, I found myself in familiar yet strange childhood terrain, with Abraham and Isaac. Kierkegaard's fictional narrator Johannes vividly evokes the silent Abraham riding across the desert (like the one in my imagination) to obey God's command to sacrifice his son, *"whom thou lovest."* Abraham's leap of faith, his embrace of what Kierkegaard terms the absurd, ultimately restores Isaac to him at the last possible minute. And not only that, but God also further rewards Abraham for his obedience, promising that his descendants will be as numerous as the stars in the sky and the sand on the seashore. They'll also take possession of the cities of their enemies. All nations on earth will be blessed by this excessive number of descendants. All because Abraham agreed to obey God's terrible command.

According to Kierkegaard, my objection to both God and Abraham's behavior meant my thinking was in the (lower) realm of the ethical and the universal where murder (filicide, to be precise) is morally wrong, as distinct from the highest realm, the religious. The ethical and the universal seemed a far, abstract cry from what I felt, which Kierkegaard might have viewed as primitive, even below the lowest (the aesthetic, the individual who lives for himself). I was, anachronistically perhaps, outraged. My childhood question, "What about Sarah?" remained unanswered. She is not even mentioned in Genesis 22, known as "the Binding of Isaac." And what about Isaac, who is portrayed as clueless about his father's intentions?

My response was not merely: killing is wrong, though *"thou shalt not kill"* is later inscribed on Moses's stone tablets. (The Most High is not known for consistency.) It was more like: Motherfucker, you lay one hand on my child, and you're a dead man. And if your God is telling you to sacrifice *my* son, I'm gonna lay him out, too, roll a boulder off a cliff, squash him like a bug.

I see that there is still a lot of heat in my response, which now comes from a mother's point of view. At twenty I was not a mother, but I had a mother I adored and depended on. Yet she was also a mother who had not defended her son, whom she loved, from terrible abuse at the hands of his father. Many times my mother had told me about my father taking my three-year-old brother into the bathroom of a summer cottage where he "beat him black and blue." There was no soundproofing in those cottages. So my mother must have heard everything. I was there also in that cabin, an infant, ten months old. As I type, my hands shake and my stomach clenches. The memory lives in my body.

Motherfucker, you lay one hand on my child, and you're a dead man.

I wanted her, still want her, to say those words. She never did.

The biblical story does not portray Abraham as an abusive father, just as someone excruciatingly, inexplicably obedient to his God who puts him to the ultimate test, the sacrifice of what he loves most. In the Lord's Prayer, some denominations translate "*lead us not into temptation*" as "*do not put us to the test.*" Doing just that seems to be one of the Biblical God's favorite pastimes. Abraham passes the test. Eve flunks (and, in my opinion, Adam is a flunky). And of course, much later, Mary passes the test. "*Be it onto me according to your word.*" And Jesus accepts the cup. "*Not my will but thine be done.*"

It strikes me that faith and obedience are often conflated. Because of his faith, Abraham obeyed God. Because of his obedience, God rewarded him. But in Genesis 18:16-33, Abraham famously bargains with God, getting him to agree to spare Sodom if he finds ten righteous people. (God destroys Sodom anyway, after evacuating Lot and his family—too bad for his wife for disobeying and looking back, getting herself turned into a pillar of salt.) It's interesting that Abraham dares to call God's moral judgment into question when it comes to smiting a city full of wickedness but makes no murmur of protest when asked to make a burnt offering of his son. Perhaps when Abraham pleaded for Sodom, he was arguing in the realm of what Kierkegaard would call "the ethical," and felt emboldened. Whereas God's demand that he sacrifice his son—a child Abraham wanted for himself—threw him into confusion, pitched him headlong into the absurd.

ANOTHER ASIDE ON FATHERS—AND GRANDFATHERS

(When my father returned from serving in the army in World War II, his father informed him it was time for him to go to seminary. My father had wanted to go to graduate school for English. Years later, he tried and failed to revive that dream. I recently read an account of my grandfather's tenure as the priest of a rural parish before he went on to a larger church in Hartford. My father duplicated his father's approach and his decisions as if he were a clone. Both were very demanding of their congregations, exhorting them to social service. But my father wasn't a clone. He was only trying to be what his father told him he should be. And not be what his father did not want him to be…an English professor? Perchance to write?

In turn, my father excoriated me for my desire to write and insisted I should be a social worker. [Women then could not be priests.] When I refused to give up writing, he predicted my failure. "You will never be published!" It felt more like a curse than a prediction. It hurt me, and it scared me, but it didn't stop me. I had been defying God and my father from an early age. I did not know till after my father's death, when we discovered letters from his father, that many of the harsh things my father had said to me, his own father had said to him, verbatim.)

BACK TO THE ABSURD

Despite Kierkegaard and RW's best efforts, I remained unable to appreciate Abraham's leap of faith into the absurd. I don't recall if I refused then to have my response relegated to the ethical and the universal. My theological development continued on its own trajectory. Years later, when writing (as it turns out) my own version of the New Testament, I told someone, with great satisfaction, that Maeve (my Celtic Magdalen) had restored the fig tree that Jesus blasted, gathered up the miraculously ripened fruit and pelted him with figs in the Temple porticoes. My listener was taken aback.

"But don't you think the withering of the fig tree has a symbolic meaning?"

"Maybe it does," I said. "But I don't care. Jesus shouldn't have blasted a tree."

And if we are talking symbolic meaning, we should consider that figs are associated with female genitalia. So of course Maeve objected to the blasting of the fig tree (or, druid-trained as she was, any tree). Maeve's bombarding of Jesus with the figs remains for me an exhilarating, fictional *fuck you.* For my theology, such as it is, includes calling out God's beloved son, too, whom I love—Jesus, that is, not his father.

As noted, Christian apologetics is a telling term. Somehow God always has to be right and righteous, despite appearing to be quite shady in some of his dealings. (We'll get to Job shortly.) Many children, no matter how badly treated, need to believe their parents are good (ergo any abuse must be their own fault). How terrifying, how life-threatening, to acknowledge that your parent/God might be unjust as well as unpredictable—even/especially if it is self-evident.

Jesus, in turn, has to be as perfect as we want to believe his Father is, despite his protest that he is not to be called good. *"Only God is good."* In researching The Maeve Chronicles I remember an exegesis explaining that the suicidal swine (into whom Jesus drove the demon whose name was Legion) represented chaos. And Jesus took command of chaos. When I read the passage without needing to prove that Jesus was always right and in control, the scene itself seemed chaotic, the exorcism possibly botched. I couldn't help but feel sympathy for the Gadarenes, who pleaded with Jesus to go away and never come back. Maeve, raised among pig-eating Celts, later makes a smart remark about how much barbecue those drowned demon-ridden swine represented.

I would not begin writing The Maeve Chronicles for another

eighteen years after my independent study with RW, but maybe I found *Fear and Trembling* compelling not for its philosophy but because of Kierkegaard's passionate engagement with a story that was primary to his own development.

LEAR AND CORDELIA

I can no longer be sure in what order RW and I read the works in our independent study or if there were other readings besides these three. But the one that comes next in my mind is *King Lear*. And I think now (if I did not realize it then) how clever it was for Wex to go from Abraham and Isaac to King Lear and Cordelia.

The tragedy of King Lear also begins with a test.

"Which of you shall we say doth love us the most?"

("How much do you love me?" my maternal grandmother would whisper in our ears when she called us over to the easy chair where she sat enthroned. "Do you love me a penny's worth?"

"No, Grandma, I love you a whole dollar's worth!"

Test passed for the moment....)

Cordelia's answer is different:

"I love your majesty according to my bond, no more, no less."

I remember sitting in RW's office. I can picture the small window, maybe a plant in it trying to catch some indirect light, his relatively tidy desk. And his question to me:

"Why didn't Cordelia just say, 'I love you heaps, Pop'?"

Why didn't she compete with her sisters, best them, avoid the tragedy that led to her father's madness and her own death, among many other deaths?

I must have attempted to answer RW's question, but I have no recollection of what I said, probably because my answer did not satisfy either of us.

Nor do I remember asking why Lear didn't respond differently to Cordelia. "Okay, fair enough. Here's your third of the kingdom.

Or better still, you can have it all. You flunk, Goneril and Regan, you sycophantic brownnosers. How stupid do you think I am?"

Really stupid, apparently. And so the tragedy unfolds with the logic of the absurd. And whatever Lear might have said, if he hadn't been an ego-driven fool, doesn't matter. Lear's test sets the tragedy in motion, yet the story hangs on Cordelia's words, "I love your majesty according to my bond, no more no less."

I recently had a counseling session with someone who has taken on the task of caring for her aging parents. She was sorting out what is her responsibility and what is not, what is a necessary (and willing) sacrifice of her time and skills and what is (unconscious) manipulation, even exploitation, on their part? Her family history is fraught. What does she owe her parents? I heard myself quoting:

"I love you according to my bond, no more, no less."

Of all the things I said, that line from *King Lear* went home. She wrote it down.

*

Why *didn't* Cordelia just say, "I love you heaps, Pop?" How would I answer that question now? I might confess that I often lack Cordelia's courage. I am still willing to sacrifice to the truth to avoid giving offense. I am still causing myself and others trouble by wanting to control how others respond. If I say the right thing, if I second-guess what they want to hear, they won't be hurt or angry—and I will be safe. That's the hard-to-admit part, that fear more than kindness might motivate me. Cordelia tells the truth, and all hell breaks loose. I find myself wondering: what would have happened if Cordelia simply said, "I love you," and left it at that. Or "I love you, and I can't or won't compare it or measure it?" Was there anger in the almost legalistic definition of her love?

Edgar, Gloucester's wronged and loyal son, sums it up at the play's end: "speak what we feel, not what we ought to say."

What if Cordelia had said, "Pop, it really pisses me off when you make love into a test."

(Actually, we tried that with my grandmother once, and she did not speak to us for months.)

As an aging parent myself, I hope I would accept Cordelia's answer from my own children with some measure of gratitude and humility. More, I hope I never ask that question of my children. I do not want to sacrifice them to my ego—or to any god's.

JOB AND GOD

If my reflections on these works were a paper for rhetoric 101, I might merit another "D." What is my thesis? Do I have one? There is a theme emerging. Each story turns on a test. Abraham's faith in God is tested. (Pass!) Cordelia's love is tested. (Does she fail or pass, or both?) Abraham and Cordelia know they are being tested. Job does not. You could also argue that it is not Job's faith in God that is being tested, it is God's faith in Job.

In any case, the test of Job's righteousness is a private bet between the Lord and Satan, what my narrative character Maeve calls a backroom deal. For the Lord God and the Adversary, as he's called in some translations, appear to be on familiar if contentious terms.

God: Hey, where've you come from?

Satan: Oh, you know, roaming throughout the earth, going back and forth on it.

God: Have you checked out my servant Job? So upright and righteous.

Satan: Why wouldn't he be? You've given him a real sweet deal. Take it all away and he'll curse you to your face.

God: Okay, you're on. I give you power over everything he has. Do your worst. Just don't lay a finger on him.

Faites vos jeux!

When God wins that bet— *"The Lord giveth, the Lord taketh*

away, blessed be the name of the Lord"—Satan ups the ante, and God's in.

God: Do whatever you want to him. Just spare his life.

Faites vos jeux!

So Job ends up sitting in the ashes, using a pottery shard to scrape the boils that cover him crown to toe. Curse God and die, says his wife. He refuses. He has something better to do than curse. Complain. At length.

Job's thesis: The wicked prosper and the innocent suffer. It is not just. It is just the truth.

(I would add that the prospering of the wicked is often the cause of innocent suffering. Children killed by an imperial power's drone attack. Whole communities getting cancer from toxic waste dumps. And on and on.)

Job has friends, called the comforters, who actually seek to comfort themselves. They need to make moral sense of what is happening to Job (although they don't seem too concerned with the widows and orphans Job cites). They argue, "you must have done something to deserve what is happening to you. You probably deserve even worse; God is showing you mercy. God is teaching you a lesson through your suffering." The comforters (like so many of us) need to believe God is good, fair, and righteous. For them, God must stay put in what Kierkegaard calls the realm of the ethical, or "chaos is come again," to quote Othello, another tragic Shakespearean king. If you're down on your luck, it must be your own fault. Job's not having it. He won't curse God, but he is calling him out, insisting that he is innocent, and one day will be vindicated, giving us the beloved liturgical line and eschatological prophecy: "*I know that my redeemer liveth, and that he shall stand at the latter day upon the earth.*"

In my life as a prayer, I have found comfort in the story of Job. As a counselor, I have told the story many times to suffering and grieving clients. I've encouraged them to make their own complaints and accusations to whatever they call God or life, whoever/whatever they feel has betrayed and abandoned them. Then listen, listen to what comes back.

I remember RW asking me if I thought God's answer from the whirlwind was acceptable or was it outrageous. After all, God does not answer any of Job's charges, except obliquely when he excoriates the comforters: *"My wrath is kindled against thee and against thy two friends: for ye have not spoken of me the thing that is right, as my servant Job hath."* (What is the thing that is right? That God is a sonofabitch who allows injustice to go unchecked?)

I can't fully explain why I love the answer from the whirlwind. Isn't it the bluster of the God I planned to squash, the one who told Abraham to sacrifice his son, who allowed Satan to wipe out Job's family on a bet? But I do love it. I once drew a cartoon of Job in the ash pit screaming, "Why!" And the whirlwind answering, "Shit happens."

Of course the voice from whirlwind is much more eloquent and vehement, evoking the neck of the horse clothed in thunder, the hawk stretching her wings to the south, the ostrich's eggs warming in the sand, the unicorn, the wild ass, the hoary frost of heaven, the sweet influence of the Pleiades. The whirlwind speaks as the creator. When I listen, I hear the voice of creation. I am a three-year-old, arms flung wide, singing ecstatically to the surf.

In Christian theology, worshipping creation instead of, or more than, the creator is considered (at the very least) an error, maybe a sin or a heresy. God's voice from the whirlwind exhorts Job to look at creation, to marvel at its splendor, vastness, and dazzling detail. How do you know a creator except through creation? Scholarly obsession with Shakespeare's identity (how could he have been a middle-class putz from Stratford, musta been an earl or something) has always struck me as sound and fury signifying nothing. Who cares who wrote the work? Read it, stage it, experience it! If there is a creator outside of creation, crafting it and (sloppily?) creating beings who cannot handle consciousness and their precious free will, the voice from the whirlwind gives us respite from the human and divine melodrama, allowing us to remember our in/significance as part of a huge and intricate cosmos we have yet to fathom.

*

When diseases borne by Lyme ticks became epidemic in my region, I would recite to myself another line from Job: "*Yet though he slay me will I cling to him.*" (Yet though *the earth* slay me will I cling to *her*.) With climate crisis (created by human heedlessness if not downright wickedness) upon us—and not only upon us, but upon all innocent life on the planet—we have little choice but to cling to earth, yet though she slay us, though we slay her.

Despite the lethal impact of my kind, I still find comfort and mercy in the whirlwind's insistent reminder that we are small and don't know much about anything at all.

UTOPIA

There is one other memory, a little hazy, from my sophomore year that has come back to me demanding mention. The culmination of our two-year program at CBS was something called the Utopia project (since renamed Capstone). Groups of five or so students had to imagine and write about a utopia and defend their vision at an oral examination with the faculty team. (RW wasn't part of my sophomore team, but I believe he sat in on our defense.) I didn't know any of my fellow students on this project beforehand. I can picture them now and have managed to recall their names. (All the best to all of you who might prefer not to be named.) We did not become friends, exactly, nor were we enemies. We were more like survivors of a shipwreck having to figure out how to stay alive.

I don't know how it came about that we decided to go with my idea. It could be that no one else had one, because I believe (hope) I would have deferred to something more appropriate. Surely we were supposed to think of how to structure a society—politics, economy, architecture, agriculture, was there a military, that sort of thing. But somehow (and it was definitely my fault) we ended up writing about a boarding house full of misfits and outcasts. Inevitably there was some sort of redemptive, sacrificial figure. What resulted, I suspect, was a badly written, poorly organized collective novel. I don't know why we were allowed to proceed with this idea, and I don't know how we passed the oral defense. But we must have. We did not flunk out, and we went on to our junior years in good academic standing.

I include this memory because it sounds a lifelong theme that began in my father's church: the embrace of eccentrics, the inclusion of people of different racial and economic backgrounds. High Valley was a school for students—and maybe teachers—who did not fit elsewhere. When High Valley came under my care many years later, as a kind of unintentional community, it kept the same quality. And fictional Maeve founded her own version of this sort of eccentric, organic utopia at Temple Magdalen.

In short, the Utopia project was my first attempt to write about the beloved community.

ALCOHOL

It may be time to say something about alcohol and its part in my life as a prayer. My father was a functional (or maybe sometimes not so functional) alcoholic who may have had blackouts, especially in my childhood. I first got drunk at age fourteen and drank after that every chance I got. And I had more chances when I was on my own at college. During my second year at school, I also experienced blackouts.

That summer I worked at a truck farm on Martha's Vineyard and lived in a tent (where I learned not to keep food unless I wanted to be visited by skunks). About halfway through the summer, after some shame-making incident, I stopped drinking cold turkey and did not have another drink for twenty-two years.

I am not the only one who has noted the linguistic connection between spirit and spiritous liquors. Unlike some protestant denominations, Anglicans (priests especially) are not known to be teetotalers. Jesus famously turned water into wine for his first miracle. And wine (either literally or as a memorial) into blood at the Eucharist.

Whatever was past or to come, I entered my junior year of college soberer than many judges and priests.

ACROSS THE CHARLES RIVER

That summer I was accepted as a transfer student to Harvard-Radcliffe, one of twenty female students in the last year Radcliffe conducted its own separate admissions. How this happened to a high school dropout with lackluster SAT scores remains mysterious. I joke that it was arrogance. I put down "location" as the reason I wanted to go to Harvard. I did have a 4.0 average as a freshman and somehow got through my sophomore year. I suspect it was RW's recommendation (which he did not show me) that made the difference. It might not have hurt that my stated career goal was Episcopal priest at a time when women could not be ordained. Also my interviewer liked me. She informed me that I was a maverick, and Harvard needed more mavericks.

I am afraid I did not fulfill my interviewer's hopes for me at Harvard. I had no impact at all on the institution, and it had very little on me. Sometimes I regret not immersing myself in whatever I imagine the Harvard experience might be. From what I observe, then and now, it has to do with an entering class living together in the Yard as freshmen, then dispersing to the Houses, each with its own character, where lifelong friendships form. Maybe I could have joined a House as a junior, but I chose to live off-campus in Somerville, then a working-class city, literally on the other side of the tracks from the affluent Harvard neighborhoods. There was a House (Dudley) for commuters with its own master (the debonair Jean Mayer). It had a cafeteria and a library. I got to know a few people there, none so well as the kindly secretary. But we didn't share a life together. I had one close friend, a fellow transfer student, who also lived on the Somerville side of the tracks. We had our own off-campus society of two. We remain friends to this day.

Mostly I was a loner. I did not join groups I might have enjoyed—theatre, chorus. I made another attempt at joining a social action group and ended up riding the trolley to Dorchester with one other student to offer our lack of skill and utter inexperience to a startup workers' newspaper. (Did they get funding by suffering our help?) It was an unmemorable activity that did not check off any of the boxes in Matthew 25.

I worked hard at my studies and mostly did well, though thanks to some deity I took the Age of Johnson (which I still detest) pass/fail. I will never forget the lecture where the famous, histrionic professor proclaimed that our age had the same problem as Johnson's. Milton had written, Shakespeare had written. There was nothing left but commentary. He had complete and utter ignorance and indifference to anyone writing outside of the white male canon, which no one at that time had significantly challenged. I remember muttering, "Speak for yourself, buddy boy."

I loved Chaucer, Shakespeare, the Bible as literature. I remember hardly believing my luck when homework for my Victorian novel class meant lying in bed and reading fiction. But the nurturing camaraderie of CBS's team-teaching was missing. I might have found some of that if I had been in the honors program. Though my credits from BU were accepted, none were applied toward my major, so I had to meet the basic requirements and did not get to take seminars with illustrious faculty members.

My strongest memory of those two years is of solitude. I was living alone for the first time in a tiny one-room apartment. My own company was available to me in a new way, because I was sober. I took long walks up and down the hills of Somerville, gazing into backyards that were mostly gardens, flower and vegetable. In almost all the yards the Virgin Mary stood in her little half-shell grotto, her arms and palms open. Sometimes, I would be greeted kindly, usually by an older woman out working in her yard. I would stand and visit a while. Walking for miles and hours is what I did instead of joining clubs or other activities. What I discovered about myself remains true: solitude, especially solitary walking, nourishes me. Exploration exhilarates me. Just as my grandmother would take turns to find out where a road might lead her, I never feared getting lost on my rambles. I would also write about or from those solitary times. I had known I wanted to write since I was ten, but I had no idea what to write. So I just wrote. The image comes to me of a butterfly's wings pulsing as it sits still. When I remember those walks, the company I kept with myself and my journal, I know that though I may have wasted opportunities at Harvard, I was also doing exactly what I needed to do and, at the risk of sounding absurdly pious, what my soul required.

I have no recollection of praying during that time. I may have experimented with going to church, but nothing took hold.

The summer between my junior and senior year, I took a short leave from my job at the farm to take an intensive summer course. I needed to shore up another credit in order to take an elective in creative writing the spring term of my senior year. Applications (yes, you had to apply to this course) would be reviewed during the January reading period.

Over Christmas break I wrote my first substantial piece of fiction, a thirty-page story (wrong length to start with) called "The Trespasser." I don't know where this story is now, but I remember the basic plot. A little girl trespasses in the wood next door to the church. She knows she has done something wrong and is terrified that God and her father (the priest) will find out. Of course she knows the story of Abraham and Isaac. They've acted it out in Sunday School. So when her remote and frightening father takes her for a walk, she is convinced he is going to sacrifice her. I don't recall how the story ends. Probably not with a substitute ram. I do remember showing some of it to my parents. My father said it was overwritten, maybe even purple. It was bad. And whoever was reviewing submissions for this course must have agreed. The piece was rejected, and I was not admitted to the creative writing course.

FAIRY GODLOVER

If I had taken that creative writing class, would I have learned how to write the sort of short story *The New Yorker* might publish? Would I have made connections that would have helped me find success in the literary world? I still wonder sometimes, and I am also filled with wonder at how rejection from this course set me on my own course.

Having gone to summer school, I didn't need to take a fourth course for credit in order to graduate. So I took only three courses and asked the section person (that's what they were called at Harvard) of my American Literature class, if he would mentor me as a writer. He agreed.

I began to write frantically, to prove that I could, pages and pages about people who might have lived in the Somerville neighborhoods I walked, people about whose lives I knew nothing. Maybe my father was right; reality was grim, and I didn't know a thing about it.

(Note: I am not a proponent of the "write what you know" school in any strict sense. I have written—convincingly, I hope—about first-century brothels and battles. It is different to write about things you haven't lived in your own era.)

I had no illusions that these attempted stories were going any-where. I had no idea how to plot them or inhabit them. Yet I showed them to my mentor anyway. It is significant that I trusted him enough, maybe trusted *myself* enough, to let him see my failures.

I can still picture his face as he sat across from me in some Harvard Square café. How to describe the look of someone who is about to tell you the truth, who is about to change your life? I don't remember what he said about the stories I'd attempted. Did he just shake his head? Somehow he indicated that the writing I'd shown him wasn't worth critiquing. Then he spoke the words that opened the way to the rest of my life.

"You need to think about fairytales. There are only five or six plots in the world."

He gave me a copy of Peter S. Beagle's novel, *The Last Unicorn*, and sent me on my way.

I went home and spent the weekend alone, reading the novel, and thinking. More than thinking, I was discovering, rediscovering my own imaginative terrain. On my bookshelf were The Chronicles of Narnia. On my wall hung a child's Map of Make Believe that I'd picked up at a yard sale. I have it still and continue to ponder it, with its compass depicting West of the Sun, East of the Moon, seas where mermaids sing and strange fishes live, impossible pinnacles topped with shacks or castles. Cows jumping over the moon, bright-eyed bears lurking in the woods.

I had bought a heather plant in bloom. I remember gazing at it till it was huge as a forest. I remembered all the tricks and gifts of imagination. And I pondered fairytales, the five or six plots of the world. I still do, whenever I lose my way in a story. Questing, risking danger, seeing through deceptive appearances, stopping to perform acts of kindness for animals and beggars, lost children, lost mothers, lost worlds, forgetting, remembering, sacrifice and redemption, death and resurrection. Enough to ponder for a lifetime.

Monday morning, on my way to school, walking down Laurel Street to Somerville Avenue, a story arrived: children who had lost their mother, and even more disturbingly, did not know who or where she was. Their frightening father had kept her a secret. I will never forget that moment, the story so vivid in my imagination as well as a heightened awareness of my surroundings. Even broken glass in the gutters and wind-blown trash remain in my memory. By the time I got to school, the six main characters had assembled, the human characters. And one who was other than, more than human: Lilith, the wild mother.

Thank you to C. S. Lewis for the intriguing mention of the one he called mother of demons and Djinns, all that looks human but is not. Thank you to Judith Plaskow for retelling of the myth of the garden of Eden with a twist, the alliance of Lilith and Eve. Thank you to Nana, my feisty grandmother, who became Ionia and Fred's Grammar. Thank you to all the influences and elements, known and unknown, that gave me *The Wild Mother*.

Thank you to my fairygodlover, for so he was.

Not long after that conversation, I wrote a narrative poem about a dragon to demonstrate the meaning of objective correlative. I have little memory of the poem, but when I showed it to my mentor, he gave me a second gift.

"You don't have write a term paper," he said. "Write whatever you want."

On spring break of my senior year, I stayed with Miss Sang. In the room with the sleigh bed, I sat at an old desk, next to the low windows under the sloping eve, and I wrote the first two chapters of *The Wild Mother*.

*

Graduation loomed. Jobs, graduate schools, careers. It seems, from reading class notes over the years, that the vast majority of my classmates became doctors and lawyers. I had no desire to fulfill my father's thwarted ambition to go to graduate school for English. I already knew that graduate students spent the first year reading the history of literary criticism. A dissertation would involve writing the same. I had a hard enough time writing five-page analytic essays.

How to make my way as an adult in the adult world? My only plan? Finish writing *The Wild Mother* in one summer, and then get a job on a cargo ship, sail around the world. Fold the map of make believe into my pocket and go.

Not long before graduation, I was sitting, curled in a deep window in Dudley House, showing a fair bit of bare leg. The master of Dudley House stopped and surveyed me.

"So Elizabet," he said in his French accent. "I understand you want to be an Episcopal minister."

"No," I corrected him. "I am going to be a writer."

He remembered, and when he called me up to receive my diploma, he kindly said, "Elizabet Cunningham, a budding writer."

CHAPTER FOUR

ANGLICAN

ADULT CHILD

LONGING

A particular memory distills the essence of this time for me.

I am sitting with the choir, now in the back of the church where the new tracker-action organ takes up the entire back wall, obscuring a stained-glass window of Mary Magdalen. We are singing an offertory anthem by Richard Shephard, "*My eyes for beauty pine, my soul for Goddes' grace.*" Light shines through the east windows. A wooden cross of Christ Triumphant gazes at us from the altar down the length of the church. This song moves me to tears that I keep unshed behind my eyes.

Pining for beauty, longing for grace, longing for a lover, longing for adventure, longing (still) to find myself stepping across some boundary from one world into another, longing to have a baby. Longing. Different threads of longing twining together, hardly distinguishable one from another, except in certain lights. Longing as an unspoken prayer.

GRACE PERIOD

I spent the summer after graduation with Miss Sang. I got up every morning at 5:30, took a walk up and down a hill, then wrote for a couple of hours before breakfast. Which she made for me. After breakfast I went back to work for several more hours. I believe I helped with the other meals. Ostensibly, I was helping by keeping Miss Sang company as she cleared her attic of generations of treasures in preparation for selling her house. Now in her early seventies, she had decided it was time to sort through everything, while she still had the strength, and move to an apartment in the village.

How generous she was to share her beloved home with me as she prepared to let it go. I hope I was a good guest and companion. Yet if there is a honeymoon period in all friendships, I suspect ours ended that summer. There were many things she could not approve of in me. "Forgive me, dear," I remember her saying, "but I think you are interested in sex for its own sake. I never was." She told me things she may have regretted telling me about her past. My tendency to question and to assert uninformed opinions must have irritated her. And I came to realize that her opinions, so long formed, were perhaps a bit rigid. She liked to say that some people were ruled by the head and some by the heart. There was a great gulf fixed between the two. She sympathized with my heart, however disordered its affections might be. But my head must have been disquieting to her.

Still, deep affection abided. I picture sitting with her in the late afternoon light listening to Vaughan Williams's "Fantasia on the Old 104th Psalm." We often read aloud to each other in the evening. I can still hear her voice intoning from *David Copperfield*, "Oh my lungs and liver, oh my eyes and limbs!" We also listened to recordings of Yeats' poems. On probably more than one occasion, I unintentionally provided comic relief. She loved to cook, and mostly I loved to eat whatever she made. One day a bright red tomato aspic appeared on the lunch table. I asked dubiously:

"Isn't that what Cleopatra killed herself with?"

"What, dear? Heavens, no!" She started to laugh. "That was an asp, not an aspic."

In gales of laughter, she began to intone dramatically.

"I clasp this aspic to my bosom."

I can still hear her laughter, and I still laugh out loud when I remember.

JUST WRITE

In September Miss Sang moved into a second-story apartment in the village of Millbrook. Even in that unremarkable architectural space, she created the same beauty and grace that had filled the old farmhouse. We continued to meet almost daily.

For it had become apparent to me that I was not going to dash off *The Wild Mother* in a summer. Wanting a semblance of independence and adulthood, I moved to a room in a somewhat sleazy boarding house on the edge of village, which may have been a front for various illicit activities. I had no kitchen or kitchen privileges; I cooked oatmeal over a sterno flame, but so many kindly people invited me to meals, I suffered no ill effects from my limited cooking. I could afford the rent on my earnings as a part-time nanny to three children (ages four, two, and newborn). I had a beautiful view of the Catskills, and I could walk across a field into the enchanted wood of my childhood, then step over the gap in the wall to the churchyard where I'd grown up.

That same month I helped sort the epic donations to the annual church rummage sale, alongside familiar adults (once "the grownups") who welcomed me into their midst. That's where I was on September 16th 1976, when I heard the news that the Episcopal General Convention had ruled in favor of women's ordination. I was jubilant on behalf of my gender—and hugely relieved. For myself. Thank God, I thought, I don't have to do it, I never have to do it, be the first woman Episcopal priest in the long line of male priests. I don't have to prove a point. I can be a writer. I can just be a writer.

NOT MY FATHER'S CHURCH

Yet for those two years I spent in my hometown, I was more thoroughly Anglican than at any other time in my life. My involvement with the church could be explained by my having no other life. No car, no phone, no friends my own age, no romance. (Except the romance of at least physical renunciation. Yes, that's a reference to the fairygodlover.) No likely prospects even for a date. It was all too easy to identify with the Anglican wives and spinsters in Barbara Pym's newly reissued novels, all of which I read. But I suspect there was more to my immersion (or re-immersion) in the church, Grace Church in particular, where my lambs had been stolen, where I had drunk the ashes of the spray-painted golden calf.

It was no longer my father's church. Though my mother still sang in the choir, my father did supply work at various area churches. Father Beaven (unlike my father, he did use that title "Father") was not my father's immediate successor. He'd arrived a few years later with his wife Margaret and their three sons; the eldest and I had both gone to school in Boston. Our whole families were friends. Now Father Beaven was, so to speak, my priest. He was also a weaver and a musician who composed settings for the liturgy. An excellent listener, not inclined to judge or give opinions, he was available for informal pastoral counsel.

I rejoined the choir as an alto. The superb organ, Miss Schultze's dream fulfilled posthumously, had attracted the excellent musician and choir director Merellyn Gallagher. Grace Church hosted many concerts with visiting musicians and choirs.

Lois Rigoulot, a fellow alto and the village librarian, offered me my second part-time job as a library assistant. In her mid-thirties, with beautiful long hair wound into a classic bun, she might have been a heroine in one of Pym's novels. She had a keen sense of humor and a particular passion for children's literature. We both loved Graham Oakley's series about Anglican church mice and the long-suffering church cat (who sometimes forgot he was a Christian).

Lois also joined the ranks of those who fostered and fed me. Every Sunday evening I read aloud to her from the novel-in-progress, benefiting tremendously from her questions and comments. Then I stayed for supper with her and her aged—and hilarious—mother, a store of arcane lore. For example, a gentleman should "never offer a lady a hot seat," that is, one still warm from his posterior. Instead, he must escort her to a cooler chair. Lois is one of the three people to whom *The Wild Mother* is dedicated.

Though my parents lived only a few miles out of town and I saw them regularly, I have almost no memories of my father from this time. The embrace of all those kindly adults, Miss Sang, Lois Rigoulot, the Beavens, must have protected me from his judgment and criticism. I joined parish committees and study groups. Without being asked or intentionally volunteering, I found myself visiting a number of shut-ins every week. I carried my weight as a parishioner. I also felt free and encouraged to explore the contemplative tradition of Christianity, defined as gazing at or being aware of the Divine— what my grandmother might have viewed as woolgathering or my father might have dismissed with contempt as preoccupation with individual salvation. Although it seemed to me salvation was beside the point of contemplation. As far as I could understand (or not understand), the quest of the contemplative was a transforming, even obliterating relationship with God, an epic love affair.

I read many books by on mysticism by the British writer Evelyn Underhill. I attempted the mystical classics, Brother Lawrence's *The Practice of the Presence of God*, the anonymously authored *Cloud of Unknowing*, Theresa of Avila's *Interior Castle*. Not that I retain much from any of those works, except feisty Theresa's famous retort to God after sliding down a mudbank in a rainstorm, "If that's how you treat your friends, no wonder you have so few." I steeped myself in C. S. Lewis's Christian apologetics, which likewise did not make a lasting impression with the exception of *The Great Divorce*. To this day, if I am in conflict with someone I ask myself whether or not I'd refuse to disembark from the bus from hell if I had to greet that person. I was delighted to learn that my favorite author had written novels for adults. I have reread *Till We Have Faces* and *That Hideous Strength* as many times as The Chronicles of Narnia.

DOUBLE LIFE

As important or more important than anything else, I was also learning my craft, immersing myself daily in the life of a story, leading two lives, something that has always been necessary for my mental health. To say that you are writing a book is misleading, it implies that you are in control, that you are acting upon your material. It would be equally inaccurate to say that the story writes itself, that the writer is a passive scribe or channeler. To write a story is to enter into a relationship with something mysterious and alive. That aliveness, quirkiness, that encounter with an other, who is both within you and other-than-you, is also how I have come to experience prayer.

One year turned into two. I moved from the outlying boarding house into basement rooms under an antique shop next door to the library. Still no kitchen but room for a record player. Room to dance to the music of Marvin Gaye, Aretha Franklin, other favorite rhythm-and-blues artists. Room to remember the life I wasn't living. Maybe never had lived but, yes, longed for. I did not know how to bring the part of myself that danced into the confines of Anglican orthodoxy. The music that moved me came from a culture and an experience I had no claim to, though it first laid claim to me at age fourteen when I worked as a volunteer at the inner-city daycare center in Poughkeepsie, the job arranged by my father. I was walking down a ghetto street, past unemployed men on stoops, when I first heard Stevie Wonder blaring from an open window and saw a little girl in a pink dress and diaper dancing on the sidewalk. My father's and grandfather's passion for social justice remained part of me, though I had no idea how to fulfill their legacy.

I began to have bouts of bewilderment and frustration over finding myself celibate, living alone in the small town where I grew up. When I visited close friends who had moved to New York City, one for a job, one to attend seminary, I sometimes felt shame at my sheltered, church-bound existence. Was I *really* an adult or was I developing a case of arrested development?

Questions and contradictions piled up about the divide between my father's social gospel and my drive to write (alone in a room doing no good for anyone!), the alchemy of sublimation, the urgent need for experience.

Among those contradictions, maybe at their root, was this one: *"The spirit is willing but the flesh is weak,"* words ascribed to Jesus. I had once quoted them to my fairygodlover. He answered, "But you have the fleshiest spirit and the most spiritual flesh." I did not know then, not consciously, that healing this split between flesh and spirit, finding God in a lover, and a lover in God would become a quest, a theme with variations that would play out in my life and work for years to come.

GRATEFUL

Looking back, I am grateful for the chance I had to know the church and religion of my childhood as a young adult. If I did not fully succeed in becoming a devout Anglican, I gave myself, for that time, to devotion, singing in the choir, taking my turn watching alone in the church from Maundy Thursday to Holy Saturday, the Passion story seeping deeper and deeper into my psyche as I entered into the yearly liturgical drama.

I did not make much progress reconciling with the first member of the Trinity. Only Dorothy Sayers ever made sense of the Trinity for me, translating it as creative process: the father as idea/creator of the whole, complete and abstract; the son, the blood, sweat, tears, and sacrifice of making it into form; the holy spirit, releasing the work into the world where it becomes part of other people's lives.

Determined to be a Creed-saying Christian, I must have recited, perhaps through gritted teeth, the first line of the Nicene Creed, "*I believe in God the Father.*" Although I no longer recite the Creed, I still admire the comma that was inserted in the last line of God the Father's opening stanza. The Book of Common Prayer was in revision during my adult years at Grace Church. I was thrilled by this debate: Should the line read, "*maker of heaven and earth/of all that is seen and unseen*" or "*maker of heaven and earth/of all that is, seen and unseen*"? The comma prevailed. Though surely the comma did nothing to alleviate human suffering, it made a difference to me, a lover of language, its sound and rhythm.

When I think of my time as an Anglican, bringing forth my first novel, I am grateful to Betty Sang, Lois Rigoulot and to all the members of Grace Church who welcomed me back, accepted me, nurtured me, and then let me go again. I bless their memories.

THE NEEDLE'S EYE

Now comes a part of this story that is hard for me to tell, that raises issues and questions I struggle with still. It also curiously and paradoxically involves my father and the only clear memory I have of him from this time in my life, one that he helped to bring to a close, opening the way to the next.

I was not the most practical person (though as I grew further into adulthood I cultivated that quality). I had no plans but to write what I sometimes called the Great American Victorian English Novel which would surely, swiftly and rightfully, take its place on the *New York Times* Bestseller List. Two years into the writing, I had discarded the idea of a cargo ship. I just wanted to go somewhere I might still have a youth and, to put it crudely, get laid. My sister was graduating from the New England Conservatory of music. There was some talk of our moving to New York City together.

I do not remember the order of events, but one day around that time of decision and transition, my father told me that my maternal grandfather had left money in trust for his grandchildren, having made a canny investment at just the right time. My father reckoned there was enough for me to be able to take a small monthly income.

I was shocked and disoriented. I had never heard about this money—though the fact that I had never worried about money or been lectured on the importance of earning a good living should have been a clue. Was I spoiled or unworldly or both? My first thought was, I have to give it all away, like St. Francis. I cannot possibly accept a privilege other people don't have, one that I have not earned. Jesus as much as said so. I would be a fat overladen camel who could not squeeze through the Needle's Eye (a narrow gate in Jerusalem), let alone enter into the Kingdom of Heaven. I am sure I made this case to my father. I thought I was speaking his language.

He was not unkind (a bit unusual), but he was unmoved. I cannot recall his counter argument or why he would make it. I wonder now if he had found himself in the same predicament, his meagre salary subsidized by my mother's unearned wealth. It is also possible that he wanted to cut the apron strings, give me a chance to manage my own finances, which I had done, but marginally. It crosses my mind that he wanted the nest thoroughly emptied, not just extended to basement rooms with no kitchen a few miles away. My mother, I believe, may have been angry (in her cold, silent way) that my father had taken it on himself to help me to financial independence. But once it was done, it was done. I had a decision to make. A conscious decision.

I kept the money. I took the income. It was not enough money that I didn't have to work, but it was enough that I didn't have to worry—which is a huge gift that so many people never get to enjoy. It meant that instead of pursuing a conventional career, I could go on having flexible day jobs while I continued to write. Paradoxically, my father's revelation and encouragement made it possible for me to pursue a vocation he continued to excoriate. And excoriate is not too strong a word.

*

My sister and I found two tiny, unbelievably cheap studio apartments on West 155 St. in a building full of musicians where a friend of the Beavens lived. There was just enough room for a single bed and a table, but there was a kitchenette, complete with cockroaches, and a window with a view of the building's armpit. Making up for the cramped quarters was the Hudson River just across the street.

We moved at the end of July. I don't remember how we moved or who helped us. I do remember what happened the day before.

HIGH VALLEY REVISITED

A couple of days before I was to move to New York City, I went to pay a farewell visit to Olga. I didn't have a car, so Paul Beaven, Father Beaven's youngest son, drove me. High Valley was always a place where people just dropped in, so we had not called ahead. As it was a hot day in July, we also planned to take a swim. Olga wasn't there when we arrived, so we swam out to the raft in the middle of the pond. In a little while, someone else splashed into the water.

It was Olga's son, Douglas. I had seen him once or twice at parties but never spoken with him. When I was ten years old, attending High Valley Camp, I had been warned by others to stay away from him, because "he snaps people's butts with a towel." Over the years I had seen his picture in the music room and compared him unfavorably with his younger cousin Bob. I had also more recently heard

Olga lament that Douglas just wasn't good with people. Now that he was getting divorced, he was going to become more and more isolated, lose touch with his daughter and everyone. Sigh...

Douglas pulled himself onto the raft. It may have taken him awhile to remember who I was (his mother's former tweeny maid). I don't remember what we talked about until I mentioned that my friend Lois Rigoulot was considering going to seminary.

"Are you a *Christian*?!" he asked, startled, maybe affronted, curious.

Bravely, perhaps recalling the much greater peril of Christians facing lions for the entertainment of Romans, I answered, "Yes."

There followed a debate, which Paul Beaven watched as if it were a tennis volley, about belief and meaning. I heard for the first time, but not the last, that Douglas's father Julian was affronted by the very idea of souls. "What is a soul, you can't see it, you can't hear it, you can't smell it...." I later learned that Douglas's grandparents had been Swedenborgian mystics. His father's rabid atheism was a violent reaction against their religion. Douglas was less insistent. He had read scientific studies that persuaded him that ESP, as he called it, might exist. But not anything that could be called God or ulti-mate reality.

"There is no meaning but what human beings make," he insisted.

So dang androcentric. I later discovered both he, and his father before him, believed only humans were capable of thought and feel-ing. But that was not my argument that day. My *coup de grace* (as I thought of it) was this:

"If there is a door, and you can't see what is on the other side of it, does it follow that there is nothing there?"

That is as much of the conversation as I recall. I do know, and it became a standing joke, that we both thought we had won the argument. Apart from satisfaction that I had bested him (I rehashed the debate with Paul on the drive home), I did not give the matter or the man any further thought. I was taken aback when he called the next day to invite me to go to Tanglewood. Eee gads, a *date*?! With Olga's *son*? Fourteen years older than me!

"I'm moving to New York tomorrow," I told him. "How about a raincheck?"

Two days later, he rang the buzzer of my new apartment.

I won't go into detail about the courtship, his blunders, my resistance, what finally changed my mind. Oh, all right, when I thought I might be pregnant—and, mind you, I always thought I might be pregnant, regardless of whether or not I'd had sex, just ask the Virgin Mary—he did not say, as I expected, "How do you feel about abortion?" He said, "I'd want to marry you." This, from a man who had recently said he wanted no more children.

An angel, a daemon, something whispered in my inner ear, "Isn't this what you've been longing for, a lover, a child?"

It has been a long more-than-forty years. But whenever I think I've made a mistake, I remember a poem Douglas wrote for me not long after we met, and I know I made the right choice.

> You live in this world
> and another of your making
> your clear eyes, double-sighted

NEW YORK, NEW YORK

After a brief, deliriously happy idyll in August, Douglas went back to Florida, where he taught political science at the University of Central Florida, and we began a long-distance relationship. My life in New York never fulfilled any of my wild fantasies. I worked all morning on revisions of *The Wild Mother*, then went to my job at the Hungarian Pastry Shop all afternoon and evening. (I was promoted from waitress to manager and had to stay as long as it took to balance cash in and cash out on my shift.) I was relieved to turn down the men I seemed to attract—an awkward seminarian and a slightly more appealing Episcopal priest in the middle of a divorce. (Did an odor of Anglican sanctity still cling to me amidst the fumes of cappuccino and hamantasch?)

Across the street from the pastry shop loomed the Cathedral of St. John the Divine. I began to see, as my therapist, an Anglican nun who'd been ordained a priest and served as a canon at the cathedral. Ginger-haired, feisty Sister Mary Michael was originally from Texas. Whenever I would describe some problematic feeling or behavior, she would lean in a little closer, cock her head just slightly and ask (pronouncing both the "w" and the "h"), "*What* does that *do* for you?"—her point being that every dysfunction also has a function. (To this day, I put on my best Mary Michael twang and address that question to clients.) My mother always accused me of liking to shock people. Mary Michael delighted in shocking me. I don't remember what we were talking about, but I will never forget her shrugging and saying dismissively, "I know lots of fuckin' priests."

I would see her on occasion for years to come. And though it is out of sequence, I find I want to remember here one more thing she said. After my first miscarriage, I was lamenting that the baby never got to live, and she said, "You cannot measure the meaning of a life by its length. Look how this life has changed your life."

*

I lived only a short time in New York City beside what I called the Great River (even before I knew the indigenous name Mahicantuck, I did not like to call it after a European explorer). Douglas and I had become serious. We wrote letters and had horribly expensive phone calls (due to his still-horrendous abrupt phone manner which took twenty minutes each time to overcome). I don't know when we decided that I should leave New York to live with him in Florida, but that is what I did the following March.

I understand better now the pain this decision might have

caused the people who had cared for me so lovingly during my time in Millbrook, particularly Miss Sang and Lois Rigoulot. The former knew I had made what she considered mistakes in the past. Now I was going to live with someone outside of, or anyway before, marriage, because eventual marriage, if not yet proposed, was on the table. It may be hard for anyone from my generation to credit, but for two years I had lived a seemingly chaste and devout life. I sensed Miss Sang's quiet disappointment and perhaps determined suspension of judgment. Lois was not quiet, and one day she shocked me more than Mary Michael could ever hope to. In the middle of the library, where I had come to visit her, and where people are supposed to be soft-spoken, she confronted me at a volume no one could fail to hear.

"DO NOT DO THIS THING."

This thing being moving to Florida to live unmarried with Douglas, who was, moreover, not a Christian. I don't remember how long the conversation went on or what, if anything, I said in my defense, but I do remember her prophetic declaration:

"YOU WILL LOSE YOUR FAITH!"

SHACKED UP

Douglas and I lived in a literal shack built on the architectural plan of a double-wide trailer. It had no insulation, no air-conditioning, and the water stank of sulfur. (We bought drinking water.) It was in the middle of commercial agricultural fields—celery and citrus mostly. Anything that wasn't cultivated or mowed was jungle. Our windows were screened but that didn't keep out the no-see-ums. When it was hot (so hot!) we had to choose between wearing too many clothes or getting bitten. Outside we had to be careful of fire ants. And the windshields of our cars (I had a used VW bug with no floor in the back) were plastered with love bugs. Still, I liked where we lived better than the suburban sprawl, heavily trafficked multi-lane highways with their disorienting repetition of chain stores and fast-food restaurants.

I was experiencing major culture shock, social isolation (though we did make close friends with neighbors at the end of our sandy road, Jehovah's Witnesses who lived in an actual trailer. They loved to tease us northern vegetarians with tales about eating rattlesnakes, possum, and armadillo). Apart from the neighbors, and until I found a day job, I saw no one. Whatever Douglas believed or didn't believe, I was still an Episcopalian. I went looking for a church. I don't remember how many I tried. I do remember I liked the drive to Sanford, an older town with houses built for the climate. I don't remember anything about the church service, whether I liked it or not. But the rector chatted me up afterwards, and I must have given him quite a bit of information. He asked if he could make a pastoral call.

One day he pulled into our yard. I can't tell you what he was driving, just that he was tall, so tall (Douglas and I are both short) and dressed in full priestly regalia, a clerical color and a huge pectoral cross that could have doubled as a lethal weapon. We invited him inside our shack, where he seemed even bigger, and our furniture too small to comfortably accommodate him. We served him tea as he ran down his agenda.

Was I a demon worshipper?

I felt confused by this question until he pointed out that Lilith (the central character in *The Wild Mother*) was a demon. Apparently I had mentioned the novel at coffee hour. I am not sure how I answered this question. Did I explain that to me Lilith was innocent, wild, never having eaten the apple? Was he reassured? Probably only of my naiveté.

Next he asked if we knew that we were living in sin. (At that point, Douglas, newly divorced, had not yet asked me to marry him.) Again, I do not remember what either of us answered.

Since I was, at least, a Christian and an Episcopalian, however errant, our guest moved on to Douglas's beliefs. Douglas confessed he was an agnostic.

"Ha!" the priest said. "Do you know what agnostic is in Latin?"

He didn't wait for us to answer.

"Ignoramus!" he almost shouted, slapping his knee in glee, and rocking back and forth in triumphant mirth. "Ignoramus!"

At that point, Douglas and I were speechless. The priest carried on the conversation unaided, confiding in us that he had received the gift of tongues.

Having run down his list of topics, he rose to leave. We walked him out to his car, at which point he turned to me and said, "I trust I'll see you next Sunday. It really hurts my feelings when people don't come back after I've called on them."

As I recall, words failed me, and I made some polite, ambiguous noises.

I did not go back to his church.

Though I was still on the parish rolls of Grace Church, my days as an Anglican were drawing to a close.

CHAPTER FIVE

QUAKER

THE WOMB OF SILENCE

We are sitting in a carpeted room, maybe a dozen or so people, somewhere in Winter Park, Florida. It's not a meeting house; I can't remember now whether it was part of a college or some other complex. There's a beige carpet, light coming in through long windows, an assortment of chairs and couches arranged so that we sit in a circle. In silence.

This is not the first Quaker Meeting I've attended. There are Quakers on my mother's side of the family. I attended her second cousin's wedding when I was a child. That meeting house, which I believe was in Philadelphia, looked more like a conventional Protestant church with pews facing forward. My mother's cousin sat in front with her groom, wearing a simple white dress. She had very dark hair held in a bun at the nape of her neck. The thing I remember most is her cheeks, so rosy, probably naturally. There was no music, no priest. Every now and then, someone stood and spoke, women as well as men.

Winter Park Meeting is a small group, a splinter from the larger Orlando Meeting. I am arrested by the face of the woman sitting across from me. The sorrow in it, the pain. It could be the face of Christ on the Cross. She is older than me but younger than many of the others. The silence goes on and on. Then suddenly speech erupts from an elderly man.

"I was reading Aeschylus at dawn." (He has a British accent and pronounces it *EEschylus*.) He proceeds to quote in Greek at some length. At last he subsides and the silence settles over us again.

Even at what Friends call "popcorn meetings," where many (perhaps too many) people feel moved by the spirit to speak, there is silence between messages. As I discovered in the weeks to come, these blasts of *EEschylus* were a regular occurrence. I still smile at the memory of an older woman with a genteel Southern accent speaking from the silence, "I'd like the translation."

The man who read Aeschylus at dawn was apparently hard of hearing, or perhaps the Spirit thought translation unnecessary, for it was never forthcoming.

*

My relationship with the Religious Society of Friends (Quakers) began in that quirky little meeting and continued for the next fifteen years. When I think of that time, I see the confluence of many streams, waterfalls, rapids, turbulence over the deeper flow of silence. From that first Meeting, I felt the power of sitting in a circle, facing others, not a priest, or a raised altar, or a cross above that. God was in our midst, God was in us, and any one of us could bring a message from the divine, a message welling up from shared silence.

Moreover, this contemplative worship has inspired Friends to active ministries of social justice for hundreds of years. Wasn't this the balance I had been seeking?

I WAS IN PRISON AND YE VISITED ME....

The woman with the tortured face turned out to be a brilliant fiber artist and poet with a wicked sense of humor. Johanna and her husband, Steve, became our closest friends in Florida. Though Douglas did not attend Quaker Meeting, all four of us completed training in a Quaker-based program called Alternatives to Violence, designed to be offered in prisons.

The training involved an intensive three days of community building and practice in conflict resolution through a variety of exercises including role play. It also featured something called the "Transforming Power Rap," created by founder Larry Apsey, a slight white-haired man in his eighties. Quakers had distilled Matthew 25 to a single sentence, "There is that of God in everyone." If you could connect with that part of a person, you had the chance to transform the most volatile situations. Conflict escalates into violence (physical or otherwise) partly because of predictable reactions. Therefore it can be neutralized or transformed by an unexpected response—humor, kindness, a willingness to listen—in short, openness to grace. Lots of principles and practice, but no formula. A practical guide to creating and sustaining the beloved community.

Before we left Florida, we joined with Johanna and Steve to facilitate an Alternatives to Violence Workshop in a detention facility for underage offenders. When Douglas and I moved back to New York State, we became part of the Alternatives to Violence community and participated in many workshops in a maximum-security prison, often cofacilitating with inmate trainers, one of whom later became our son's Godfather.

It was not difficult to see "that of God," Jesus himself, in the inmates we met. Prison is constructed physically and psychologically to intimidate, humiliate, depress, and debilitate, and it often succeeds too well. The wonder is that it also fails. I don't think the exercises, raps, and role plays mattered all that much in themselves except that they created a container for expression and witness. I witnessed what my father would have called "grim reality," even though I would never experience it directly. I witnessed the injustice of what the inmates called the criminal "just us" system, referring to overwhelmingly disproportionate numbers of black and brown people in prison. I also witnessed brilliance, humor, passion, talent, and humanity that survived, despite having been locked up for the sake of what has become a for-profit industry.

MEETING

Douglas and I got married in December 1979 during his winter break from teaching, nine months after we moved in together in Florida. We returned to Millbrook for our wedding at Grace Church with Father Beaven and Sister Mary Michael presiding. We used the Order for Marriage from the Book of Common Prayer. At Douglas's request, Father Beaven reluctantly omitted references to Father, Son, and Holy Spirit. Douglas's few experiences of attending the Episcopal church made him feel like "an anthropologist observing a strange cult." The pastoral visit from the Floridian priest hadn't helped. Inspired by my attendance at Quaker meeting, I asked if we could arrange the pews in a circle. Father Beaven's three sons did all the heavy lifting before and after. I can still picture how beautiful the church looked with facing pews.

Six months after our wedding, we moved back to Dutchess County, Douglas having decided not to pursue tenure he felt he was unlikely to be awarded at a university where he had never fit in well with students or faculty. We rented a house from Olga. I went to work at High Valley as a drama teacher and part-time cook. Douglas began a long, varied career as an adjunct professor at several area colleges, including teaching at correctional facilities as well managing the land his mother had placed in a state forestry program.

Not long after we returned, Douglas and I both began to attend Bullshead Friends Meeting, located in an old schoolhouse in a grove of pines, about a fifteen-minute drive from our home. Larry Apsey and several others active in the Alternative to Violence Program were members, so we were greeted by familiar faces. A larger meeting than the one in Winter Park, Florida, about thirty people attended meeting each First Day (as Sunday was called). I can still picture all their faces and remember their voices. I probably closed my eyes sometimes, as many Friends do during silent worship, but I must have kept them open much of the time. I don't think I stared. Everyone was so present in the silence. To sit in expectant shared silence is a rare and deep way to come to know people.

When we first arrived, the old schoolhouse was the only building. Monthly Meeting for Worship with a Concern for Business, as it was called, was also held there with Friends eating their bag lunches together as the clerk of the meeting presided—the clerk being whoever had agreed to serve when requested to do so by the nominating committee. I soon learned the Quaker joke, "God so loved the world He did not send a committee." Unlike some programmed Quaker meetings, silent meetings have no paid clergy. All members are responsible for ministry. There is a committee for everything: ministry and counsel, faith and practice, peace and social justice, hospitality, buildings and grounds, finance, and more. Each committee makes a report at Monthly Meeting for Business. No decision is made without "a sense of the meeting." The secular term is consensus process. For Friends, it is more than human consensus. A core tenant of Quaker faith and practice is corporate discernment of Divine will. Meeting for Business is as sacred and divinely guided as silent worship

Though I sometimes felt impatient with the leisurely pace of the clerk, which I later recognized as consummate skill, I soon developed a fascination and respect for this nonhierarchical, egalitarian decision-making process. The clerk's first task is to ensure that every person is heard. There is no interrupting, no cross talk, no repetition by any individual of a point she's already made. The voluble and verbally facile don't get to dominate, and the reticent don't get to hold back. No action is taken until everyone consents to a decision.

*

The Quaker practice of corporate discernment dates to Quakerism's founding in seventeenth-century England. As colonists in what became the United States, the early Friends must have encountered indigenous nations with similar practices. The Haudenosaunee, also known as the Iroquois confederation, made decisions by consensus. In the early days of settlement, Quakers generally had a better relationship with indigenous peoples than the Puritans. I wonder if their common approach to decision-making created an affinity. And of course Quakers did not see indigenous people as Godless savages but as bearers of the Divine light that is in each person.

Before attending a Friend's Meeting for Business, I had only participated in groups run by Robert's Rules of Order, the procedure whereby a group makes a motion that is put to a vote. Democracy, the rule of the people, is in fact the rule of whoever is in the majority. There is always a winning and a losing side, and the losers are usually unhappy, to say the least, and don't have the same stake in the outcome as the winners. It is hard to imagine a large nation making decisions by consensus. It remains a radical idea and ideal. In my time with Quakers, I was to witness and participate in the challenges of consensus process even in a relatively small and homogenous society.

From Friends' long history of corporate discernment come turns of phrase that I still treasure:

> That Friend speaks to my condition.
> I have a Stop in my mind [a way of expressing a doubt not quite formed].
> Waiting on the Spirit.
> To stand aside [a means of expressing reservations but not blocking a decision].

To stand in the way [one person alone can block the
whole group if conscience dictates].
To labor with [what Friends do when someone stands
in the way].
And my favorite expression: Way will open.

*

I wonder now if the people who had welcomed and nurtured
me at Grace Church felt that I had abandoned them. I could as
easily have driven to church on Sunday morning as to Bullshead
Meeting. I still visited Miss Sang, the Beavens, and Lois Rigoulot,
but I was no longer part of their community. I suspect I was also full
of young adult satisfaction. I had found a place of worship where
my "ignoramus" husband was willing to join me. Though Quakers
began as a radical Christian sect, there were, at that time, plenty of
universalist Friends, even a smattering of atheists. In Meeting for
Worship, finding God in the faces of those around me, I felt safe
from the God looming in the darkness over the pulpit, and from the
thundercloud God of the desert. My grandfathers in heaven, if not
exactly smiling, surely could not frown upon the Religious Society of
Friends with their passionate commitment to justice. I gave myself
wholly to Bullshead Meeting, where I became a member and took
on full responsibilities as such.

The only one of my Episcopal family and friends to visit
Meeting was my father. He did supply work at smaller churches and
had a free Sunday now and then. I will never forget his one visit.
How strange and wonderful to see my father sitting on one of the
back benches in the little meeting house, in the shared silence, the
light filtered by the pines coming through the plain windows. How
warmly Friends greeted him afterwards, some of whom had met
him in various places over the years as fellow activists. I thanked him

for coming, and he said, dismissively, "The silence didn't do anything for me. I just recited the liturgy in my head."

I don't remember how or if I answered my father. My own head is rarely without words. More experienced Friends would talk about how they quieted their minds. I could sense it happening in the meeting house, the silence deepening like a leaf falling slowly to the forest floor. Maybe, without knowing it, I learned to watch the thoughts come and go. I came to recognize when a spoken message wanted to come through me by how it felt in my body. And I would wait to see if the signs would subside before I spoke. Sometimes I resonated with other people's spoken ministry, and sometimes I didn't. But I always appreciated that the offerings were born of some trembling necessity. (Yes, quaking!)

I do have one wordless memory that I will translate into words. My eyes were open. I remember the dust motes in the light. I had been noticing one of the children, nestled in her mother's arms. The wind outside rose and fell, now and then a bench creaked. I felt in my body the passage of time, life moving through me, generations of life. How swift life suddenly seemed, how continuous, how intimate and impersonal all at once.

My father's words have stayed with me, not because they were belittling, but because over time they revealed something about what happened to me in Meeting for Worship. In the wordless, creedless womb of silence, something began to gestate in me. This change, not coincidentally, coincided with my childbearing years.

CHAPTER SIX

THE MOTHERS, THE GODDESS
LOST AND FOUND

When I was fourteen years old, I had a dream. I was pregnant and riding a donkey through a landscape, all golds and browns, hills crowned with ancient trees. I arrived at a monastery where monks with brown hands helped deliver my baby. From that time on, I longed to have a child.

*

My first pregnancy ended in miscarriage. I was devasted. Not only had I lost my longed-for baby, but I realized I had always taken my body for granted. Despite illnesses and injuries, I had assumed my will and my body's health and strength were one. Now I knew in my own flesh that I was not in control; doing all the right things (thinking all the right thoughts) could not save me from sorrow. I sat in my own small version of Job's ash heap.

Over the next few years, I heard many stories, told in sympathetic murmurs, from older women. I learned that one in four pregnancies (maybe more) end in miscarriage. The medical term is spontaneous abortion. Many miscarriages do not complete themselves. Mine didn't. To prevent potentially life-threatening infection,

I had to have dilation and curettage, a procedure that in this post Roe v Wade era, will be or is illegal in many states. Although reproductive rights were controversial then (almost forty years ago), I could not have foreseen a time when a woman could be convicted of manslaughter for miscarrying, something that has happened more than once in the 2020s.

But I knew something was wrong, something was missing. I remember leafing through the pages of The Book of Common Prayer looking for a ritual to "speak to my condition." Its pastoral offices include "Thanksgiving for the Birth or Adoption of a Child" but nothing about loss of a pregnancy through miscarriage or still-birth. The Thanksgiving Office used to be called "the Churching of Women," an echo of the ritual purification of women prescribed in Leviticus. Jesus's presentation at the Temple marks Mary's observance of this rite, though theologians have argued that the Blessed Virgin incurred no impurity when she gave birth to him. I used to wonder about that as a literal-minded child; even if she had conceived by the God through a messenger angel, how had her hymen stayed intact through childbirth?

Such were the unspoken (of) mysteries of the body, of women's bodies.

*

During my childbearing years, I experienced another subtler but more bewildering loss.

"You can't write and have children. You will have to choose. You cannot do both."

I was at lunch with Miss Sang and her best friend Eileen, the former army nurse and mother of two adult children. I was taken aback both by Eileen's pronouncement and her anger—a woman I had experienced as affable and easy-going. I don't remember if I argued. I don't remember whether Miss Sang agreed with her, but

I do know she did not defend me, perhaps because she had not raised a child herself. Yet she was my fairy godmother. That is how I thought of her. I had begun writing *The Wild Mother* in her home. I missed her championship keenly.

Other older women added their voices to Eileen's. When I was pregnant with my son, a woman from Quaker Meeting called to plead with me to give up writing, as her own mother had not, apparently causing great harm to her children—and lasting bitterness.

In my own generation, many women were raising children and working outside the home out of necessity as well as choice. Was it the choice that was the problem, that I *wanted* to write, though so far I had no publisher? I don't recall anyone saying, "You will have to quit your job at High Valley when you have children." Nor had anyone questioned the effect of my writing on the stepdaughter I had been helping to raise since she was eight years old.

I remembered the women of my childhood; only one divorced mother worked outside the home, i.e. for pay. The rest of them, as far as I could see, ran everything: the rummage sale, the altar guild, the portion supper, the needle guild, the garden club, the PTA. My mother volunteered her skills as an architect to help design the new centralized public school. They were not paid, so however hard they worked, they were not working for a living. Their families came first; their families defined them. Anything else, these women had given up, as my grandmother had given up her career as a concert pianist, as my mother had given up her desire to be not an architect but an artist.

You cannot write and have children. You have to choose.

You cannot bring a life into the world and have a life of your own.

You have to choose.

You have to choose between a child's life and your own.

(The same argument that is made in the radical anti-choice movement. Once she conceives, a woman's life is not her own.)

There are plenty of rational and anecdotal arguments I could make, and probably did make, to insist that I did not have to make this choice. But the mothers (later, devastatingly, my own mother included) had spoken. And no matter what I thought, their words hit hard, below the belt. Moreover, the mothers, individually and collectively, had once been allies of my writing, contradicting the maledictions of my father, and his fathers before him.

From whence cometh my help?

*

When I was pregnant with my son, Miss Sang, now approaching eighty, decided to move to Arizona to live near her nephew and his family. "Blood is thicker than water," she said. I was sad that her connection with me and my family felt thin and watery to her. Just before she left, my pregnancy quickened and she was able to feel the baby kicking. I treasure that memory.

Early in my pregnancy, perhaps to assuage the impending loss of Miss Sang, I began writing another novel, *Murder at the Rummage Sale*, set at the church of my childhood, the detectives modeled on Miss Sang and on my father, the two poles of Christianity, contemplative and activist. I attempted to cast my father as a comical character, maybe to neutralize his power in my life. I discovered I was not ready to write about either of them. Nor was I ready to write about a church I had only recently left. Just before my son was born, I set the novel aside…for thirty years.

STRAW INTO GOLD

A vivid memory: I am eight months pregnant and have been put on bedrest for the duration of my pregnancy because of high blood pressure. The bed in question is a foldout couch in the living room that sags in the right place for my huge belly. There's been an April snowstorm. The power is out. Douglas is away at an Alternatives to Violence workshop. I am alone in the house.

I can still remember the silence, no refrigerator hum, no heat, just the crackle of the fire burning low in the woodstove, maybe the click of the dog's nails on the wooden floor.

I could be afraid. I could be lonely.

I am not.

The sun comes out, and I spend the day watching a daffodil in a vase track the light. That is how still I am.

A rhyme comes into my head:

> Take the pain and make it power
> Take the dung and make it flower
> Let your own fear make you bold
> Take the straw and spin, spin, spin the gold

The next day, propped up in bed, I began to write a narrative poem about the nameless woman who was the real spinner of gold, not Rumpelstiltskin, as we've been told. No, not a poem, a short story! No, not a short story, a novel, that I began writing just before my son's birth and completed three and a half years later, just six months after my daughter was born: the story of an outcast woman who became a healer, midwife, wise woman, witch.

(Years later I read aloud the story to my children, who were maybe seven and ten years old. I remember them leaning their heads on my shoulders. The novel was as yet unpublished. They asked me to rename two of the characters after them. So I did. The book is dedicated to them.)

Maybe that April day of solitude and silence—two things in short supply for mothers of young children—was a prayer, or an answer to a prayer.

*

After my son Julian was born, I gave up writing for four months. Then I split the writing week with my husband, who taught in the evenings. Throughout my children's early childhood, I wrote two to three mornings a week, for two to three hours a morning, six to nine hours a week total. All the other hours belonged to my children.

Though my mother adored being a grandmother and loved to spend time with my children, I never regained her support for my writing. She was also critical of me as a mother, as her mother had been of her, though for different reasons. She expressed her fear that my son would stop breathing and I wouldn't notice. Or when he was a toddler, that he would drown in the pond at High Valley because I wasn't paying attention. She could not see me as the attentive, responsive mother I strove to be.

You cannot be a writer and a mother. You have to choose.

And if you refuse to choose, you must be a bad mother.

When I was pregnant with my daughter, my mother made her most direct pronouncement:

"I don't see how you can go on writing when you have two children."

I understood, even then, how unbearable my choice to write *and* be a mother must have been for her, how it called her whole life into question. Yet I felt betrayed and bereft. Because of my choice, or refusal to choose, I had, in many ways, lost my mother.

*

(A note from the present: All our children are long since grown. I made my own mistakes, well-intentioned or oblivious. I have some regrets that stay with me and some sorrow over hardships I could not prevent. I also have many happy memories of them as children. I admire who they are as adults. In writing this book, I want to respect their privacy and independence.

It strikes me that children, at whatever age, are in the foreground of the parents' picture. Parents are meant to be a background for their children, a boulder or a tree, a reassuring landmark, even as we go through our own changes. I hope that whenever they need to, my adult children can look back, know I'm there, and get their bearings as they go on their way into their own lives.)

THE GODDESS FINDS ME

Between the birth of my son and the birth of my daughter, I had a second miscarriage. The signs that something was wrong were subtle at first. I drove myself to a doctor's appointment, hoping to be reassured that everything was all right (though I already sensed it wasn't). En route to the office, perhaps to distract myself, I pondered why it was that I had never written about the church, or Christianity.

Then…

I turn onto the main street. I glance at an old clock tower, and there she is, superimposed against it, huge, big as the sky, vast as the earth.

Then I hear her voice:

You have been searching for me all your life.

She speaks inside me, all around me.

The wild mother, the witch in the wood. You have been searching for me all your life.

*

And now I had found her. Or she had found me. She was with me; she had been with me always. She was with me when the doctor could not find a heartbeat. She was with me later when I was sedated and wheeled into the operating room for a second dilation and curettage. She was with me as I grieved. She had always been with me, and I would never again be without her.

When I recovered from my miscarriage, I went on a brief solitary pilgrimage to the sea. Hadn't I met the Goddess there before at age three when I sang ecstatically to the surf, the same summer I plotted to kill God? I spent a day walking the shores of Block Island, breathing the salty air, the woman-scent of low tide, listening to the rhythm of the waves, the same rhythm as labor contractions, the tides and women's bodies, both responding to the pull of the moon. All life comes from the sea, and the Goddess is the mother of all living, all that dies, all that is reborn. All these mysteries, I knew in my own body. I needed no scripture, no teacher, no preacher. I was surrounded by the Goddess, and the Goddess was within me.

She spoke to me again that day, *You will have a daughter, and you will name her Marina.*

And I did.

*

It is strange to think of now, but in 1985 I had never even touched a computer. I wrote two hand drafts of every manuscript and then typed it up using carbon paper, whiteout ready at hand, and often in tears when too many errors meant I had to retype a page. I could not Google the Goddess. I knew a little about ancient goddesses, Greek, Roman, and Egyptian. But the Goddess that had come into my life was both vaster and more intimate than those.

I also knew some of the history of the Church, the Inquisition, the witch hunts, what happened to people like Joan of Arc, even if they were sainted later. Despite my liberal Episcopal upbringing, where mention of hellfire was considered in poor taste, I knew that there was no room for any God but God, his only begotten son Jesus, and the Holy Spirit, who were all One. I knew that some Christian feminist theologians saw the Holy Spirit as the feminine aspect of God. And Holy Wisdom was called Sophia. But the Goddess who came to me did not strike me as one third of the Christian Trinity, nor could she be identified by one virtue. So who was she? What did she want from me? If I embraced her, was I damned?

In the wake of my first ecstatic encounter with the Goddess came terror, sorrow, and bewilderment. I remember the Anglican writer Evelyn Underhill saying that Christianity, like a cathedral, could only be fully understood from the inside. Now I was outside, looking back at the huge, hulking edifice, its stained-glass windows opaque. Worse than my unprecedented fear of damnation, was my fear of abandoning—and losing—Jesus. I am sure I did talk to trusted friends and Friends, but there was no one who shared my peculiar predicament.

I turned to C. S. Lewis, rereading *That Hideous Strength*, one of my favorites of his adult novels. Much of the plot turns on the awakening of the Arthurian magician Merlin (sometimes called the Devil's son). Merlin has been sleeping in a sacred wood one day to awaken. In the novel, both sides (the good and the evil) want to enlist Merlin. Which side will find him first?

For Merlin, there is no question. Once wakened, he goes straight to Arthur Ransom, the latest Pendragon, to whom Merlin has sworn allegiance. He offers his magical pagan powers. But Ransom refuses them. The universe, Ransom explains to Merlin, is coming to a point, a moral point, sharper and sharper, narrower, more defined, with less and less room for ambiguity. In Merlin's time it was possible, though questionable even then, to be a neutral agent. Now it is not. Everyone must choose. C. S. Lewis resolves this choice in the novel and in his life by saying that the pagan (the old gods and goddesses, the earth spirits he loves so much) must be baptized, refined, put into the service of (the one true) God.

But I did not want to baptize the Goddess, as if I could.

And I did not want to choose.

So there I was, where perhaps I have always been, between the churchyard and the enchanted wood, at the gap in the stone wall.

*

Two years passed, maybe a little more. As foretold, my daughter Marina was born. My son Julian went to nursery school at High Valley, where I told stories several times a week. I finished writing *How to Spin Gold.*

What do you want from my life? I kept asking the Goddess.

What do you want? she must have asked, silently, persistently.

What I always want. To write a story, of course, this time the story of the Goddess returning, coming to life in the lives of ordinary people, taking them by surprise, overwhelming them as she had me. And all at once, I knew I could do it; I knew I had to do it. In my mind's eye, I saw Esther, a minister's wife, sitting on the back steps of the rectory (yes, just like the one where I grew up) with her two young sons, playing with homemade playdough.

> The shape was profoundly female: global breasts resting on thighs drawn up in a squat. Her feet were strong, broad, like the hands spread over her round belly. Her face merely suggested features, a pinch here, a hollow there. Who was this figure? Where had she come from? How had her homemade playdough and her own fingers conspired to bring this figure into being?
>
> "It's the Lady," Jonathan stated.
>
> "The Lady?" Esther repeated.
>
> "And look," pointed David. "Her belly is the world."
>
> Sudden, silent tears astonished Esther. They ran in streams on her cold cheeks. She put out her tongue and tasted them.
>
> —from *The Return of the Goddess*, edited for brevity

As soon as I started working on the novel, synchronicity kicked into high gear. One of the four narrative characters of the novel, a Black ex-convict (based on someone I had known in prison and included with his blessing and permission) was a tarot reader. I went to a bookstore looking for books on tarot and there was Vicki Noble's *Motherpeace: A Way to the Goddess Through Myth, Art and Tarot.* At the same store, Margot Adler's tome *Drawing Down the Moon: Witches, Druids, Goddess-Worshippers, and Other Pagans in America Today* fell off the shelf and almost landed on my foot. The index of Margot Adler's book led me to *The Spiral Dance*, the ovarian work by Starhawk, Goddess worshipper, witch, and activist.

I was not alone! There were others who knew the Goddess. Over and over, in the years to come, I heard stories like mine, like Esther's, of the Goddess returning, unannounced, into lives she turned upside down and inside out, the initial encounter unmediated by books or workshops. A bumper sticker I began to see everywhere summed up this phenomenon succinctly:

"The Goddess is alive, and magic is afoot."

That summer Starhawk came to Omega Institute, three miles from my house, offering a workshop called "Myth, Mask, and Ritual." I signed up.

*

Some forty people stand on a circular wooden platform under a tent top. Starhawk, pacing, drumming, invites us to call in the qualities that will make our circle strong and safe. Then we call the elements air, fire, water, earth. We call in the Goddess by many names. We sing simple rhythmic chants, easily learned, chants that invite harmony and improvisation, chants that move us to dance, chants that lead us to enchantment. We dance, we weep, we laugh, we embrace.

My fleshy spirit and my spiritual flesh rejoice, united at last.

*

I had grown up steeped in the rituals of the church, their comfort, power, and beauty, but with the priest apart from the congregation. I loved silent Meeting for Worship, sitting face to face with Friends. Now here was ritual in a circle, words and music, but without the need to hold—or defer to—a book. Here was ritual that could be unabashedly ecstatic.

There are many pagan groups whose structure is hierarchical, complete with high priestesses and priests and degrees of initiation. Some have liturgies as formal as any church's. Starhawk's approach was egalitarian. Everyone is a celebrant contributing to a shared experience. Yet her rituals were not formless. She taught us how to create a structure with a focus, an intent—for example a rite of passage, or a mythic or cyclical story—that left room for spontaneity. She was what I came to call a deep priestess, the ritual equivalent of the Quaker Clerk, not presiding over the ritual but opening the way for it to unfold. The deep priestess is conduit, protector, observer, a responsive partner with the mysterious, living whole that is greater than the sum of its parts.

That long weekend with Starhawk in the open-air tent was an initiation for me. I knew that whatever else I might be, I was—or was becoming—a priestess.

CHAPTER SEVEN

AM I A QUAKER?

WOMEN'S RIGHTS/RITES COMMITTEE

When the tide is turning, ebb tide to rising, high tide to ebb, there is a span of time when it is hard to tell which way it's going. There are moments of churning and chaos. Then, so fleeting you can only catch it if you've been watching and listening intently, an almost imperceptible lull, like the one between an inbreath and an outbreath. One of my favorite places on earth is a tidal island on the coast of Maine. When the tide rises, the waves crisscross, weaving over and under each other until they merge in high tide. The pebbled passageway between the worlds, home to mussels and clams, vanishes completely to be revealed again when the tide ebbs.

These images come when I think of my life as a prayer, a beautiful chaos, with its own rhythms and mysteries, changes that I could not always perceive, let alone predict.

*

For ten years after the Goddess returned to my life, I remained an active member of the Religious Society of Friends. Surely there was room for the Goddess in the silence. Surely I could go to Meeting and also explore the Goddess on my own, in my home and backyard with a small circle of friends. Maybe I was no longer a Creed-saying Christian, but I was a Quaker, serving on committees, attending Monthly Meeting for Business. Bullshead Meeting was my beloved community. Everyone knew everyone well. When anyone was sick or in need, care and casseroles abounded. More children were born into the Meeting. We now had a building next door for Sunday School (or, as Friends call it, First Day School), events, and potlucks for every occasion. After Meeting for Worship there was always coffee and home-baked cookies and cakes, a basic tenet of my children's faith.

I was especially fond of a number of the older Friends in my Meeting, agemates with my parents. In the early days of my encounter with the Goddess, I confided in a few of them. They heard me with kindness, patience, and some bewilderment. The idea of a deity having a gender seemed odd and unnecessary to them. They had not grown up saying, "I believe in God the Father and his only begotten Son." I do have a particularly sweet memory of a conversation with one of the men. In Meeting, I could never tell whether his eyes were opened or closed. When I think of him now he strikes me as a Quaker Buddha, amused and serene. I do not recall anything he said about my revelations, but I have seldom felt so heard and received.

It turned out I was not the only one going through changes or questioning my spiritual identity. Friends, not just at Bullshead Meeting but in the Religious Society as a whole, began to go through what one Friend called "a Quaker identity crisis."

A longstanding question, often quiescent, resurfaced:

Are Friends Christian or Universalist? Historically, Quakers are without doubt Christian. George Fox famously said, "There is one, even Christ Jesus, who can speak to thy condition." Quakers never rejected Christianity; they just practiced it more radically. Oddly enough, I rarely heard Friends speak of Jesus. They much preferred the Light, perhaps synonymous with Christ, the Divine Light, the Inner Light, the Ocean of Light that overcomes the Ocean of Darkness.

(I do not recall being moved to speak from the silence about the Goddess. I was no proselytizer. But I do remember speaking about the dark, the darkness of the womb, of the earth, the darkness that reveals the stars.)

I sensed that many of the older Friends would have preferred to sit quietly, leaving others to sort out their own relationship with God. It was the Quakers of my generation, many of them birthright Friends (that is, born into Quaker families) who began to press the question. Some of these young Friends were my close friends. Our children had played together since they were babies. I loved and respected them, but the divide between us was growing.

Related controversies arose.

Abortion. Friends held strong convictions on both sides, some believing that abortion violated the Quaker principle of nonviolence. At the time, there was an attempt at the New York Yearly Meeting to include a minute of support for reproductive rights. Friends could not come to a Sense of the Meeting.

(Note: As of this writing, there is still no consensus on abortion among Quakers, but in the wake of the Dobbs decision in 2022, Friends have a renewed commitment to corporate discernment on the issue.)

Homosexuality. Should Friends sanction homosexual unions or any sexual expression outside of heterosexual marriage? Homosexuality was a particularly intense issue for one of the younger Friends in my meeting, who once got to his feet and declared. "The finger of the Lord is upon me. Homosexuality is an abomination in the eyes of the Lord." At the other end of the spectrum, one woman declared herself *try-sexual*: "If it's sexual, I'll try it."

As Friends, we did not debate in any conventional sense, we did not shout, interrupt or commit any form of verbal violence (or we earnestly endeavored not to). But we did hold many special called meetings within our Monthly Meetings and at Yearly Meeting. There were weekend conferences to explore hot topics at Powell

House, the Quaker conference center. In a format called "worship sharing," a meeting focused on a topic or question, Friends spoke passionately, always allowing that sacred moment of silence between speakers.

I threw myself into the heart of every controversy, abortion, sexuality—and belief. I even wrote an article positing that Quaker genius lay not in belief (couldn't we just leave it at "there is that of God in everyone?") but in practices that could embrace differences, make a place for everyone at the potluck feast.

*

When my children were old enough, my family attended New York Yearly Meeting, a weeklong gathering of Friends from all over the state on the shores of Lake George. There were activities for children all day. Meeting for Worship with a Concern for Business convened every morning. In the afternoon there was a plethora of interest groups.

And lo, the second year I attended, there was one on the Goddess, facilitated by a venerable white-haired birthright Friend who identified herself as a witch!

Some twenty women signed up for this group. And yes, we called the elements, we called the Goddess, we sang chants, we danced in a circle.

The Goddess had returned to—or arrived at—New York Yearly Meeting. Nor was her presence confined to a weeklong interest group. That winter there was a Goddess conference at Powell House, sponsored by the New York Yearly Meeting Women's Rights Committee. Not long after that gathering, I was nominated to serve on the committee, and I accepted.

During my third summer at New York Year Meeting, the Goddess eclipsed all other controversies, took up most of every

Meeting for Business. She was beyond the pale of Universalism. Was it all right for Quakers to worship a/the Goddess? A pagan (possibly Satanic) deity? I don't think that question was even posed. It was too huge, too disturbing. As I recollect, the focus of the Yearly Meeting became the Women's Rights Committee (which we not-so-jokingly called the Women's Rites Committee). Had the committee acted improperly, had we exceeded the bounds of our authority by sponsoring interest groups and conferences within the purview of Yearly Meeting? I don't recall the Sense of the Meeting, if there was one, except that the Women's Rights Committee was to be called before Yearly Meeting's Ministry and Counsel.

I was present at that meeting. I retain an impression of a drab room and severe-looking faces. And the questions that shocked me:

"Do you call on the name of demons?"

"Do you sacrifice animals?"

"Do you consort with spirits?"

What?! *No!*

*

That interrogation was a turning point for me. It crystallized a concern that I began to articulate. Which issues require corporate discernment and which do not? I had no attachment to Quakers as a corporate body embracing Goddess worship. I could see the objection to the Women's Rights Committee sponsoring workshops under New York Yearly Meeting's aegis. I would have stood in the way of anyone who wanted to replace the tradition of silent Meeting for Worship with a Goddess circle. But I did not want anyone telling me how I could conceive of the divine.

Quaker tradition has a name for people who do not defer to the corporate discernment of the Meeting: ranters. Historically, ranters were extreme in their beliefs and publicly disruptive. How to distinguish between behavior that affects the group and that which doesn't? I felt this distinction had gotten lost in the frenzy over the Goddess.

During these years of controversy, Friends liked to remind each other that it took our Quaker forebears one hundred years to reach consensus on opposing slavery. During those one hundred years, the Society was divided; some Friends were active abolitionists while others continued to be slaveholders. Finally, corporate discernment of Divine Will became clear to all. And Friends as a body took a stand against slavery.

I began to ask myself: would I be willing to wait for the Sense of the Meeting on abortion, homosexuality, what was and was not acceptable belief? Was I committed to corporate discernment of Divine will? Did I even believe in it?

In short, was I a Quaker?

I was Quaker enough to wait for my own internal sense of the meeting.

*

The silence of Meeting for Worship can be a silence deeper than any religious construct. In that silence, I began to see feet, brown as earth, walking on the earth. I was missing Jesus, not the theological overlay, but the story of an incarnate god who joked with friends, who sometimes lost his temper, who wept. I loved him, but I could not go back to his church. Gradually, it began to dawn on me: if I had to make a choice it might not be, could not be, between one religion and another, between silent worship and formal or ecstatic ritual. *I could not choose between Jesus and the Goddess.* "A witch's love song to Christ," those words kept repeating themselves in my mind. I wanted to sing that song.

One day in Meeting for Worship, I heard these words: *Your path is to make a new path.* Or maybe not even a path. For the path that beckoned me, I didn't need a machete, just a willingness to turn off the main road, or even the side roads, to see an opening in the trees, a faint impression laid down by deer. "A new path" did not translate in my mind to a new religion or tradition that others might take up. It just meant that it was time for me to go, to follow a flash of golden mane.

Not long after that, I asked my Meeting's Ministry and Counsel to convene a clearness committee for me, something Friends did when they faced an important decision. I wanted to go through the whole process. After meeting with the committee, I requested formal release from membership. Ministry and Counsel brought the matter to Monthly Meeting for Business. There was no objection, no blame, or recrimination. I was released with Friends' love and blessing. And I left them with mine.

CHAPTER EIGHT

ONGOING DOUBLE LIFE
COMMUNITIES OF IMAGINATION

Everyone has an inner and an outer life, conscious or unconscious. We breathe in and out, a necessary interchange, sometimes an alchemical one. My formative memory of attempted deicide is purely imaginative, though it affected how I experienced the world. Likewise, all the stories I heard in church or read in books, all the things that happened to me in my daily life shaped my imaginative world. This tendency to lead a double life became more pronounced when I began writing novels. I can still see the broken glass in the gutter on Somerville Avenue as all the characters of *The Wild Mother* took hold of my imagination.

Things keep happening, one damn thing after another, as the saying goes. During my last years as a Quaker, my children started school. I took a job at an art cinema that gave me an eye-opening experience of community based not on belief but on passion for an artform. High Valley School closed (or was closed by the state because Olga ignored one too many regulations). There was a crisis in my family of origin that affected me and my family of generation for years to come (and worked its way into novel after novel). While life went on, as it does, the four narrative characters of *The Return of the Goddess* inhabited the landscape of my childhood, saving the enchanted wood next door to the church that had, in actuality, been razed for condominiums long since.

The time spent putting words on paper—or screen—is only a small portion of this double life. There are scenes unfolding while you walk, or shower, or wake in the night. Many of them don't make it to the page. It is living in the story that matters. The characters of *The Return of the Goddess* became another kind of community. Before beginning a new chapter, I would convene a meeting with them to discuss what happens next. Their ideas often surprised me. I would usually follow their lead. No matter what was happening in my outer life, these imaginative, collegial relationships sustained me.

When I finished writing that novel I was both deeply satisfied and bereft. I felt that I had said everything I had to say. I had no more words, no more stories. (And though I remained determined to find one, still no publisher; sending the fruit of my imaginative life into the outside world was an initiation yet to come.) An artist friend suggested I take up drawing or painting for a time—visual art being a form in which I had no experience, skill, and best of all, no ambition. I dabbled in paint and charcoal but soon reverted to magic markers, my childhood medium.

One day a line drawing in brown marker took shape. An ample woman sat naked at a kitchen table having a cup of coffee. The round clock on the wall read a little after three in the afternoon. (The same time of day I was born, I realized later.) She told me her name was Madge.

(Later I reflected on that name, the sound, a syllable in key words: magic, imagination. No wonder magic markers brought her to life.)

Her next portraits took on color. She used up many peach markers for her abundant flesh. She chose neon orange for her hair. She had green eyes. She soon needed speech balloons and headings.

In one early drawing she lolls in the bathtub, over her head the caption:

"Madge listens to Christian radio on the theory that amoral indignation keeps you spry."

Balloon from the radio: "We are all members of the body of Christ. Some of us are hands, some of us are feet, some of us are…

"Kneecaps," thinks Madge.

She goes on to wonder about other members of Christ's body, the twelve-year-molars, the colon….

I might think I had nothing more to say, but Madge was just getting started. She sprawled naked in a red velvet chair (it was always difficult to get her into clothes) and pontificated about the meaning of life while eating chocolates. She was an unsold, unsung painter (hmm, I could relate) who invented the whole-body-no-holds-barred school of art. Since painting did not pay very well, she supported herself as a prostitute.

I was enchanted with Madge. Surely she would star in my next novel.

"Maybe," said Madge.

I began to ransack my mind for plots.

"How about," I said, "you're a retired prostitute, who moves to the coast of Maine to paint."

"Honey," she answered, "I am not ready to be a *retired* anything. First, I want my own book of cartoons. Then we'll talk."

That Christmas a friend gave me a bound book with blank pages. On the first page, along with a peacock feather and some other decorations, I wrote: *The Book of Madge, Her Book*. In early 1991, as I listened to the Congressional hearings about the First Gulf War and followed the unfolding news, a novel-in-cartoon came into being featuring Madge, the Peace Prostitute, founder of TWAT (Tarts with Attitude Triumph) and WITCH (Women Inclined to Create Havoc). And POWER (Prostitutes Opposing War Everywhere Rise).

Magic marker, in my hands especially, is a crude medium. Though I had no skill, and once affixed a hand to an arm backwards, somehow with a slant of an eyebrow or the jut of a hip, character and humor came through. I also discovered the pleasure of sharing the latest drawing with friends and acquaintances. Unlike a daunting pile of painstakingly-typed manuscript pages, a cartoon can be taken in at a glance. Most people were as charmed by Madge as I was.

"But," one woman objected, "you can't make her a prostitute!"

(Not that I *made* Madge a prostitute. I was never closer to being a channeler than during my brief stint as a cartoonist.)

"Why not?"

Because: prostitutes are products of and enable the patriarchy. I think that was the gist. They play to male fantasy (now called the male gaze), wear too much makeup and skimpy garments. They sell their bodies (as distinct from their minds?). All the things feminists stand against. The goal of feminism should be to end prostitution. And it is undeniable that many women, children, men, and people of all genders are victims, trafficked in a brutal, global industry that exploits their poverty, oppression, and desperation.

I didn't know any prostitutes at the time. As soon as Madge mentioned her profession, I began reading books by prostitutes. Many of the sex workers (their preferred term) I encountered in print and later in person define themselves as sex-positive feminists, the other side of a divide that endures to this day.

Sex work is a complex issue, running the gamut from slavery to agency. I have written about it from both extremes. How did a privileged Episcopal priest's daughter become so absorbed in the subject of prostitution? It might go back to the near-abduction, what could have happened to me. Yet long before that trauma, I used to break into the parish house with my friends and mime doing a strip tease act on the upstairs stage.

I had also heard the story of my father and his clergy friends going to a strip joint while at a conference in some city. I gather they sat in the front row. All at once, the stripper stopped in the middle of her act, and exclaimed, "Father Cunningham! What are *you* doing here?"

And then there was Jesus himself who allowed a woman of dubious reputation to bathe his feet with her tears, who preached in the Temple porticoes, "*Verily I say unto you that the tax collectors and the prostitutes are entering into the Kingdom of God before you.*"

For her part, Madge was not in the least apologetic about her day (or night) job. She was not given to apologies—or apologetics.

As the Gulf War went on and the pages filled up, *The Book of Madge* became a witness for peace. My artist friend encouraged me to submit it to the Center for Book Arts in New York City. It was accepted and displayed in a show called "War and Peace." That novel-in-cartoon was my first public, if not conventionally published, book.

I had more than met Madge's conditions.

One night I had a conversation with my husband about Mary Magdalen. I don't remember why or any details of what we said. It was late February 1991. The moon was full, and the temperature unseasonably mild. After dinner I went outside to moon gaze. The air was so balmy, I took my clothes off and lay naked in the moonlight.

All at once, it came to me that the name Madge and Magdalen had many letters in common. With her flaming hair. Madge could be…a Celt!

"How about that?" I asked her. "A novel starring you as the Celtic Mary Magdalen? Would you be in *that* novel?"

"Yes!"

I had found my witch, ready to sing her love song, her passion story, full throat.

I did not know on that moon-flooded February night that I would spend the next twenty years of my life researching and writing her story, but I did know:

It would be *her* story, not just Jesus's story through her eyes.

She would be his lover, *not* his follower.

She might become a prostitute, but she would never, *ever* be a repentant one. (A distinction few of the outraged understood. "But she was a disciple, a spiritual teacher, his true successor!")

Now I realized: I had been missing not only him but *her*, the goddess incarnate, a mortal woman whose dusty feet would also blister, who would know suffering and joy, who would undergo her own apotheosis, just like her beloved.

*

In the midst of my exhilaration, I knew I had set myself a daunting task, not to mention an undeniably heretical one. I was already in the habit of talking to Madge (soon to become Maeve). It occurred to me that, out of courtesy, I should give Jesus a heads-up. That may have been the first of many conversations that continue to this day.

"Jesus?" I began, without liturgical preliminaries. "I'm going to write a novel about this wild Celtic witch, who turns out to be Mary Magdalen. And, um, and you're going to be in the story. Is there anything you'd like to say?"

There was. The answer was prompt and succinct.

Please don't make me a prig.

I did my best to honor his request.

*

I had never written a series of novels. Early on, it became evident that Maeve had too much story to fit into one volume. I figured there would have to be at least three novels, a good Celtic number, a trilogy, a trinity. (Surprise again, by the end, there turned out to be four!) Calculating how many years it would take me to finish writing all these tomes became a new form of procrastination.

"I'll be writing this story into the new millennium!" I protested.

"So?" Maeve said, unimpressed. What's a new millennium to

someone who has waited millennia to tell her story her way? "Have you got something better to do?"

Something better than writing the story I believed I was born to write? Uh, no.

For that is how it came to seem to me. I had to write my way to dawn in the Resurrection Garden or else reincarnate as a writer and start again.

*

Though I did not know it at the time, I had happened upon the method of St. Ignatius of Loyola: entering into the Gospels imaginatively, engaging all the senses, experiencing the Gospel as directly and vividly as if you are there, not as a passive but as an active witness, a character in the story. Participating in the story is called "imaginative prayer."

Maeve's journey to and then beyond that Garden is a long and perilous one. She lives her own gospel. Exiled by the druids, Maeve survives slavery and forced prostitution in Rome by making common cause with her fellow whores and creating an unlikely community that comes to include whores, priestesses, and onetime enemies. When she wins her freedom, everyone goes with her to Jerusalem and Galilee to support her in her search for her beloved, but he remains elusive. At last Maeve and company settle together at the outskirts of Magdala, founding their own holy whorehouse—a new iteration of my long-ago Utopia project.

> ...We were whores; we took all comers, whether they
> were suppliants seeking the embrace of the goddess or
> homeless laborers seeking work and shelter or sick people
> seeking healing. People came and went. There were sel-
> dom more than we could handle; for there was a built-in

self-selection process: the censorious, the self-important and the humorless tended to leave in a hurry.

Here Maeve welcomes a widow who has lost her home:

> At Temple Magdalen we are all exiles.... We don't come from the same places; we don't have husbands or families, just each other and this place to be for now. I want the people who come here to be able to eat if they're hungry, heal if they're sick, rest if they're tired. I want us to be able to dance together and sing. Can that be? I don't know. I only know you are welcome here....

As welcome as a Samaritan knocking at Temple Magdalen's gates one stormy night, seeking help for a wounded man.

Double life might be an inaccurate term. The imaginative life permeates the life we live in this world, each one affecting the other, each one a form of prayer.

CHAPTER NINE

INTERFAITH SEMINARY

STANDING IN MY LINEAGE

I am ready, I am ready, I am ready
I am ready, I am ready, I am ready
I am ready, I am ready I am re-eh-eh-eh-dy

In a conference room, on New York's Upper West Side, Rabbi Joseph Gelberman is leading some hundred or so students in song. Born in Hungary in 1912, now in his eighties, compact, vital, he sings, rolling the R of "ready" with gusto. I picture him getting to his feet, snapping his fingers and dancing. It is that sort of song. His joy is contagious, triumphant. The determined joy of a man who lost his wife and child and all his relatives in the Holocaust. He founded the New Seminary to create interfaith alliances and understanding. We sing with him.

To do the good and the beautiful
I am ready, I am ready, I am re-eh-eh-eh-dy

We sing this song at the beginning of each class. It is an expression of Rabbi Gelberman's favorite Hebrew word: *Hineni.* Here I am. What Abraham said in response both to God, who commanded, and to the angel who halted, the sacrifice of Isaac. When God called to Moses from the burning bush, he likewise responded, "Hineni!"

Here I am. I am ready.

It is an answer to divine calling, to crisis, to life.

Hineni.

*

Twenty years before I enrolled in the New Seminary, I had rejoiced that the Episcopal General Convention had ruled in favor of women's ordination. I did not have to be a rebel or pioneer. I did not have to continue the priestly lineage of my paternal line. I would serve only one mistress, the muse. I would have only one vocation, writing. Everything else from being a waitress to working at the cinema (where I blurred some boundaries by writing essays on film) was a day job only.

Now here I was in a two-year program that would culminate in my ordination as an interfaith minister and spiritual counselor. Not quite the same job description as all those ancestors, but close. How had my path doubled back leading me to this new yet familiar place?

WHEN ONE DOOR UNHINGES...

With High Valley no longer a school, the buildings had fallen into disuse, their contents unsorted, gathering dust and mouse droppings. Olga had created a not-for-profit organization with a broad mandate called the Center at High Valley, which was so far inactive. I left my job at the cinema with the intention of helping to answer the question: what next? What about turning High Valley into a retreat center as well as a place for hermitage? In my naiveté, I imagined this enterprise could support the property *and* generate several salaries. Olga bankrolled renovations of the classrooms and part of the main house, the latter resulting in three rooms with a shared kitchen.

Not enough privacy for hermitage retreat and not enough space for group retreats or conferences. Our plans for expanding into another building ran into zoning and building code obstacles, as well as the restrictions written into our own conservation easements.

Nevertheless, for a couple of seasons, we rented the rooms to overflow guests from Omega Institute. We could not afford to hire any help, so I would spend hours waiting to greet arrivals, who would never give an ETA. (Hard to imagine now, but most people did not have cell phones then.) I cleaned and made beds, scrubbed toilets and showers. Though some people were easygoing, others had limited tolerance for Olga's flock of roosters (not a hen among them) who decided to crow at dawn outside the guest bedrooms. Refunds for irate guests seemed only fair.

In short, this aspect of High Valley as a retreat center was not a success. When we had the chance, we rented the rooms as an apartment to a man who became a core member of the community that would take us all by surprise.

I again faced the question of right livelihood. Though I had at last found a publisher for *The Return of the Goddess* and *The Wild Mother*, fame and fortune (i.e. my rightful place on the bestseller list) remained as elusive as Ahab's white whale. Was it time to consider a second profession? I had always been drawn to counseling but pursuing a master's degree in psychology or social work (my father's Rx) seemed incompatible with writing.

Then I heard about the New Seminary and Rabbi Gelberman's motto: "Never instead of, always in addition to." I knew he meant maintaining our own religious tradition as we gained knowledge of others. I had my own personal translation:

"Never instead of writing, always in addition to."
Hineni!

SEMINARIAN

Once a month I take the train to New York City, gazing out the window at the river, watching the light and seasons change, the mountains on the west side rising up and receding. I spend the night in New York with my sister and attend all-day class at the New Seminary. Then I take the train home, absorbing the day's teachings and conversations to the soothing sound and rhythms of the train as the light wanes and night falls. This contemplative, solitary journey, the counterpart to joyous participation in diverse community.

*

The New Seminary was affordable, flexible, and rigorous enough to be challenging and thought-provoking if not academic. Our first-year studies included Judaism, Christianity, Islam, Hinduism, Buddhism, and Taoism. We also studied indigenous traditions and syncretistic ones like Santeria. It was, of course, a whirlwind tour. What saved our curriculum from being merely superficial was our individual and collective passion, openness, and determination to expand our knowledge and experience.

As well as the New Seminary's own faculty, we had visiting teachers from different faith traditions. I will never forget the Tibetan Buddhist monk. One student asked him if monastic life wasn't hard and full of sacrifice. The monk threw back his head and laughed—and laughed!—for what seemed like five minutes. Then he made some astute observations about our lives, which he considered ridiculously complicated and difficult compared to his.

Our second-year curriculum in counseling was likewise an overview of different schools of psychology: Freudian, Jungian, as well as Neuro-Linguistic Programming and other therapeutic techniques. Not that we would ever be practitioners of any of these without further education. We were carefully taught the limits of our training. We were not to call ourselves therapists, but spiritual counselors. I have always had a distaste for the word spiritual, as it implies some things are spiritual, others not. Counselor unadorned seems adequate. Ethics were thoroughly discussed as well as recognizing when to refer a client to a psychiatrist or other professional. For those, like me, who wanted to focus on counseling, the New Seminary offered an additional year of supervision.

Along the way, we also wrote our own wedding, funeral, and baby-naming ceremonies as well as sermons, and a personal creed—everything we might need to serve as interfaith ministers to anyone who crossed our paths.

At our first class, we were told to form study groups, which would also meet monthly between classes. Our group, the Merry Ministers, continued to meet once a month for twenty years after ordination. (We still remain in touch, though increased age and geographic distance make our meetings less frequent.) From the outset, though we engaged in serious discussion and heated debate, we were a bawdy, irreverent crew, given to laughing till we cried. I don't think we ever met without telling jokes.

For me, the essence of the New Seminary was camaraderie with my classmates in the presence of a very human teacher who was wise and fallible, charismatic yet with no aspirations to be a guru. I never attempted to develop a close, personal relationship with Rabbi Gelberman. It was a new and salutary experience for me to be content to sit in a middle or back row, not to feel compelled to distinguish myself. Maybe because I was both relaxed yet alert, bits of wisdom have stayed with me for more than twenty-five years.

"Trouble," Rabbi Gelberman would often say. "When you're dead, maybe you don't have trouble. As long as you're alive…trouble."

And then he would shrug. Trouble was no trouble. It was life.

I always enjoyed his story of visiting a Catholic church and having a conversation with Jesus.

"Rabbi Joseph," Jesus greeted him from the cross. "What are you doing here?"

"Rabbi Jesus," he shot back. "What are *you* doing here?"

On the subject of conversing with deity/ies or, um, hearing voices, someone once asked Rabbi Gelberman how to know whether such voices were real or not, good or bad. As someone who hears voices (internally, anyway), I pricked up my ears.

"Simple," said the Rabbi. "You know the tree by its fruits. If you hear a voice telling you to go kill someone, not God. Don't listen. If what you hear helps you or tells you to help someone, maybe you can trust it. Look at the fruits."

One day I asked a question. It came out of a particular, emotionally charged circumstance, but boiled down to knowing when to say no.

"Simple," said Rabbi Gelberman, "you give what you have. What you don't have, you don't give. Otherwise, it's the same as writing a bad check."

I have repeated this wisdom to myself and others many times.

I liked our deans, as they were called. They administered the program, read our papers, served as advisors and occasionally taught a class. One day Dean Diane Berke, who went on to found her own program, spoke to us about her approach to counseling. To illustrate the difference between confrontation and compassion, she told the old story of the North Wind and the Sun. Which one could get the man to remove his coat? The North Wind was sure he could tear it off the man. Though the North Wind blew and blustered, the man only wrapped his coat around himself more tightly. All the Sun had to do was shine, and the man took off his coat himself.

Since then, I have told this simple story many times.

Another lasting lesson from that time came to me not in class but in the hospital. My mother had been admitted with severe emphysema. I made myself very busy, trying to get her moved to a better room, trying to figure out what she needed to have in place when she went home again (which she never did). I wanted to be useful, to help, to fix something that could not be fixed. I wanted to *do* something. At one point my mother said, "Just sit with me."

I listened. I stopped everything. I just sat with her.

Not long after that, she did move to a quieter room with a view of a tree.

In my last memory of her, she is propped up in her hospital bed with the tree filling the window behind her. She smiles at me. The North Wind vanishes as it if never was, the Sun comes out. Everything else falls away, like an old coat we don't need any longer.

ORDINATION

Eight months after my mother's death, my classmates and I were ordained in the Cathedral of St. John the Divine. My father was there as well as my intrepid aunt and uncle, who had once wanted to reform me but had long since given up on that with good-natured amusement. We all wore clergy robes. Dreadful garments, mine with a white rope tied around the waist. (You can be sure the Merry Ministers made lewd jokes about that.) Olga gave me a gorgeous, woven stole from Guatemala. My artist friend sewed a golden ankh (in honor of Maeve, who had by then become a priestess of Isis) onto the back of my robe. She later painted a picture of me in the cathedral, the columns turning into trees, the ankh floating above me. The portrait hangs in my counseling room, far more impressive than my diploma.

After innumerable speeches and songs, my class rose and went to stand in a circle around the altar for the official ordination. We were anointed and/or blessed by the rabbi, an imam, a Roman Catholic priest, and many others—everyone, it seemed, except an Episcopal priest. No matter, I was being ordained in an Episcopal cathedral. I had taken my place in the lineage, albeit with an Escher-like twist.

BEGINNING MINISTRY

I don't remember if my father congratulated me or what he said about this unorthodox ordination. At my request, he looked over the first marriage certificate I filled out to make sure I had checked all the boxes.

I officiated many weddings in the early days of my ministry, some fairly conventional, others that required interfaith skills. One wedding involved the bride's Presbyterian family and the groom's Jewish family. The couple were pagan and wanted pagan elements in the ceremony—but ones too subtle to be recognized by their parents as such. We included both families' traditions. In the course of designing the ceremony, I discovered how easy it is to incorporate pagan elements. Literally. Earth, air, fire, and water. I didn't need to cast circles or invoke deities with strange names. I simply needed to remind people where we are, standing on earth, breathing air, under the sun, our blood and tears echoing the salinity of the sea. Most of the weddings I perform do not take place in a church building. Honoring the elements serves as recognition that the earth *is* a sacred place, always and everywhere.

It was at funerals and gravesides that I was most aware of standing in a lineage. I never forgot my father officiating at the funeral of a woman I had known in grade school. A young mother in her thirties, she had died drinking wood alcohol, whether as an attempt to kill herself or because she was a desperate alcoholic, I don't know. My father was by then rector emeritus at Grace Church. He had been called to do the funeral because he knew the family well. I don't remember what he said except for a fragment of a sentence: "the body of a young man on a cross." Somehow, not just with words, but with his presence, he contained all the terrible grief in that church.

Not long after my ordination, a couple who had stayed several times at High Valley, asked me to officiate the funeral and burial of their newborn baby. The funeral was somewhere in Queens in a vast hall that was filled to capacity. I can still see and feel the collective grief and anguish rushing towards me, a towering wave. I knew my task was to gather and hold that wave, if only for a moment. And I knew I could, not as an inexperienced newly-ordained minister, but as part of a long lineage. Knowing how to meet immeasurable grief was in my blood.

After that I understood, whatever religion I was or wasn't, whatever creed I professed or didn't, I was a born priest.

BLESSING

My father lived six years after my mother's death. During the first three years, he came to dinner at my house at least once a week. For the last three years, he lived in Maine, about an hour away from my brother, at a retirement community he and my mother had already chosen.

When my father moved to Maine, he succumbed fairly quickly to dementia. He was not really qualified for his independent living unit. My brother bore the brunt of all the issues, having to have his stove turned off, his driver's license taken away. Eventually, my father moved to assisted living and then to a nursing home.

Not long before his death, I spoke with him at length on the phone. It was like speaking to someone who is in the middle of a dream. He was hashing over some complicated pastoral problem.

At one point he stopped and asked, "What would you advise me to do?"

His account hadn't been coherent enough for me to follow, but I knew it involved parishioners in crisis. I decided to offer reassurance.

"I think the way you're handling it sounds just right."

There was a pause, and then he said.

"Will you give me your blessing?"

I don't remember the words I used, but I did it.

I gave my father my blessing.

COUNSELOR

Not long after my ordination, I opened my counseling practice, "Companion at the Crossroads." I made a business card with this tagline:

"All faiths welcome; all doubts, too."

I have been in private practice now for twenty-five years. Counseling is a second vocation; or maybe it is another aspect of the same vocation. Writing and counseling are both about listening for the story.

In some therapeutic circles, story is dismissed or judged: "You're in your story. That's just your story. You need to get out of your story." As a lifelong reader and writer of stories, I see story as a primary way we make meaning. If a story can harm, a story can also heal. When it seems as though someone might be stuck in a story, I often say, "That is one way to tell the story. Can you think of another?" Part of the work of counseling is detective work, with story as a way into mystery.

That said, I don't have just one approach. My first task is to pay attention to how each person gains access to her own wisdom. There's a similarity to what educators identify as learning styles, visual, aural, kinesthetic. How does this person know the world? How does she know herself? What works? What might be in the way, and how can the way be opened?

I have counseled people of all ages, all genders, all religious backgrounds and none. It has been an honor and an adventure to work with each one. Over the years I have created a number of meditations and exercises that I keep handy if they are useful. Some of them I've named:

"Root Memory" also includes a journey to the future self. "Standing on Threshold" means turning to look at the landscapes behind and ahead. "The Place Between Lives" is about contemplating choices our souls might have made.

Other meditations arise for a particular person at a particular time. I like to reassure people that they don't need to have a literal belief in order to engage in imaginative exploration.

One of my favorite exercises is one I call "Who's at the Table?" or internal consensus process. Just as in a group of people, most of us have parts of our personality that dominate and parts that hold back. When we make decisions without the consent of the whole self, we often end up sabotaging ourselves. Internal consensus process can go on for many sessions, especially when an individual or couple is facing a major life decision.

The other Quaker practice that remains with me is leaving room for silence. It is especially powerful when couples speak from silence, not answering each other, but revealing themselves. Silence is an ally in one-on-one sessions as well. When someone comes in frazzled or dispirited, not sure of how to begin, we just sit for a moment in silence. Silence is useful at any point in a session. I would say its effect borders on the miraculous.

All the techniques I've learned or developed are secondary to simply being fully present to another human being, to receiving that person without judgment as far as humanly possible. When that happens, both the counselor and the one seeking counsel are in a sacred time and place together.

One of our assignments at seminary was to write a prayer for ourselves as counselors. Here's mine. I don't always say it aloud, but it is always with me. It is addressed to Divine Mystery.

This is [the name of the client]

Whatever is useful in me, use it. Whatever is not, set it aside.

Help us to go to the place where the wounding and the healing live to do the work you have called us together to do.

Let me be a way for you to be present to her and let me touch your presence in her.

At the very least, let me do no harm.

Amen.

CHAPTER TEN

HIGH VALLEY
UNINTENTIONAL COMMUNITY

THE EVE OF MAY

The sun has set, the sky is that indeterminate dusk color. A first star appears, or maybe the crescent moon. Some seventy people fan out over the playing field, holding hands in a circle around the Maypole. The drumming, chanting, and laughter have given way to a hush. The Beltane fires that we have leapt or passed between burn brighter as the light wanes. Keeping fresh at the edge of the lake, flowering boughs wait, forsythia, quince, apple, dogwood, shadblow. Soon we will sing and drum again, gather the boughs, bring in the May. Still chanting and drumming, we will bedeck the lakeside room of the barn. Then we will crown each other monarchs of May.

Holy body, holy earth.

We will chant till our song becomes wordless, till our voices raise the rafters, and silence falls again and we fall, giving back to the earth the joy that has come from the earth.

Merry Meet, Merry Part, Merry Meet Again. Blessed Be. And, as we always say, "Blessed *Bees*," because bees and other pollinators are a blessing to all life.

*

From the time I took it into my head that something ought to happen at High Valley, Olga was supportive. She loved seeing the place being enjoyed or put to profitable use (as when she once blithely granted permission to a former student to turn the classroom attic into a cannabis farm). She relished lots of coming and going. She would have preferred to see one layer piled on another to create a more interesting archeological ruin. We could only clear spaces for the center's use (with her permission but not her blessing) when she went on vacation.

Olga twice moved friends at loose ends into the center's office for stays of indefinite length without informing me. During the time we rented rooms, she failed to see why I scrupled about saying we had handicapped accessible rooms when we didn't.

"Well, just tell them we do!" I remember her saying when we received an inquiry about accessibility.

"But we don't!" I pointed out.

Why was that a problem? Nothing was a problem for Olga. She just laughed and said "C'est la vie!" (pronouncing *vie* to rhyme with *lie*).

Many things were problems for me. In my eighteen years as volunteer managing director, I never stopped trying to figure out what to do, how the Center at High Valley, the not-for-profit organization, could find a way to sustain High Valley, the place. I wrote unsuccessful grant proposals and held fundraisers; over the years, we rented High Valley for workshops, picnics, and events. But what came to define the Center at High Valley, to give it meaning and beauty, happened organically, as when a seed falls on fertile ground and takes hold.

*

In August 1995, I went with several friends to a Lughnasadh ritual at the Linden Tree in Poughkeepsie. Afterwards we ended up in a spontaneous drum circle in the parking lot. The neighbors were cheek by jowl with Linden Tree, so the drumming could not go on for any length of time without risking complaints. As the impromptu jam wound down, I approached Gary Siegel, the director of Linden Tree.

"I have a place where we can drum as long as we want," I told him.

Soon Linden Tree and High Valley began cohosting celebrations at High Valley. Linden Tree had a full a calendar of events and classes. One day Gary said to us, "You take the Wheel of the Year." Not a steering wheel, just the wheeling seasons that follow the waxing and waning sun, the blossom, fruit, fall, quiescence of life here in our little bit of northern hemisphere. Eight celebrations, two solstices, two equinoxes, and the four Celtic cross-quarter days.

Many of the people I came to call the Usual Suspects (as in: round them up!) were present at Linden Tree for that Lughnasadh celebration. For me, that event marks the beginning of what became a loosely-structured, unintentional community at High Valley, one with its own organic life that lasted eighteen years until our last Lughnasadh celebration in 2013.

*

As the High Valley community evolved, I often felt bemused to think that I had ended up (like my forbears) ministering (so to speak) to a worshipping (so to speak?) community. Though I was a presiding priestess, the Center at High Valley was not a traditional parish or church. What I had learned in ritual circles with Starhawk stood me in good stead. We were all celebrants. Everyone was welcome, no matter what their path. Our common ground *was* the ground—the Earth and its seasons. We had no creed, no belief system, no official pantheon, though the Celtic Goddess/Saint Brigid did take us under her spacious mantle. Our celebrations were ecstatic and often profound, offering communal connection and release.

Unlike my forebears, I failed to create any institutional structure. People helped in many ways, taking turns facilitating rituals, setting up and cleaning up. But there was no program committee, no hospitality committee, no finance committee, no buildings and grounds committee, no committees at all. (Maybe Goddess so loved us....) Though the not-for-profit had a titular board, there was in effect no decision-making body or process. Many times, especially in the early days, I called together the Usual Suspects for a meeting thinking that I/we ought to institute such systems and structures.

It never happened.

Other things, maybe better things, did happen. Many of the Usual Suspects organized groups around their interests—a monthly drum jam, a poetry group, a singing circle. One year we built a labyrinth from field stones we gathered. We hosted juke joints and evenings of storytelling. When *The Passion of Mary Magdalen* was published we had annual Passion readings, complete with drumming and singing. One Usual Suspect directed her own original adaptation of *A Midsummer's Night's Dream*. For many years High Valley flourished as a center for celebration and homegrown arts. In a time when entertainment is mostly consumed, we created our own, as if High Valley were a community back porch where everyone could pull up a chair.

UTOPIA?

When the community at High Valley began to take hold, I was writing *The Passion of Mary Magdalen*. Perhaps my hope for our community derived from my vision of Temple Magdalen as a place where conflicts could be resolved by airing them in song. At Temple Magdalen, people of all backgrounds not only coexisted but celebrated together.

High Valley faced problems more easily resolved in fiction. Thanks to Paulina (Maeve's Roman matron frenemy), Temple

Magdalen had financial backing. Moreover, Paulina's newly acquired husband was an architect and engineer (no problem with buildings or maintenance, a perennial concern at High Valley). At Temple Magdalen there were beaucoup whore-priestesses in residence as well as others on staff tasked with caring for anyone who showed up in need.

The Center at High Valley was not a well-endowed, well-staffed holy whorehouse (though we joked about becoming a strip joint with a neon sign flashing Live Nude Old Ladies). But I did like to believe that our unintentional community, like High Valley School before it, welcomed people who might have been misfits elsewhere. I liked to think that High Valley was, in current overused parlance, safe space.

The Center and the place High Valley were technically two entities, the Center presiding over events, High Valley itself being the land and buildings belonging to Olga. There was a small, equally unintentional, residential community, some of those residents connected with the Center, some with the property. If these two conjoined yet separate aspects of High Valley seem confused and confusing, they were.

THE SHEPHERD IS TIRED

In 2007 Olga had a health crisis from which she never fully recovered. Her short-term memory, already faulty, was completely shot. She got lost in her own house. She needed round-the-clock care. Douglas hired caregivers, which was costly in many ways. After two years, Douglas found a small, cozy adult home, with only six residents, run by a family of mother and daughters, all RNs. I was terribly resistant to the idea of moving Olga. I could not imagine her separated from High Valley. To my surprise, Olga found it a relief.

In one of my early visits, Olga confided in me, "I seem to be in charge of a lot of people here, and I...I just can't anymore."

I reassured her that Pam was in charge, and she did not need to take care of anyone.

"Thank God!" she said.

In another conversation I will never forget, she told me,

"The shepherd is tired. There are so many sheep. But the shepherd is tired."

I was struck by her imagery. Despite having been born Roman Catholic, Olga was areligious. Mass, in her childhood, would have been in Latin. How had shepherds (or the Good Shepherd) taken up residence in her psyche?

"The shepherd can rest," I assured her. "The shepherd deserves a rest."

And Olga did rest for several years, deeply and peacefully. When she still had the strength, she opened the sliding common room door and went out to the deck overlooking the creek. (She once scandalized Pam by removing her shirt.) I often sat outside with her. Once, eyes closed, Olga tapped her feet and waved her hands. She seemed to be dancing to some music in her dreams.

THINGS FALL APART

The center cannot hold. Not only the Center at High Valley but High Valley, the place, the people. Olga was the center of an equilibrium more precarious than anyone knew. Without her, the subterranean conflicts of interest we had all ignored or denied began to surface.

Our resident Usual Suspects, beloved core members of the unintentional community, decided to buy a home of their own. I don't know exactly when, how, or why it came to me, but with Olga's house empty and in need of repair, it seemed logical for Douglas and me to sell our house and land. We could move into the newly vacant upstairs apartment at High Valley and put all our efforts into preserving the core property. I persuaded Douglas of this folly-masquerading-as-wisdom, and we made the arduous and ultimately disastrous move.

Looking back from the distance of a decade, I can see the archetypal elements of our predicament. I offer a brief fairytale as the best way to express some of what happened.

THE BEAUTIFUL REALM

Once upon a time there was a great Empress who ruled over a beautiful realm of diverse people. Her subjects got along because all of them loved and revered the Empress. They regarded each other as friends and neighbors.

One day the Empress, who had grown very old, went away to live in the Land of Dreams. No one knew who was to rule in her stead, and no one agreed on how her realm should be—or could be—supported and maintained.

The Empress had long been served not only by her son and heir but by a knight. These two had been friendly, jocular rivals while the Empress reigned. With the Empress gone, the disarray of the realm became more apparent. The knight might have come to consider the heir unworthy of his inheritance. The heir could have begun to regard the knight as a usurper.

Who knows?

In this realm there was also a priestess. She was married to the son and heir. Though she had no desire to rule, she believed that she had inherited from the Empress the task of making sure everyone got along and was provided for. She trusted that all conflicts could be resolved, and she prized her skills not only as priestess but as peacemaker.

She failed.

Many meetings were held, many of bottles of wine shared. Still, no one ever agreed on anything. At last they decided that the realm should be divided. Although this division eventually came to pass, the legal affairs of the realm were so complicated, the decision did not bring peace. In fact, it made things worse. It was not long before the enmity between the heir and the knight, and the unhappiness of the priestess affected the whole realm.

Endings turn into beginnings and beginnings lead to unexpected endings.

For the rest of her days, the priestess prayed that everyone would find a way to live happily ever after.

UNSUCCESSFULLY SUCCEEDING OLGA

Until she was too infirm, Olga used to enthrone herself outdoors in an Adirondack chair right next to the walkway up to the house. She had a view of the parking lot, and anyone arriving for any purpose stopped to pay court to her, as was only fitting.

I had enjoyed the unannounced comings and goings that were always part of High Valley's ambiance when I lived a mile away in my own house. Once we moved into the upstairs apartment, I often thought of my mother's comparing life in the rectory to living in a fishbowl. High Valley was where I *worked*. But now I could no longer go home. We had made the apartment as comfortable as we could, but it felt like a rabbit warren, all hall and separate rooms with a living room-kitchen in the middle that had no direct light. Our bedroom had once been Olga's. It was a lovely room with a picture window. I would wake at night and in the morning and always know the weather by the light or rain on the bark of the copper beech.

But it remained Olga's room, and I remained...not Olga.

I had planned to generate extra income for the Center by renting the downstairs for events and a small room off the kitchen to paying guests. Now and then events happened. Now and then guests occupied the room. My most vivid memory of life in Olga's house is of cleaning and dusting unused rooms, still filled with Olga's things.

UNEXPECTED GIFT

Douglas had always had a vegetable garden wherever we lived, but I had never kept a flower garden. Olga's innumerable gardens were all overgrown. I had no idea what to do with them, but I found myself drawn to them. I weeded, added plants, pruned, brought a dying rosebush back to life, had the derelict tennis court planted with wildflowers. I asked questions of experienced gardeners, looked things up (gardening by Google), came to know most plants by name and all by sight. I did not become a skilled gardener. I was, and still am, an amateur.

But I fell in love with plants (all plants, cultivated and wild, native and invasive), and I learned something that astonishes me still. The gardens came back to vibrant life, not because I knew what to do, but because I began to notice everything. I paid attention, and the plants responded. In tending Olga's gardens I also came to know her more intimately. I shared her joy in the green, flowering world.

THE WHEEL OF THE YEAR IN A RUT

Not the actual wheeling of the sun and seasons. We went on gathering to celebrate the cross-quarter days, but I noticed a change. In their heyday, the energy of the celebrations was so high, so alive. We all created it together and we were carried by it together. In the last couple of years, the energy dragged. I felt sometimes like I was tethered to it and had to pull it with my own strength and will. Pull it like a heavy cart or a sore tooth tied by a string to a closing door.

I can think of many reasons for this winding down. The resident hosts of the post-ritual parties had moved away, though they usually came for celebrations. Douglas and I were tired and tense. I suspect the rise of social media as a source of community may have been a contributing factor. The gardens also taught me—and continue to teach me—that everything that grows and flowers in due season also dies back.

I made another discovery during this painful time. We hosted an event for a visiting poet who worked in a form he called American Ghazal, descended from but very different than the form that originated in seventh-century Arabia. The American form, made famous by Robert Bly, had twelve syllables to a line, three lines to a stanza, six stanzas (each able to stand alone), with the poet often addressing her/himself in the last stanza. When I could not concentrate on any other writing, I found that counting syllables soothed me. Syllables became my prayer beads.

Here is a ghazal from what turned out to be our last autumn at High Valley.

...bear witness back, be here

frost in the night, shining at dawn, melting at noon
flowers give up the ghost on black funeral stalks
I come with the clippers and cart away my dead

light shining through windows and cracks in the old barn
makes patterns with the beams, the weathered boards, the dust,
draws my attention, turns me to some mystery's heart

the tender of an empty shrine, that's what I am
the gods may be here, though the devotees have gone
still the sleeping ground is alive, birds feast on seeds

hawks roll over on the wind as if on a bed
big spruce lies on the lawn, a dogwood crushed beneath
in the same storm's wake, downed trees, playful birds of prey

some are planters, some tenders, others harvesters
of a field, a time, a place. after the fall falls
who watches, sings, and sweeps until it's time to sleep?

Elizabeth, the land is your wordless witness
forms pass, trees and buildings fall, people come and go
stop trying to stop them, bear witness back, be here

—from my collection of poems,
So Ecstasy Can Find You

FAREWELL CELEBRATION

There were many factors that went into our decision to leave High Valley and sell the part of it that was still ours. In summary, our life there had become untenable.

Lughnasadh was High Valley's farewell celebration, a poignant event. It was a beautiful August afternoon when the light itself is ripe and golden as corn. A friend made a video, not of the ritual itself, but of people speaking before and after about what High Valley, the community and the place, meant to them. At my request, she took her camera around to all the gardens. The video was beautiful, and I am grateful it exists. I confess I watched it only once. As I recall, people said, over and over, that High Valley felt like home, they had never been so welcome anywhere, so free.

Thank you to everyone who participated in the transitory beauty of the High Valley community. Gratitude to all the Usual Suspects, who remain my dear friends.

PARTING PRAYER

Moving is always hard. In leaving High Valley, we were leaving a place where we had thought we would live until we died. We had felt responsible for the land and for the people who lived there. And now we were leaving, and everyone else had to leave, too.

What has happened to the core property at High Valley, and the people who now live there, is no longer my story to tell, though the place and all the people who called it home are in my daily prayers. Thanks to Olga—who lived to be 101!—and Douglas, the land remains in conservation easements and cannot be sold for development. By whatever name, High Valley, Tall Trees Farm, the Old Munsee Place, the land has its own spirit. I trust that spirit will prevail.

*

Just before we left, I had learned the Hawaiian prayer Ho'oponopono. In English:

> *I love you, I am sorry, please forgive me, thank you.*

On moving day, I walked all around the buildings, the pond, the gardens, reciting the prayer over and over until it was time to go.

I love you.
I am sorry.
Please forgive me.
Thank you.

CHAPTER ELEVEN

HERMITAGE

THE COMMUNITY OF MY BACKYARD

THE DAY WE FIND OUR HOME

We've been looking at houses all day. In the late afternoon, we turn into a long, wooded driveway. The blue house at the top of a rise looks unremarkable. Then I see a gigantic Oaktree on the far side of the yard. I walk straight towards what we later learn is a three-hundred-year-old white oak, with a hollow big enough to stand inside, where black snakes like to leave their shed skins. Four or five people holding hands could ring its girth. I don't even need to go inside the house to know.

We are home.

In a place that was once home to the Lenape peoples.

It is April, and the yard is full of daffodils. The owner of the house is a weekender. When our offer is accepted, I take to stopping by during the week to absorb the peace of the place. When the daffodils finish blooming, I deadhead them, also noting the location of the poison ivy when it comes up. In short, I begin tending the gardens. I soon meet the other guardian trees: a cottonwood in the east with a heart-shaped crown; a red oak (in the fall we will see how red) in the north; a towering pine in the west; and the great white oak in the south. There are also many junipers, shag bark hickories, spruce, a maple, a pear tree (where a black bear will stand on its hind legs to pluck the last pear of the season), three apple trees, overgrown fenced vegetable gardens. The house is on its own small ripple of a ridge. Beyond the yard rises the Shawangunk Ridge. To one side of the yard is a hayfield that still feeds cows we can sometimes hear lowing in the distance.

The house turns out to be just right, not too big, not too small. We call our place the Happy Hermitage.

We move in September, a month after the last High Valley Lughnasadh.

HOW AM I A HERMIT?

If a hermit is someone who lives alone in a secluded cabin, I don't qualify. I live with Douglas. I see friends and have an active counseling practice. In the first few years, I experimented with volunteering at various local organizations, but nothing took. Between writing and counseling, I often work six days a week with maybe one afternoon off during the week. I simultaneously feel I ought to be doing more (for/in the world) and that I am doing too much. The conundrum may be my current version of *"We have not done those things we ought to have done, and we have done those things we ought not to have done, and there is no health in us."*

So how am I a hermit?

For the first time in my adult life, I am not part of a church, Quaker meeting or any kind of community that gathers for ritual. For other people this lack of affiliation might not be noteworthy. For me it remains new and questionable. I hear cautioning whispers from Anglican ancestors, Quakers, even C. S. Lewis who somewhat reluctantly acknowledged that believers must belong to a corporate body. Anchorites, like Julian of Norwich, had anchorholds attached to a church; they participated in the rite of Communion through a window.

Maybe I am only a hermit in the early morning. In my backyard I enter into communion with *"all that is, seen and unseen."* I have a daily practice that includes motion and stillness, silence and praying out loud. I walk around looking at everything, light, weather, birds, the daily changes in the plants. I always stop at the bee enclosure to bless the bees. Blessed bees. Sometimes I go out into the field to watch the play of mist and mountain. Yet I can't say that my practice is solitary; I am never more aware of how we are all connected, the living, and what we call the dead, animals and plants, microorganisms and stars, rivers, seas, mountains, rocks, soil, light and dark.

Like many of us, I am painfully aware of the impact our kind is having on the earth. I often wake depressed and anxious. When I go outside, greet the day and am greeted in return, I am amazed by grace. I also know that not everyone gets to live in the midst of such beauty and abundance. During morning prayer, gratitude momentarily overtakes chronic existential guilt. Courage, even joy, rises in me.

Part of my daily prayer is for guidance to do and be what I am here to do and be (even if I don't know what it is). I pray not to miss it. One day in the midst of my fretting over all I should be doing and don't do, I hear:

What?! You don't believe your prayer is being answered?

Could it be that getting up early each morning and wandering around the yard is an answer to that prayer? Could it be that my delirious joy when I have an afternoon free to walk on the ridge is part of my purpose? What *do* I actually do? I listen to people. I listen for stories. I write and rewrite sentences. I notice beauty. Could that possibly be enough?

Whether it is or it isn't, that's what I do amidst all I don't do. That is where doing slips over some edge (a waterfall, a rocky precipice) into being.

ALL THINGS PASS

In 2020, a little over seven years after we first met the Oak, it fell. So quickly, so slowly. It was a warm, sunny afternoon in early May, perfectly still. It had rained for days before. The ancient oak was sending water up to its tiny, shining baby leaves. The weight of the crown was too much for its hollowed-out trunk to hold up. Moments before, a friend of mine had been sitting under it. Then he walked back to the picnic table where I was helping him with some paperwork. (We were working outside because of the pandemic.) The tree fell, not where he had been sitting, but where he had just walked. We saw it fall together.

"Was it loud?" people asked.

Loud, soft, slow, swift, all of that.

Firewood from the crown kept us warm all winter. But the body, ever more dragonesque, remains where it fell. The snakes still come to shed their skins in the now horizontal hollow. The chipmunks scurry in and out of the same knotholes. Snowdrops and daffodils still bloom around the great fallen trunk. Dead, yes. But what does death mean for a tree? It is gathered up by all the life around it, part of an ongoing change.

Next winter the huge pine tree fell in a windstorm at night.

Yes, it was loud, the house shook and went dark. We went outside to look. The world was full of horizonal tree, its branches filling the yard between the house and the gazebo, taking a bit of siding and an eyebrow roof over a door, but leaving the roof, the windows, the gazebo, and our lives intact. So gracious, so benign as it fell, just like the oak.

Now two of the four guardian trees have fallen. The western sky is empty of pine branches, like the southern sky where I used to trace the serpentine windings of the oak branches whenever I woke. We are also changing, aging.

Is it time, is it time to go, to let go of this place? Five to ten good years, I kept thinking when we found the place. Five to ten good years. Is it time to go?

It took a long time to clear away the pine. We couldn't leave it where it was as it had fallen across the driveway and on the electric line. Its branches blocked a door and filled the upper-story windows. The electric lines, improperly repaired, shorted out, sparked, and almost started a fire.

Is it time? Time to go? We kept asking all that winter.

Then spring came again. We can see where the trunk of the pine tree lay, but the rose bushes came back alongside the daylilies and all the tangle of briar and brush on the steep bank.

Not time to go. Not yet.

The milkweed we planted to encourage monarchs is spreading. Douglas's bees survived the winter. Everything is coming back to be raked, weeded, tended, loved. How can we not plant this year's vegetables, sunflowers, marigolds, zinnias?

Another round begins.

One more year at the hermitage with all its beginnings, all its endings, all its slow and sudden changes.

Amen and Blessed Bees.

PART TWO

A WAY OUT OF NO WAY

ORIENTATION

"God can make a way out of no way" is one of my favorite recurring lines in Gospel music. I imagine a desert or a wilderness, interior and exterior, with no clearly-marked path. Nothing but attention, intention, and a compass tucked away in the heart of my heart.

During my years as a backyard hermit, I have continued to explore prayer, often off-trail, but sometimes on pilgrimage routes that many have walked before me. The chapters that follow are varied, self-contained, and do not need to be read in any particular order. They differ in tone, some philosophical, some poetic, all reflections on prayer, the fruits of my life as a prayer. Take what is wholesome and helpful for you.

I am not the one with the map, not the guide. Sometimes I forget, and I pray what I call bossy prayers where I go on at some length about what this one or that one needs or what I need, what the planet needs. Then I catch myself and say, "bossy prayer." I remember that I "see through a glass darkly" like everyone else. Then I remind myself of another way to pray.

> Pray for courage
> in each moment
> not false cheer through gritted teeth
> but the bravery to howl
> in grief and then put the kettle on
> feed whoever has to be fed.

Pray for the courage of hands thrown up
hands held out and open.
Pray for the guts
to give way to laughter
when by grace it comes.
Pray for tears when you need them.
Pray for anger to be brief and fine
and burn away leaving no trace
of resentment.
Pray for a hand to hold
even if it is only your own
Pray for your life and your death
to bear good fruit.

—from my *journal*

CHAPTER TWELVE

CHANGING, UNCHANGING

HOLDING ON, LETTING GO

"Hold to God's Unchanging Hand" is the title and refrain of a Gospel hymn by Jennie Wilson. It conjures for me not so much an image as a sensation. I remember a powerful hand holding mine just after my daughter was born while I labored to deliver the placenta. Still in pain, I held to that hand, a source of strength. When I turned to see whose hand held mine, I saw with wonder that it was not the midwife or my husband. It was my newborn daughter.

How could I experience the grip of an infant as the hand of life itself? But that is how it felt to hold to her hand, a hand that would inevitably grow and change.

*

"What if God changes?" my friend Tom recently pondered. "As our changing consciousness, the changing universe becomes part of whatever God is, maybe God changes, too."

Once a guest speaker at Quaker Meeting also posed that question, pointing out that Jesus changed in the course of his life on earth. She cited the story in Matthew 15 of Jesus's initial refusal to heal a Canaanite woman's daughter. *"I was sent only to the lost sheep of Israel,*" he dismisses her. When the woman persists, he is even harsher, "*It is not right to take the children's bread and toss it to the dogs.*" (Which really, seriously, isn't a very nice thing to say, though Christian apologists continue to try to spin it.) Desperate, determined, the woman boldly extends Jesus's metaphor, pointing out that even dogs get to eat the crumbs from under the master's table. Her faith, as he calls it, changes his mind, changes him, changes his understanding of his purpose. God incarnate, if that's who he is, changes; he is changed.

I find the idea of a changing, changeable Divine inspiring if also unsettling. I held to the hand of my newborn. I suspect there is also a newborn or very young child in all of us who wanted and needed to hold to a mother's or father's hand. How all-powerful for good or ill those primary figures are. How inevitably they fail us. How we long for someone or something that will always be there, unchanging. Yet deity, at least as depicted in scripture and story, can also be changeable, even abusive. Because that thought is unbearable, we often blame ourselves, we so need to believe our parent, or our God, is perfect and unchangeable.

TO THAT ROCK I'M CLINGING

Like many people, I turn to what we are apt to call "nature" (as if it were separate from us, and we from the world around us) for comfort, reassurance that there are rhythms and patterns greater than us, and there are. But most of us can't deny that we are in a period of cataclysmic climate change caused in large part by our own kind. We are, to borrow a phrase from the prophet Hosea, "reaping the whirlwind." Sometimes literally.

I like to visit the stone people (as I call them) in the Shawangunks for solace. For now, the rocks are apt to be there, where I last saw them. "No storm can shake my inmost calm, while to that rock I'm clinging..." is a line from an old hymn, possibly of Quaker origin. But stones change, too.

> we could teach you lessons
> of catastrophe, the violent heave,
> the deafening tumble, then
> the silence, the silence,
> endurance, the slow sweetness
> and sorrow of water shifting
> our shape, finding our faces.

—from my collection of poems,
Tell Me the Story Again

With the Shawangunk Ridge to the east of my yard, I have a great view, especially in winter, of the sunrise moving along the ridge north to south and then south to north. The full moon also makes a journey I can track. When Venus is the morning star, she rises over the ridge at dawn. These seasons of sun, moon, and stars are relatively unchanging and predictable. Yet the tilt of earth's axis is slowly changing. There are mysteries in what C. S. Lewis calls Deep Heaven that our human minds cannot yet fathom or predict. Is the universe expanding? If it is, will it contract?

When my mind boggles, I come back to the body. Our hearts expand and contract, our lungs do, too. Heartbeat and breath, we hold to them as long as we live.

THE BENDING ARC

Collectively and as individuals, we resist change and we also struggle to create it. We feel powerful and powerless by turns. Barack Obama chose as his theme song Sam Cooke's "A Change is Gonna Come."

Martin Luther King Jr. drew on the thinking of transcendentalist minister Theodore Parker when he invoked the long arc of the moral universe bending toward justice. We cannot see very far along the arc, Parker said, so we have to take the trajectory to justice on faith.

Most Westerners were raised on the idea of progress. The world will get better, we will get better. There may be struggles along the way, but we are following a more or less linear path that will lead to something better. We are now witnessing the apparent reversal of progress with rights we thought had been won under threat or lost, wars we thought settled erupting again. Hatreds, violence, atrocities we might have wanted to believe had been relegated to the past now excruciatingly present.

On a smaller scale, I often hear clients exclaim in dismay, "But I thought I had already dealt with this issue. How can I be here again?" Wherever that issue may be: insecurity, rage, despair, betrayal, unfulfilled longing.

The model of a linear path or even an arc is faulty. Our very DNA spirals. I suggest to my clients that whatever they are encountering, the dilemma is in a different place, deeper, higher, whichever image they prefer. They have a chance to resolve the issue or heal the wound at another level.

Or it could be that life—and our psyches—are not even as orderly or progressive as a spiral. I have often marveled at how wires or necklaces get tangled and knotted without my ever touching them. I look at the beautiful chaos of once-mown fields growing into meadows and forests. A purposeful chaos however wild and random it may appear. Life coming back, healing over, making new, changed and changing.

If the world is changing, if the universe is changing, if even God is changing, what is unchanging? What do we hold to?

HANDS ARE MADE TO DO TWO THINGS

In *How to Spin Gold*, my fairytale novel, the narrator, a mid-wife-in-training, complains to her teacher that her hands are empty again and again. She has no child of her own. The wise woman tells her, "Hands are made to do two things, hold fast and let go."

Of course hands do many other things, everything, but holding on and letting go are essential to how they work.

I think of the allemande in many folk dances. You take a hand, turn, release, and take another hand. At some point in our lives, we swing out of the dance into a beyond that the other dancers cannot see. And someone else swings into the dance, and the dance goes on, with the dancers coming and going, holding fast and letting go, the dance itself changing and unchanging.

I remember walking hand in hand with my daughter when she was three years old. We were crossing a stream into a wood on the other side.

"I want to see the Goddess," she said.

"You can," I answered. "She is everywhere, in everything."

My daughter was quiet for a moment and then she said, gazing up at a tree,

"Those are the branches of the Goddess."

She looked down at our clasped hands.

"And these are hands of the Goddess."

And so they were, and so they are. Hands that hold us, hands we hold to.

Hands that also let us go.

CHAPTER THIRTEEN

PRAYING RAGE, GRIEF, AND DESPAIR

I KNOW HOW IT IS

I am in a yurt. Which may or may not be relevant, but it is the location of this memory. I raised funds for this yurt when I thought we might have a camping ground at the Center at High Valley complete with a composting toilet (for which I failed to get a grant). The zoning board said: no camping. So the yurt is near my house at the other end of the property, beside a natural spring where snakes come out of hibernation and bask on a rock. It is a lovely round structure. The wasps like it too. Even though I have a phobia of insects, I have tried to communicate with the wasps. I notice they are gentle and seem to have heard my request that they not build a nest inside the structure. You might think I would be happy and peaceful here. Sometimes I am.

Not today.

I have just received another rejection for another novel.

Rejection has been my recurring fare for more years than I care to count. I won't go into detail, and I know my story is not unique. I continued to write novels and submit them to publishers. I have often reflected on the word submission; it implies masochism, except that there was not even perverse pleasure in the process. I just gritted my teeth and subjected myself to the process again and again, hoping for a different outcome (insanity?) and, yes, praying with all my might. Each rejection also stirred up a lacerating litany of questions:

> Did my lack of success mean the answer to my prayers was no?
> Or that I was being tested in some way?
> Or that I did not think the right (positive) thoughts?
> Or, as I understood Buddhism then (and hated it), that I was too attached to my desires?
> Ergo that my suffering was my own damn fault?

I was voluble at an early age, making speech-like sounds before I could form words, but according to my mother, I was not given to tantrums. Having witnessed her responses to my siblings' rages, I discovered it was much more effective, when I was angry or hurt, to retreat silently to my room and wait for my mother's guilt and anxiety to kick in.

*

On the day I retreated to the yurt, I thought maybe I'd have a quiet cry, even though of course my mother wouldn't come, no one would come. I was completely and utterly alone in my despair. No one would hear me. (Except for the wasps.)

I am not sure how it occurred to me to speak out loud. Speak? Say, rather, scream, wail.

*

I am turning the full force of my rage on God, a high-volume, full-body rage. I don't care who or what God is or if God exists. It is still God's fault, my pain, my suffering. (At such moments, you need that three-letter word in upper case.) I rant on and on.

I can't remember all I hurled at this deity. Here's the gist:

How could you, how *could* you give me this gift (because in the midst of my fury, I believe in my gift as absolutely as Job believed in his innocence) and no way to give it, no one to receive it. No place for it in the world. How could you! Why did you! *Why!*

I rail and howl until I am spent. And then it occurs to me, maybe for the first time ever, to let the accused have a chance to answer.

No whirlwind.

It is very quiet. Maybe a wasp buzzes, or maybe the wasps are silent, too, stunned by their inadvertent witness. A heavy, palpable warmth envelopes me. I am translating here, because the answer is as much image as word. For a moment, I glimpse the creation, its vastness and intricacy, life forms still unknown to my kind, beauty still unseen. So much beauty, so much fierce, tender brilliance.

I know (I hear, see, feel), *I know how it is when your gifts are not received.*

It is not a reproach; there is no judgment. It is not reassurance that everything will be all right. Maybe it is resonance. Whatever, whoever answers me expresses and contains my small bitter, angry sorrow, gathering it into a greater sorrow, ongoing, unfolding, unfathomable yet intimate.

LOSING THE THOUGHT POLICE

Letting loose in the yurt may have been my first experience of uncensored prayer. When you repeat over and over that you have "sinned in thought, word, and deed," that there is "no health" in you, it is easy to become frightened of yourself, your strong emotions, your errant thoughts. No wonder I have reacted with fear and anger to some New Age teachings that reinforce this message. For example (as noted above), you must think positive thoughts or else you might draw negativity to yourself. Thoughtforms create reality. There may be some truth to these beliefs, but I have not found them helpful. The thought police I have already internalized do not need backup.

Perhaps for many people of my background—WASP, middle class—any form of loss of control is a source of shame that extends not only to behavior but to emotion. Lots of isms (racism, sexism, classism, to name only a few) have at their root despising the Other as out of control, emotional, lacking in self-restraint. Though my parents, in particular my father, took a stand against all forms of prejudice and would never have stereotyped any person or group in this way, emotions in our family were not something any of us understood or knew how to handle.

My father was given to unpredictable, displaced rages. My mother's anger was cold and silent, never directly expressed. She was clinically depressed and kept a lid on all emotions. She feared and despised my father's anger. My more expansive emotional range also disturbed her. "I wish you could learn to be on an even keel," she told me over and over. I never did learn, but as I grew older, I strove—and strive—mightily for the appearance of self-control in all interactions with other people, unless they are trusted intimates.

When my parents had both been dead for more than a decade, I returned to writing *Murder at the Rummage Sale*, this time setting it in the era of my childhood, and giving characters based on both of my parents a narrative point of view. In writing Anne, I discovered the red-hot molten core of my mother's cold anger. In writing Gerald, I found my father's fear and vulnerability beneath the rage. Whether my depictions are accurate or not, writing from the point of view of my parents was revealing—and healing.

THE MOTION IN EMOTION

Emotions are not good or bad in themselves; they just are. In *That Hideous Strength*, one of C. S. Lewis's characters remarks to another that there is no bad weather, only weather. The effects of weather can be devastating, but the weather is just doing what weather does in response to a complex set of variables that now include rapid global warming. Emotions are similar. They come; they go. They seek release; they can wreak havoc.

How apt that *motion* is part of the word emotion. When I am experiencing a quandary that stirs up sticky, uncomfortable feelings, I pray at the beginning of a walk or bike ride for the motion of my body to help move the emotions. (If mobility is limited, singing works just as well. Or listening to music.) Emotions live in the body and often, without our even knowing it, they get stuck there. Then a simple emotion becomes complicated, like a secondary infection. If emotions are held in, tamped down, denied, then eventually they will out, in a slow corrosive leak or a sudden explosion. We've all heard expressions like "the dam burst" or "the floodgates opened" to describe pent-up emotion that can no longer be contained.

Of course it takes more than a long walk to move some emotions that are so vast and unwieldy, they are like mountain ranges, tidal waves, gaping cracks in the earth, lightning strikes. We need help—from a friend, from a counselor, sometimes from medicines. Seeking help is a prayer. Railing from the ashpit, howling inside a yurt are prayers. Listening for the voice from the whirlwind, from the silence amid the gentle buzzing of wasps are prayers. Anything that breaks our isolation is prayer. Connection, reconnection is prayer.

SHAME AND SIN

The words *shame* and *guilt* are sometimes used interchangeably. A chronic, anxious sense of guilt regardless of what you have or haven't done is probably shame. If you do something to harm someone or something, and you can face it, then you can make amends. Shame is more pervasive; its origins are deep-rooted. The abused often take on the shame of the abuser. The abuser sometimes abuses because he or she can't bear to face his own shame. Addictions and addictive behaviors are ways to avoid the pain of shame. Any loss of control, acting out, passing out, lands us back in shame, which is so unbearable that we repeat the cycle.

I have discovered that if I can find the courage to feel the shame, it can burn itself away. *Burning with shame* is not an idle expression. It is a bodily sensation. Tolerating it takes all my concentration. I no longer have the energy to ricochet between self-judgment and self-justification. All I can do is breathe. When I can stay with the pain, it consumes itself. What's left is something like the sun, shining, bringing clarity to whatever was the occasion for this particular bout of shame and the possibility of resolution.

Original sin and shame are also intertwined. Adam and Eve ate the forbidden fruit and were immediately ashamed of their nakedness, scrambled to cover it, hid from God as he prowled around the Garden. There is more than one Hebrew word for sin. *Hattah* means missing the mark. *Pesha* means rebellion, a willful violation of God's law. Adam and Eve disobeyed willfully, though of course most of the blame and shame got heaped on Eve.

The old English word synn, whose meaning includes all sorts of transgressions from mischief to offense against God, can trace its lineage back to the root -es, a root, if I am understanding correctly, that is common to both Germanic languages and Latin. It means "to be." So in *es*sence (same root), being itself is the origin of sin (original sin). And if we exist, whose fault is that?

EMOTION AS SIN

Emotions have not escaped the scrutiny of the Church Fathers.

Wrath (anger, rage) is listed among the Seven Deadly Sins.

Grief gets a pass. Maybe because it is easier to understand. Who has not grieved a loss? Jesus wept outside the tomb of Lazarus. The women wept at the foot of the cross. The history of wearing black as a sign of mourning goes back in Western culture to the Roman empire. The outward signs of grief were visible and respected, whatever anguish the mourner may have kept hidden.

Despair (not mentioned among the Seven Deadly Sins) is considered "a sin against the Holy Spirit." According to Thomas Aquinas, despair is one of six such sins. It earns its place because it "consists in thinking that one's own malice is greater than Divine Goodness." It is deemed unforgiveable. Reading various Roman Catholic commentaries, I gather despair is particularly bad, because it is a willful refusal to believe in/receive God's grace. As such, despair is viewed as presumptuous. The sinner can always repent, but if you die unrepentant, you can be unforgiven (damned) for all eternity.

I find it presumptuous and, frankly, enraging that the Church Fathers feel entitled to decide who can and cannot be forgiven for what. Recent Roman Catholic teachings, perhaps to keep up with the times, have decided depression is not despair, because it is not willful. I do not find this distinction helpful or instructive. Whether you are in despair or diagnosed with depression, you are suffering. You don't need judgment, you need compassion.

More than once, I have heard clients say, "I am angry with God, but I can't be angry with God. It's not right. I'm afraid God will be angry with me." I assure them, you *can* be angry with God, you can be whatever you are. Whoever, whatever God is, God can take it. Who better to rage at, who better to receive our tears, who better share in our despair?

I know how it is....

sacrifice (to make sacred)

The gods/God will accept as sacrifice
whatever we bring to the altar
fears, shames, rages, despairs
things we have hidden or denied.

The gods do not despise these gifts
the gift of what is wounded in us
the courage it takes to lay ourselves bare.

—from my collection of poems, *Wild Mercy*

RAGE, GRIEF, DESPAIR FOR AND IN THE WORLD

There is much suffering I have never known directly: poverty, exile, living in a war zone. I have never been stuck at a border camp in horrific conditions. I have never faced not being able to feed my children or fearing for their lives, or my own, because of racism. Or not having access to clean water. I have never been disenfranchised. I have not been incarcerated or lived without shelter. I have not had my life or livelihood threatened. I have not lost anyone to a mass shooting. Or to the pandemic. I have not lost everything to fire or flood, hurricane or tornado.

Then there is other-than-human suffering. Exhausted salmon trying to swim up dammed, overheated rivers. Whales starving because the salmon are disappearing. Polar bears and other arctic inhabitants, including humans, watching their habitat disappear. Coral dying for lack of oxygen. Wolves gunned down from airplanes. Marine birds with their feathers coated from an oil spill. Forests clear cut or burning. Impossible to list all the forms of life facing cataclysmic changes.

People often say the world has always been a tough place, difficult and dangerous, (although many cultures have stories about a time when it was paradise and people lived harmoniously with their own and other kinds). It's true that throughout our recorded history, humans have suffered and perpetrated terrible things. And humans have had an environmental impact wherever they lived. For example, Romans deforested hills, in part to heat their baths, causing erosion that silted over their harbors. And they knew it was happening. In

Ephesus, I read the translation of a public plaque posted about this problem. It was never solved. I gather it was too late and/or the Romans lacked the collective will to make the necessary changes.

I see three differences in our own time. We now have the largest human population in our history. We have global communication that can spread (dis)information at the speed of a click. And we know, unless we are in determined denial, that human agency is heating the whole planet with consequences for all life. I also hear people say, the planet will be fine, it's just us who won't be. The planet no doubt will go on evolving. But what *is* the planet? Isn't it everything, all that is living, dying, changing, including our own kind?

*

Collective rage, grief, and despair can erupt as rioting and/or generate mass movements for social change. People often condemn the former and laud the latter. Maybe the distinction is not so simple. It is easy, too easy, to pass judgment if you are looking on from the outside.

No matter how Jesus is viewed—son of God, prince of peace, savior, social revolutionary, ethical teacher, Messiah, failed Messiah, someone who possibly did not exist, on and on—his story, as it comes down to us, has him on record as starting a riot, aka cleansing the Temple of Jerusalem by driving out the money changers.

As a child, I did not know what a money changer was. When I was older, I had an image in my head of currency exchange at the airport. I knew there was selling going on, and I gathered Jesus didn't approve of making the Temple into a marketplace. Maybe he was a radical, anti-capitalist—or at least he was not pro-business.

Not until I was doing research for The Maeve Chronicles and read the Reverend Bruce Chilton's *The Temple of Jesus: His Sacrificial Program Within a Cultural History of Sacrifice* did I understand why Jesus was so enraged. According to Chilton, when peasants brought their own animals for sacrifice, they had to be inspected by Temple priests who were apt to find an unacceptable blemish, rendering the homegrown offering unacceptable. The peasants, who might have traveled for days or weeks from places like Galilee, paying for a place in a caravan, were then forced to buy approved Temple livestock for sacrifice at jacked-up prices. It was a racket, or, as Jesus put it, "a den of thieves."

Jesus wasn't having it. He made a whip with knotted cords and drove out the money changers along with their sheep and cattle. No doubt there was property damage, too, overturned tables and spilled coins. The Bible doesn't say so, but Jesus probably didn't act alone. He had his posse of disciples and very likely the fed-up peasants joined in too. Not exactly a nonviolent demonstration. I include this reminder not to be prescriptive or proscriptive but as an example of rage at injustice. Jesus's rage.

Jesus is notoriously hard to peg, speaking in parables, answering questions with questions. When I did research on the feeding of five thousand, I learned that some scholars considered the miracle not to be the multiplying loaves and fishes but the uniting of the various factions of the House of Israel, all gathered to see what Jesus would do in the wake of John the Baptist's beheading. According to the Gospel of John, afterwards the people wanted to seize Jesus and force him to be "king," i.e. a political leader of the militant resistance to Roman rule. In the three Gospel accounts of this event, Jesus disperses the crowds and goes off alone to pray. You could make a case that in refusing to be king, he chose the path of nonviolence.

Whatever tactics he approved or disapproved, Jesus was outspoken. The powerful, the self-serving and the hypocritical felt the rough side of Jesus's tongue. He got himself into what the late John Lewis might call "good trouble" by eating with sinners and other outcasts, healing on the Sabbath, and telling stories featuring a Samaritan (a group despised by the Jews) as the good guy.

Jesus's life and teachings inspired leaders like the Reverend

Martin Luther King Jr. In his "Letter from Birmingham Jail," King challenged white clergy to support nonviolent direct action. My father answered this call, organizing local clergy to join demonstrations in Washington, DC, and Montgomery, Alabama. At his memorial, in lieu of a eulogy, I read aloud my father's sermon account of the march in Montgomery.

STANDING ROCK

In 2016, fifty-three years after Martin Luther King Jr. wrote his "Letter from the Birmingham Jail," I saw a video of a Lakota elder calling on clergy of all faiths to come to Standing Rock, North Dakota, and join the Standing Rock Sioux Tribe and other indigenous nations in opposing the Dakota Access Pipeline. I don't know if the elder deliberately echoed King's letter, but that is what I heard.

And I heard the echoes from my father's life. And yes, I did think—or maybe it was not so coherent as though—at last, I will follow in my father's footsteps, stand in his lineage without shame.

A close friend also felt compelled to go. Encouraged by each other, we made our plans. Since we would be flying and unable to donate supplies, we each held a fundraiser so we would not arrive empty-handed.

We went in mid-November, not long after the presidential election and just before President Obama, in the final days of his presidency, issued a short-lived executive order to halt construction until the Army Corps of Engineers could conduct a long overdue environment impact study. Which is still not complete as of this writing. Nor did construction ever halt.

From my 2016 journal:

> We are welcomed by men from the Sioux tribe and drive
> down an avenue of tribal flags, tents and teepees every-
> where rising from dusty ground, milling people, camp

fires, sacred fires, clusters of porta-potties, horses and dogs, the gleam of the Cannonball River on the camp's far side. Signs for a medical tent and counseling center. We look for the legal tent where they tell us we will need to be vetted to participate in direct action. A woman is filling out the direct-action form; her last known address, a homeless shelter in Austin. A member of the legal team says he's got to go to a meeting. We should come back at noon with our donation.

We begin our meander through camp.

"Hello, relatives!" booms a voice from a loudspeaker every few minutes, calling out whatever anyone needs, a ride to Bismarck, tools for fixing a truck. "Hello, relatives!" each announcement begins. We offer our services at the counseling/medical tents, where we are told that only people planning to stay two weeks can work. We go to the volunteer tent and are directed to sort food and help organize a refrigerator car.

Later we took training for direct action:

We are surrounded by mostly white people. An exuberant young man volunteers a prayer. Two indigenous women from different tribes go over the Lakota principles of nonviolent direct action. They give us details about what to expect, how to protect your eyes from tear gas, how to protect your hearing from the sound boom, how to link arms to form a human barricade. We practice a formation. (Link arms and grasp your own wrists.)

"Who do you put on the frontline?" the instructors ask us.

White people? Elders?

No, the elders are too vulnerable. People move my

friend and me inside the circle. Me, an elder?! Still a surprise. All I know is I am short and can only see the middle of people's backs in any crowd.

A member of the volunteer legal team talks to us about arrest. Write the team's phone number on your body. You are likely to be strip searched, have your belongings taken and not returned. You may be jailed anywhere in the state till your bail is posted. You will have to come back to North Dakota to stand trial. Don't give anything but your name and address. Demand a court-appointed lawyer. Refuse blood or DNA tests.

My friend and I, here only for a few days, short elders other people would be obliged to protect, know we are not prepared for the frontlines. We go back to doing support work, sorting donations of clothing and food.

I cannot say I answered the call as my father answered Martin Luther King's. I did not organize a contingent of clergy. I was never in danger from the militarized police. I was not on the frontlines. I did not place my body in the way of machinery. I was never arrested. I did not go to jail. The only thing I know is that being at Standing Rock changed me.

After returning home, I kept up with what was happening there. Veterans arriving to stand with the water protectors and to make ritual amends for the history of genocide against First Nations peoples. Water hoses, tear gas, rubber bullets turned on unarmed water protectors at the Backwater Bridge. The storms and floods endured by the people who stayed through the winter. The water protectors choice to burn the teepees before the camp was closed by force in February 2017. I followed the cases of the people who were arrested and tried for felonies.

Days after he took office, President Trump reversed President Obama's order to suspend construction until the Army Corps could submit an Environmental Impact Statement, not that Energy Transfer Partners had ever complied with Obama's order. In July 2020 the United States Court for the District of Columbia ruled that the Dakota Access Pipeline must cease operation pending the completion of the Environmental Impact Statement. The temporary shutdown order was overturned by a US appeals court on August 5, 2020.

Meanwhile oil continues to flow, now at double volume, through unceded treaty land underneath Lake Oahe, the source of water for the Standing Rock Sioux Tribe and millions of people down river. The pipeline has leaked at least five times. It is notable that Lake Oahe, a reservoir in the Missouri River created in 1958, also violated treaty rights. When the river was dammed the Cheyenne River Reservation lost 150,000 acres of land and the Standing Rock Reservation, 55,993 acres, most of their prime agricultural land.

Treaties with Indigenous nations broken by the United States government is a recurrent, ongoing story, many of these treaties made after tribes were forced onto reservations, food sources, like buffalo, hunted nearly to extinction. To date, all of the more than 500 treaties have been violated by the US government. For more information, I recommend reading *An Indigenous People's History of the United States* by Roxanne Dunbar-Ortiz. For updates on ongoing indigenous resistance to pipelines in North America, become a member of the Lakota People's Law Project.

*

During my childhood, in the 1950s and 60s, children used to call each other "Indian giver," meaning: you gave me something and now you want it back. Maybe the term originated with the indigenous understanding that the land was not owned; use of the land could be negotiated between peoples. Use, not abuse. That childish taunt is staggering to me now—what egregious projection. The US government "gives" the tribes land until it discovers minerals to be mined, or wants to construct a dam, or build a pipeline—or some multinational corporation does. Who would not respond with rage, grief, and despair to this ongoing history of betrayal, which is a mild word for attempted literal and cultural genocide?

Yet over and over, indigenous peoples declare: We are still here. We are still protecting water and land, we are still following the Original Instructions passed down from the Creator, the ancestors, the elders on how to live a life in harmony with the Earth.

Standing Rock was founded as a prayer camp, an ancient and ongoing indigenous tradition. The Dakota Access Pipeline has not yet been shut down, but the prayers go on. *Mni Wiconi.* Water is Life. Who knows how the prayers will be or are being answered. The prayers are a way of life. They are a gift.

May this gift be received!

Heart Prayer

You can only pray what's in your heart

so if your heart is being ripped from your chest
pray the tearing

if your heart is full of bitterness
pray it to the last dreg

if your heart is a river gone wild
pray the torrent

or a lava flow scorching the mountain
pray the fire

pray the scream in your heart
the fanning bellows

pray the rage, the murder
and the mourning

pray your heart into the great quiet hands that can hold it
like the small bird it is.

—from my collection of poems, *Small Bird*

CHAPTER FOURTEEN

FORGIVE US
AS WE FORGIVE
KNOWING/NOT KNOWING WHAT WE DO

"I forgive you."

These words make my teeth buzz the way the sound of chalk squeaking on a blackboard does. I can vividly recall my sister and myself, as children, saying these words through clenched teeth. The only other words I hated as much were "I'm sorry," which I was also forced to say through clenched teeth. Oddly enough, I cannot recall my older brother being told to ask my forgiveness when he and his friend Jon pummeled me for their amusement. That fell into the category of "you egged them on." But my sister and I were supposed to be nice to each other.

Every day of my childhood we spoke—or sang—the words, *"Forgive us our trespasses as we forgive those who trespass against us."* I did not have any faith in God's forgiveness of me no matter how many times I prayed for it. I did not know what it meant. For me as a child, trespassing meant sneaking onto private property without permission, so I didn't know quite how my quarrels with my sister resembled trespassing. Yet she was the one I was most frequently required to forgive and to ask for forgiveness, all without leaving the rectory, let alone stepping over any gap in a wall into a mysterious forbidden world.

I also cannot remember my father asking forgiveness for any of his excesses and abuses, except possibly once when I was sixteen. He was very drunk and pulled me into a rare, excruciating, and seemingly interminable embrace as he whimpered "I love you so much," which I doubted given his customary behavior towards me. I am not sure if that qualifies as an appeal for forgiveness. If it was, I don't think I gave it, not in that moment.

HEALING AS FORGIVENESS

As a counselor, I've worked with people who have suffered extreme abuse (rape, incest, physical and emotional violence). Premature or willed forgiveness can be damaging in itself. It keeps the focus on the perpetrator of harm; it can be another way of caretaking that person at the expense of yourself.

Here is an alternate method of forgiveness: healing. To give a crude, literal example: if you stab me, I don't have to say (through clenched teeth), "I forgive you" as I stand there bleeding. I must tend the wound, wash it, bandage it, keep it free of infection. When the literal (or figurative) wound heals, the harm is undone, and I am free to hold you harmless. That is what I think of as an unforced, organic form of forgiveness.

Some wounds are mere accidental scratches; some go to the core of our being and may take a lifetime to heal and even then can leave scars. We can choose to heal our wounds, regardless of whether or not the one who wounded us did so knowingly or unknowingly, regardless of whether or not that person is sorry, regardless of whether that person is alive or dead. The harm done to us often renders us powerless. Healing can restore our agency. Healing as forgiveness is not so much a moral imperative as a practical one. It is a process, one that can and sometimes must include acknowledgment of anger. If we do not judge anger as a shameful negative emotion (indicative of moral failure), in most cases anger will pass when it has served its purpose.

Forgive and forget is an axiom I heard frequently while growing up; alliterative and easy to remember. Does forgetting mean literally not being able to remember the harm someone has done? If so, forget it. I wonder if healing can be considered a form of forgetting. I can remember many things that hurt me, but these incidents no longer hold a charge. I can move in and out of different perspectives, see things in different lights. Most of all, I don't have to dwell in these memories. They are past. When a wound goes unhealed and untended, the past is still, at any given moment, present.

I've been speaking as one harmed, but of course I have done harm—the harm that comes of not understanding what my children are going through, the harm of imposing my will, to give just a couple of examples in broad strokes. We all hurt people, usually unintentionally, even unconsciously. In my experience, both perpetrators and victims of trauma can lose access to memories that are unbearably painful, terrifying, shaming, or all three. Remembering can be essential to healing.

The events in *All the Perils of This Night*, the sequel to *Murder at the Rummage Sale*, are entirely fictional, but the emotional terrain of trauma is not. In the character of Gerald, I explore the phenomenon of alcoholic blackout, repression, and recovery of memory. When Gerald remembers what he did to his daughter Katherine, he seeks out a priest for the rite of personal confession. After he confesses, the penitent reads aloud from the Book of Common Prayer:

> *"For these and all other sins which I cannot now remember, I am truly sorry. I pray God to have mercy on me. I firmly intend amendment of my life, and I humbly beg forgiveness of God and his Church, and ask for your counsel, direction, and absolution."*
>
> Gerald looked up again.
>
> "But I'm not ready for absolution. I don't even know

if I believe in it any more. Can you give me a penance? I need help. Help me. Please help me."

Later Gerald faces the daughter he harmed. The scene is from Katherine's point of view.

> "Katherine," said her father.
>
> Thank God he had stopped sniffling.
>
> "I don't expect you to forgive me."
>
> "Good," she said.
>
> "But I still have to ask your forgiveness. I do ask your forgiveness."
>
> She sat for another moment. There was a world outside, fields, trees, sun.
>
> "Thank you," she heard herself saying. "I'm going to take Bear for a walk now."
>
> And without rushing, she got up and went outside, closing the door quietly behind her.

For me, as a novelist, these scenes are the beginning of healing. Gerald recognizes that he has done something he considers unforgivable. And who is God to forgive him for what he did to Katherine? (Though of course theologically Katherine is one of the least of Jesus's brethren.) But Gerald is beyond theology in the realm of raw, emotional truth. When he does ask Katherine's forgiveness, he makes it his obligation to ask forgiveness, not hers to grant it. He releases her from responsibility for him. And she is free to go outside and take the dog for a walk, free to begin her own road to healing, short or long, winding or direct, hers.

WE KNOW NOT WHAT WE DO

"Father, forgive them for they know not what they do," is the first of Jesus's seven last utterances from the cross. Is he simply doing his best, even in extremis, to reconcile us with the Father? Don't be mad at them, Father. Don't visit your legendary wrath upon them. In one sense, they (whoever they are, and that's tricky in itself. Are they the Romans, the Sanhedrin, the soldiers carrying out their orders?) certainly do know that they are torturing a man to death. Is the implication that they don't know he's God's only begotten son, or in the Trinitarian doctrine yet to come, that he is God [him]self, which makes it worse than torturing, say, a thief?

In human history, before and after Jesus's crucifixion, there have been so many atrocities, so much church or state-sanctioned torture and genocide, so many murderous mobs. So much human violence and perpetration of misery that seems unforgivable. Sometimes we can separate the victims from the perpetrators. Sometimes, knowing or unknowingly, we are both. Who can forgive us, how can we forgive?

What if Jesus cried out for his Abba to forgive because in that moment it was beyond his suffering human self? The question, "If there is a God, how could God allow the Holocaust, the Middle Passage, the murderous conquest of whole continents?" continues to resound. If we acknowledge that human beings have authored all this suffering, then who, what, and where is God? Is Abba a negligent and/or abusive parent? Is God with us, within us? Or are we, God help us, on our own?

Forgive them, forgive us, we know/we don't know what we're doing.

*

In *The Coming of the Cosmic Christ*, Roman Catholic theologian Matthew Fox, who was once silenced by the Vatican, sees our current ecological crisis as Christ crucified again, Christ as Mother Earth.

We are on the knife edge of knowing/not knowing what we do to the earth. To give just one example, what did we know/not know when we sprayed pesticides all over crops and even residential neighborhoods in the 1950s, utilizing chemicals developed for warfare in agribusiness? When did we know that we were poisoning ground water and killing pollinators—and sickening ourselves? Was there originally a benign intent, such as increasing productivity to end famine or was it all profit-driven? Same for damming rivers for irrigation, drilling oil and gas for electric power. Someone or ones were/are getting obscenely rich. Did we ever believe, do we still persuade ourselves that it was/is for the good of all?

I am often on the knife edge of blame and shame, hating my own kind, which leads to hating myself. Even when we know what we have done and are doing and take what steps we can to reduce our carbon footprint (reusable shopping bags, planting pollinator gardens) we are caught up in a system that seems as out of control and driven as the sorcerer's apprentice's bucket and mop.

What gives me hope is watching how the earth adapts, how it heals itself, given a chance. I live in an area that was once completely deforested for industry, mill stones, barrel staves, cement. When those industries died or raw material was found from other sources, two Quaker brothers bought up vast amounts of land along the Shawangunk Ridge and hired local people who'd lost their jobs to build winding carriage trails and, yes, hotels, one still extant, one lost to fire. Less than two hundred years later the forests have grown back, no doubt they are different than they once were, but they are adapting, changing, living.

stone mountain song

can you hear my voice?
you come to me for silence
for wind in the pines

for water running underground
for the slow wheeling of vultures
over my bare height
for blue sky beyond shadow
in the strong hot light.

it was not always so.
I remember the violent din
when you stole me piece by piece
to make millstones and cities,
stripped of trees, a barren place
where only berries grew, you
stole those too, took them to your tables
miles and rivers below.

now I have taken back
mist and tree, moss and fern
and mystery. bears and snakes sleep
deep in hidden winter warmth
and wild cats roam. stay. I will
chide no more, small one,
forgotten, forgetting, alone.
cling to me now, I will be your home.

—from my collection of poems,
Tell Me the Story Again

(A note here about preservation of land: The founding of
National Parks displaced many indigenous tribes, often to the det-
riment of ecological systems. One example: all over North America
indigenous peoples practiced controlled burns to manage forest
and prairie land, a practice which is now being reintroduced. Land

doesn't need to be void of human inhabitants to thrive. It needs humans who know they are part of the land, not separate from it, humans who have passed down Traditional Ecological Knowledge (TEK) for generations.

Forgive us our trespasses. That should be the prayer of all colonial governments. The original English settlers, land-hungry because of the Enclosure Acts, came to this continent and trespassed against whole peoples, making into private property land that once belonged to all life.)

*

If healing is forgiveness, then the earth is forgiving. It is tempting to look at cataclysmic storms, floods, and fires as punishment, the earth taking revenge on us. Or, if we deny culpability, to see natural forces as malevolent, or to see catastrophe as an "Act of God," an actual legal term in insurance policies. But retribution is an androcentric view; it is not only humans who suffer in a hurricane. Plants, animals, whole ecologies can be devastated.

I once had a painful injury to my back and hip that was taking what seemed to me a long time to heal. I groused to my Friend, "So what happened to *'only say the word and I shall be healed'*?" An answer came back that I have never forgotten:

Obviously, this is what healing looks like.

Not so obvious to me at the time, but I continued to ponder. I am still pondering. It could be that storms, floods, fires are what healing looks like for the earth. In the midst of what we experience as devastation and destruction, the earth may be seeking to balance what is out of balance. What if we align with this healing? What if we change how we live, where and what we build, how we grow food, how we treat each other and all life? If we shift from not knowing to knowing, it could happen. In fits and starts, here and there, it is already happening. We may not be able to see the whole picture, but we can pay closer attention. We can begin to make amends, repent, as in turn, turn around, choose a different way.

Perhaps we can begin to forgive ourselves and be forgiven.

Great oak song

hush now, small one.
I have not spoken yet, though I have grown
in silent rings three hundred years,
though I groan in wind that gives me
voice as light gives me
new limbs and earth opens to me
its depths where my roots taste truth
in rock and water.
Come into the shelter of me
and lay down your despair,
come into the shelter of me
and be silent.
Come into the shelter of me
and remember
you are a child among elders.
Small one, you've forgotten your task,
small one, you're forgiven before you ask.

—from my collection of poems,
Tell Me the Story Again

CHAPTER FIFTEEN

BEAUTY SINGER

THE HOLINESS OF BEAUTY

I am walking in a springtime wood and spot a trout lily, the small yellow flower, its petals trumpeting open, curling back, revealing its red stamen and delicate green pistil. Its speckled leaves, which give the plant its name, blend in with the forest floor when the flower is not in bloom. I remember the delighted shock of my first sighting. I know the plant's name, because I went home and described it to, yes, google. I don't carry a field guide with me, and I don't always succeed in finding the names of what I see (in which case I make up a name). I know people now have apps on their phones that will identify plants. I don't carry a phone or a camera, but I do like knowing names. It seems friendly. Naming helps us to see. When we know the names of trees, we can see particular leaves and needles, instead of an undifferentiated mass of green. I am not a scientific observer, though I am grateful to those who are for helping me to see more clearly and distinctly. I am not an artist or a photographer. I am a lover, an amateur in every way. I am a prayer.

The title of Alice Walker's novel *The Color Purple* comes from Shug Avery's feisty declaration: "I think it pisses God off if you walk by the color purple in a field somewhere and don't notice it." Conversely, when you do notice a color, a slant of light, a flash of wings, maybe it rejoices whatever God is, gives God heartsease.

That is, of course, pure speculation, perhaps fanciful, but if so, it is a persistent fancy. Sometimes when I see a wildflower in the woods where other humans seldom walk, it occurs to me that many beauties come and go without a human witness. Most likely it doesn't matter to the trout lily blooming for its own purpose or the purposes of a pollinator. What is a flower, or any being, to itself? Even (maybe especially) humans, who invented mirrors and gaze into them, have little idea of their impact on the lives of others, the life around them.

When I am walking around looking at things, listening, breathing a scent, I think *this* is why I'm here, this is why *we're* here. To take in the world, exclaiming, silently or out loud. Oh! Look! Listen! Why do we do anything else? Oh right, survival, food, clothes, shelter. Yet maybe meeting those needs is not the reason for our existence, if there indeed is one.

*

I have an early childhood memory of staying overnight at my aunt's house in Redding, Connecticut. Early in the morning, maybe before breakfast, she took my hand and led me outside.

"Listen to the birds!" she said.

All at once, I was overwhelmed with sound. The air was dense with it. I can hear it now, the songs of so many birds. I can more than hear. I can remember the moment when the sound began, with her naming. Whenever, wherever I hear that sound, it still holds the intensity of revelation.

The summer I was ten years old, I inexplicably developed insomnia. My distress, even panic, intensified it. My mother consulted doctors, dosed me with Benadryl, became anxious herself. Such preoccupation with her children's troubles generally irritated my father. Our emotional enmeshment must have seemed impenetrable to him. He was hardly sympathetic. Yet, one night, very late, maybe my mother had finally given up on me, my father sat with me in the room I shared with my sister in a summer cabin by a lake.

"Listen," my father said. "Listen to the sound of the wind in the pines."

And I did. It was soft, strong, melodic, rhythmic. Surely I had heard it before by that age. But now I listened intently.

"It's because you're awake that you can hear the wind," he said. "Listen."

He must have left the room shortly after that, left me listening to the wind in the pines until I went to sleep. Whenever and wherever I hear the sound of wind in the pines, the sound holds the memory of that rare tenderness and peace.

I don't know if I bequeathed such moments to my children or if someone else did or some circumstance, but I do have memories of witnessing beauty with them.

There are things I remember
like watching the stars come out
with my children when they were young.
How quiet and still we were.
The bats came out, too,
black and beautiful against
that transient sky—you couldn't
call it purple or blue—doing
their sonar dance with the bugs
while the birds gave a last twitter
or two. Sometimes the coracle moon
would be setting, the last light
lapping it silently.
We would watch together,
my children's mouths small
gaping nights and their eyes

that same dusk color
with the first stars floating in them.
And when I remember I know
I have not wasted my life.

—from my collection of poems, *Small Bird*

THE EYES OF THE BEHOLDERS

When I am tempted to think that noticing beauty is our uniquely human purpose, I remind myself that we know directly only our own ways of perceiving. I boggle my mind wondering what the world looks like—or feels like, sounds like, smells like, tastes like—to other creatures, and not just other mammals. We have some awareness of dogs' keenness of smell and cats' sharp hearing. What about raptors or a murmuration of birds, what about earthworms and all the life under the sea. What about microscopic life in the soil, in our own bodies. Everything alive, including humans, seeks to survive and reproduce. How can we be the only beings who ponder or praise or play? I have seen ravens turning somersaults on the wind. In the song of the scarlet tanager, I hear solemn, intricate joy. Can this sound fill the air only to court a mate or mark territory?

My husband is a beekeeper. I do not tend the bees, but outside in the gardens, I am constantly in their company. Bees have three single-lens eyes on top of their heads, enabling them to see colors as ultraviolet light, as well as two compound eyes with thousands of lenses, which their brains swiftly organize into a mosaic view of their world.

Long before my husband joined a local beekeepers society, where he continues to learn about the lives of bees, he noticed that each hive has a different personality. The hive is the person or the being. (It's tempting to make puns about apian *beeings*.) We suppose every bee we see is an individual, and maybe it is, but it is also an expression of the hive. (We suppose we are individuals, but maybe we are more like hives, with myriad different buzzing parts.) My husband tells me each bee does all the tasks in the course of its life. First it cleans up the cell from which it was born, then it nurses other bees. Making bread from pollen and honey from nectar comes next, and then the task of gathering pollen and nectar from the flowers. The last job is as a scout, finding what's blooming, sometimes a couple of miles away, mapping the way and returning to dance the map for the gatherer bees who learn the way by touching the scout bee while it dances the route.

Bees gather nectar and pollen to make food to survive. (And because they do, *we* survive!) When I was commented to my husband on the amazing psychedelic vision of bees, he said, "Well, that's just how they see. But who knows, maybe when the bees come on a swath of flowers (like the beebalm in my garden) it looks beautiful to them."

Maybe beauty is not superfluous to survival. Maybe it is integral. Modern western human beings are not as close to their sources as bees are to flowers. But in times and places where we were—or are—we sing planting and harvest songs, dance for rain or sun. We hold feasts in gratitude, making our offerings pleasing to the eye. Prehistoric cave art is full of beautiful, moving images of animals hunted for survival. When we were hunters and gatherers, surely we wandered around, our senses always on the alert for sustenance and beauty. Look, we said silently or aloud. Listen, smell, taste, touch.

HUMAN-MADE BEAUTY

We now think of the arts as something distinct—and maybe they are distinct in a world where many things are mass produced and where only a few artists are recognized and rewarded. Museums display remnants of ancient pottery as artifacts of history but also for their beauty. Utility and beauty were not always separate or at odds. In some times and places everyone participates in the arts. When we visited Trinidad, where Olga grew up, a woman told us, "At Carnival everyone is an artist, making costumes, playing music, dancing." There is no separation between creator and consumer and what is created.

(I am not qualified as an art historian, but I have an impression that the artist as individual may be a concept that dates to the western Renaissance and has d/evolved to its present idolatry of celebrities in a global capitalist system.)

Just before I turned fourteen, when I fell thirty-three-and-a-half feet from a tree, cracked three vertebrae and an ankle, I was in the hospital for three weeks, flat on my back. I can still picture the face of one nurse who was especially kind. I also remember a volunteer bringing around an art cart. I selected a print of a painting by the Quaker artist Edward Hicks, part of a series called "The Peaceable Kingdom." The painting I chose has a prominent lion beside an ox with various lambs and children scattered about. In the distance, First Nations people meet on the shore with colonists. The Quakers of Hicks's time, among them William Penn, did seek to maintain more peaceful and equitable relations than other European settlers, and the painting reflects that aspiration. I did not know or think about any of that then. I just gazed at the painting, which I now find so quiet and still, as perhaps I had to be then. It is one of my few memories of contemplating a work of visual art, my memories of music and words being more prominent. When I was confined inside a room for weeks, the painting became my landscape.

There is another painting vivid in my memory, one that I saw in Miss Sang's house. Giotto's "Saint Francis Preaching to the Birds." To me, it always looked like he was feeding the birds, because of his openhanded leaning towards them and their alert expectancy. I do know he is supposed to have preached to the birds, among other brother and sister creatures. As a child, I loved an illustrated book that recounted the story of Saint Francis and the Wolf of Gubbio.

Unafraid of the ravening beast, Francis went outside the village walls to meet with Brother Wolf, who agreed to stop eating villagers in exchange for being fed by them. Maybe it was because of the story that this painting made such an impression on me. Or maybe it is the golden background, the leafy tree bending toward the saint, in contrast to the skeptical-looking fellow monk standing back, hands raised in a sort of "Now what?! Really?" kind of gesture.

The gold, the brown of the saint's robe, the green of the tree, the blend of colors are in the same family as the colors in the Peaceable Kingdom. They are also colors I associate with my mother and with my long-ago dream of riding on a donkey through a golden-brown landscape to give birth, assisted by monks wearing habits like the ones in the painting. Both paintings show a world where humans are connected and at peace with fellow beings on this earth. Hicks apparently believed that all creatures, not just humans, share in the Divine inner light.

WORSHIPPING BEAUTY, BEAUTY AS WORSHIP

Hicks, a recorded Quaker minister and preacher, made his living as a decorative painter, an occupation not looked upon with favor by some of his coreligionists. He eventually gave up his ministry to devote himself to painting, though his themes continued to express his convictions as a Friend.

Plainness was a prominent Quaker value from the beginning. Plain speech (the use of the familiar form "thee" for everyone instead of "you") and plain dress, plain meeting houses. There is a Quaker anecdote about a new member arriving at meeting impeccably dressed in expensive grey linen, looking down her nose at a woman wearing apparently cheap (and rather colorful) calico. At the rise of the meeting, the woman in calico welcomed the newcomer, noting "Thee speaks well, but thee dresses too fine."

The prohibition against graven images goes back to the Ten

Commandments. The Israelites were at pains to distinguish themselves from pagans who worshipped, in groves or among unhewn dolmen, multiple deities, gods of sun, moon, stars, love, fertility instead of the one God *"immortal invisible, God only wise, in light inaccessible, hid from our eyes."* Despite the splendor and riches of the Temple of Jerusalem, the Holy of Holies, entered by the high priest once a year, was an empty unadorned chamber.

The term iconoclast literally means a smasher of icons and dates back to the 8th century when the Byzantine Emperor Leo III made a decree prohibiting the depiction of religious figures. Pope Gregory III declared iconoclasm heretical in 730 and the Second Council of Nicaea in 787 made his ruling official in Byzantium. The Protestant Reformation took up the cause of iconoclasm with a vengeance all across 16th century Europe.

Islam also has a prohibition against depicting the divine in form. And so they created exquisitely beautiful geometric designs as well as calligraphy and vegetal images. Most religions have constructed architectural wonders.

Is worship of beauty, natural or human-made, a form of idolatry? Is this question perennial?

My early memories of church are all of beauty, the sonorous words of the most terrifying prayers, the light coming through the stained-glass windows. Candles and evergreen boughs on Christmas Eve. I remember a canticle we sang during morning prayer in the church of my childhood.

"O worship the Lord in the beauty of holiness."

Maybe beauty is holy and holiness is beauty. I was ordained in a beautiful cathedral where the pillars rose like trees in a forest. I have sat in Quaker Meeting on beautiful, handmade wooden benches, watching the light come in through plain windows. I have danced the Maypole under a crescent moon in a dusky sky.

All these ways of worshipping are beautiful.

The holiness of beauty is not limited to formal worship. Ritual may be a way of remembering what is always present. The Navajo Beauty Way is a way of life. Beauty above us, below us, before us, behind us, walking in beauty, every step. A Celtic prayer attributed to St. Patrick has the same rhythm: "*Christ with me, Christ before me, Christ behind me, Christ in me, Christ beneath me, Christ above me....*"

I think of Miss Sang setting a table, cooking a meal, creating beauty with a gesture or a glance—her essence, beauty.

SINGING BEAUTY

Beauty is not a luxury, a frill, a pretty bow decorating and distracting from what my father might have called grim reality. A grim reality like the maximum-security prisons I used to visit. I have always wondered, and still do, if the ugliness of prisons is deliberate, punitive. I may be only projecting how I would feel to be confined in a clamorous, crowded place, cells stacked on top of each other, no quiet, little natural light or dark, no sky except what you can glimpse from the yard, no beauty except what you can find in your own mind or maybe witness in someone else's hard-won peace or kindness. Even if I am projecting, I believe we all need beauty of some kind, in some form to live, wherever we can find it or create it.

In my fairytale novel-in-progress, the wealthy elite live inside a completely artificial domed world. Fountains flow; gardens bloom; images of sun, moon, and stars move over the vast dome that is their sky. The Outsiders they exploit live in something like a prison yard or refugee camp. They are the slaves of the Insiders, who keep the Outsiders' conditions as marginal and miserable as possible. Among the Outsiders there is a secret band of women known as Beauty Singers. Every morning at dawn they roam the streets singing beauty, their voices clear and piercing as the stars. If they are caught, they know they will be executed. Beauty singing is their defiant risk, their offering, their revolutionary act.

Many of what we call the arts require some means to purchase materials, some expensive, some as simple as pen and paper. But singing is part of our body, our being. So is rhythm, our heartbeat and breath inspiring handclapping, foot stomping, dancing. From the workers on the slave plantations came call-and-response field hollers, spirituals, a way of worshipping and also a way of coding and passing along information. The blues went from backyards to juke joints to record labels to influence every subsequent American musical form.

As long as we are alive, we can sing. Even if we think we can't, we can sing.

Song is the other side of silence, rising invisible from the body, returning there, residing there. It is a way to pray, it is a way to comfort and encourage yourself and others. When you sing you are filled and emptied at once. I don't know where I read that in Aramaic, Creator and/or Creation can be translated as Singing Radiance. I can't find any confirmation of this memory but it stays with me. One of the most beautiful passages in the Chronicles of Narnia is Aslan singing Narnia into being.

*

Back to wandering around, noticing beauty. A spider's web beaded with dew shining in the early light. A bee gathering nectar from the dark center of a sunflower. Does it matter that someone witnesses? That I do? How is it useful? Who or what does it serve?

Don't fret so, child, said one of those inner voices. *You are a beauty singer.*

I hope I am. I believe we all are.

Why else are we here?

CHAPTER SIXTEEN

HELP! HELP!

HOW SOME PRAYERS ARE ANSWERED

"Help," I prayed, "help." (Help, help is one of the best prayers I know. You just have to be prepared for some bizarre responses.)

—from The Maeve Chronicles' *Bright Dark Madonna*

Maeve is praying after she flees the Christian communal house where Peter has just blasted Ananias (causing him to drop dead) for hiding some of his personal wealth from the ecclesia. People being struck dead is not the sort of prenatal influence Maeve wants for her unborn—and already contested—child. The answer to her prayer comes in the form of her frenemy Paulina, the Roman matron who used to own Maeve as a slave. Maeve hears Paulina loudly haggling in the market place, demanding strangled meat (unkosher to Jews) for a dinner party she's hosting. Paulina is delighted to have a chance to save Maeve's life or at least hide her from the apostles and smuggle her out of town, pronto.

More often than not we don't know how or if prayers are answered, prayers for other people, prayers for the world. Maybe we can't know. Every now and then I have had some unmistakable—and yes bizarre—answers to my own impromptu prayers for help.

MIRACLE AT THE MALL

(Note: The following memory is more than twenty years old and is shared here with my daughter's permission.)

Shopping. At the mall. Or rather, I am not shopping, I am taking my teenaged daughter shopping. This is not a happy thing as it may be for some mothers and daughters. This is a fraught and woeful thing. At least today. She is not happy, maybe not happy with herself, certainly not happy with me. She does not speak much. She doesn't need to. She emanates. Or maybe she isn't emanating. Maybe my perceptions are skewed by my own anxieties. I can't honestly say I know what she is thinking or feeling. I only know how I am feeling.

Desperate.

At one store I sit down on a step that divides one level from another while she stalks the racks of clothes. *Help*, I pray, *help! I don't know what to do, I don't know how to be. Help, help!*

I don't know how many stores we go to or whether we find anything she wants or needs or not. At some point, we look for a restroom, following the signs to one of the mall facilities. It's small, only three stalls. The middle one is occupied, so we take the stalls on either side.

In the middle stall is a mother and small child, who needs… help!

"Come on, now, go," sings the mother at top volume. "Go out the door. Just turn around now, you're not welcome anymore…."

I start to shake with silent laughter. We emerge from our stalls, wash our hands, the mother still singing with gusto. Out in the hall, my daughter and I burst out laughing together. My daughter has the best laugh in the world. We laugh and laugh all the way to wherever we're going next. And for the rest of the day we have fun. Together.

To this day, I do not doubt. That was the answer to my prayer.

"Come on now go, go out the door…."

A mother coaxing her child to poop.

I never saw the mother or child. She could not know that she had provided the best family therapy ever. Such is the mystery of prayer.

SHOWING UP AT THE TABLE

For years (many of them while I was writing *The Passion of Mary Magdalen*) I went on hermitage retreat at Villa St. Dominic, which was run by a small group of Roman Catholic Dominican nuns who called themselves the Sisters of Corazon. The sisters lived in the main house, a huge, sprawling three-story building with a big, winterized sun porch. Here they hosted group retreats. Some wealthy Catholic man had donated the property to the Catholic Church (perhaps some sins were expiated?) and it included a mile of riverfront property and another large house, Villa St. Joseph, where nuns went on holiday. (I visited there once and found the nuns drinking iced tea and playing cards.)

The Sisters of Corazon had built two little hermitages some distance away from the main house. They were close together (probably because they shared a septic tank) but angled for maximum privacy. The hermitages were simple: one room with a small, complete kitchen and a bathroom. There was a skylight and a huge picture window overlooking the Mahicantuck (aka the Hudson River). The big house and the hermitages stood on a bluff just above the river facing east. Each hermitage had a porch complete with a rocking chair. No matter what time of year I was there, I never missed a sunrise.

Most of the people who stayed in the hermitages were nuns and priests. There was a journal where guests left entries about their stay, the peace, the beauty, the weather, the birds, and animals they had seen, and their gratitude to the sisters and to God. When there were two hermits in residence, we would nod and smile and keep silence.

How close and companionable silence with another hermit can be. I spent a lot of time walking by the river (and in summer I swam naked) and never saw another person. Another cause for gratitude to this small, devoted band of sisters.

Hermits and other retreatants (I was often the only one) were welcome at daily Mass. I usually attended at least once during my stay. I liked Father Julian, one of two priests who led the services. Probably in his sixties, he lived in the nearby village and cared for his aged mother. He would always give a seemingly extemporaneous homily, standing in the center of the tiny chapel, his palms turned up, his eyes squeezed tight shut, his heart open—his words always came straight from there.

I did not realize till later, when my visit coincided with a group retreat, that lay people were supposed to sit in the living room, a step down from the chapel. So, not knowing the protocol, I initially sat with the nuns and sang along with the recorded music they used to lead singing. I also received Communion after asking permission from Father Julian. I told him I had been baptized but was not a Roman Catholic.

"How's your relationship with Jesus?" he wanted to know.

"Good," I answered.

"That's all that matters," he said.

One day, after I'd been making annual retreats for several years, Sister Peggy confronted me after Mass.

"You shouldn't be taking Communion," she said angrily.

I was taken aback.

"I did ask Father Julian—"

"Father Julian!" She cut me off, snorting derisively. "He shouldn't allow it. You're not Roman Catholic. This is a very conservative congregation."

I didn't argue with her, as I had once argued with one of my father's successors at Grace Church after a service where he'd said, "all baptized Christians are welcome at the Lord's Table."

"So," I had challenged him, "Jesus couldn't take Communion here?"

I don't know what John the Baptist was doing when he dunked Jesus in the Jordan River, but I don't think he was baptizing him in the name of the Trinity.

"Well," said the priest, "it's the Church's rule."

"The kind of rule Jesus tended to break," I pointed out.

I am happy to say that the next time I attended Grace Church, this priest said, "Everyone is welcome at the Lord's table."

But Grace Church was my home church. I was a guest at Villa St. Dominic, and I wanted to be a polite one. Sister Peggy had already turned me away. I didn't take her rebuff personally. Mostly I felt badly that I had offended her. I liked attending Mass as a way to pay my respects to the community. But my blissful solitude, the sunrises, the rambles by the river, would remain unaffected. I continued to be a happy hermit.

The next time I made a retreat, I decided I would not attend Mass. I saw no reason to ruffle feathers. As noted, I was content on my own.

But Jesus had other ideas.

I want you to go to Mass today.

(Yes, I do talk to him. I suppose the conversations began in Quaker Meeting when I informed him that he would be a character in a possibly heretical novel. Who knows whether I make it all up? I have come to recognize and trust what seems like a distinctive voice, pithy, often humorous, inclined to answer questions with questions, but always ready to cut straight to the heart of the matter. That day I had not started the conversation. Or asked his opinion. I had already made my decision.)

"No, really," I answered. "I don't need to go. I'm fine. I don't want to upset Sister Peggy."

He was not interested in what I wanted or didn't want.

You. At my table. Now.

He was so clear and insistent, his directive so contrary to my own inclinations, that I went. And against my better judgment, I took Communion.

After Mass Sister Peggy embraced me and held me close. And I understood. She had likely been reproaching herself for almost a year for telling me I was not welcome to receive Communion. Maybe she'd even confessed her rebuff of me as a sin. She might have prayed for a chance to make amends. Now, whatever harm she feared she had done had been undone. Jesus's insistence that I go to Mass had been not for my sake but for hers. Ever after, Sister Peggy could not have been warmer or more welcoming to me.

Their numbers dwindling and their years increasing, the sisters retired to the Mother House in 2015 in Sparkill, New York. With no younger nuns to take their place, and no doubt a dearth of funding, they sold the property to Scenic Hudson, a nonprofit organization devoted to preserving and protecting land and communities along the Hudson River. It is still possible to hike the trails along the river, and the Falling Waters Preserve in Glasco, New York has become a popular spot. I miss both the sisters and the solitude I was lucky to enjoy for years and years of hermitage retreats.

ANGELS, FAIRIES, AND DEVAS

I believe that far more often than we can know, we are the answers to prayers we know nothing about, we play the part of angels in disguise. We are or can be angels to each other. That is very particular and perhaps off-putting language for many people. You could also call these moments synchronicity or flow or being in the right place at the right time. You don't have to believe in God or gods or angels. You don't have to call it prayer, but if you ask for help, however you do it, sometimes there's an answer. The trick is to recognize when you have been answered—and perhaps when you *are* the answer.

A client once gave me a book about angels that she had found helpful. I don't remember much about the book. I don't think I read it all the way through. I did not get caught up in angelology (yes, there is such a field). It was her summary of the book that stayed with me.

"The angels are there," she said, "all the time, ready to help with even the most trivial things. But you have to ask. They can't do anything unless they are asked."

I thought of all the angels, standing around, twiddling their thumbs, or filing their nails, frustrated and bored. Under-employed.

"Wot the hell, Archy, wot the hell." I quoted Mehitabel (the cat in *The Evening Sun* columnist Don Marquis's cat and cockroach pair).

I decided to help the angels out.

I don't know why I began addressing them as angels, fairies, and devas. People more familiar with otherworldly beings might look askance at my lack of distinction. No doubt angels, fairies, and devas come from different cultures, times, and geographies. But when I ask for help that's how I speak to whoever they are. Maybe I don't even speak with commas in between. (Yes, I address them out loud.) For me, they are a benign and collective entity.

I began by asking for help finding lost things, socks, coffee cups, keys, gloves—the list is long and varied. Usually within a few moments I find my gaze directed to the missing item. No more frantic, anxious searches. If it is taking a little longer than I'd like, and I find myself getting frustrated, I stop and say, "It's all right. I don't need whatever it is right away. Just sometime soon." And I stop looking and go on about my business. Within hours or sometimes a day, I see whatever it was (once a prized pair of socks had fallen out of the laundry basket into a wastebasket). Sometimes a memory will return that shows me when and how I lost whatever it was and directs me where to look farther afield—under the car, for example, in the case of missing gloves.

I am aware that there are other explanations for this method of finding things. I calm down; I shift into another mode of thinking and perceiving. Instead of looking manically over and over again in the same places where I think something should be, I am relaxed and open, my vision more apt to be wide-angled. If addressing invisible helpers facilitates this state, why not? I am willing to accept a rational, scientific explanation. I also reserve the right to believe in angels, fairies, and devas. Who is to say this frame of mind is not, in a sense, angelic?

It is very happy-making to find a lost object in this manner. I always give the angels, fairies, and devas profuse thanks. I tell them they are my dear friends.

*

One day I took a walk through a wood that has no path. It is only passable in the winter, because the barberry (which harbors Lyme ticks in summer) is so dense. Following the course of the winding stream, I came to waterfalls flowing over flat rocks. On the way there I walked on the bluff above the stream. On the way back I wanted to stay closer to the water. Here the barberry was even thicker in places. And after passing through some grassy, muddy flood land, the stream came up against the steep high banks. The way through was not evident.

It occurred to me that if the angels, fairies, and devas could help me find my socks, they might help me find a path through the swampy thickets. So, I asked them, politely and out loud. Then I stood still and waited. In a moment I saw how I could take a few clear steps. So I did. Then I stopped and waited again until another opening appeared. When I say "appeared," I don't mean that invisible beings with invisible machetes cleared a path where there hadn't been one before. What cleared was my perception. In this way, little by little, I walked through the swamp between the stream and the steep bank, coming closer to a beavers' dam than I ever had before.

At last this way out of no way guided me to a gentle, open slope that led to the field.

Over the years I have come to ask for other kinds of help. "Angels, fairies, and devas, I have lost my temper, please help me find it again." When I work in the garden I ask for guidance. I also do due diligence, looking up the needs of various plants. But it is different being out there with all the living beings of the yard. I ask the angels, fairies, and devas to guide me to make the best choices as I prepare soil, prune, plant, and weed. (As to the weeds—the ones that would leave no room for other plants, I also speak to them. I say, "You are a fine plant, strong and resourceful. You have many places to grow, just please not in this garden.")

I also often pray to all beings kindly to the Earth, including the angels, fairies, devas, deities, some of whom have walked this earth. Help us! I pray out loud. Help us! Help my kind wake up and love this Earth! Help us to cease our harm. Help all life here on this Earth—rooted and leafed and spored, winged, finned, scaled, feathered, boned, boneless, huge and microscopic—and all that gives life: air, rivers, oceans, mountains, soil. If you need someone to ask you, I am asking. I am praying.

Help! Help!

CHAPTER SEVENTEEN

AN ELEMENTAL MEDITATION

EARTH, AIR, FIRE, WATER

Where are you right now? Even if you are indoors, beneath the floor or floors; under the plane, if you are flying; under the water, if you're on a boat; beneath your feet whenever you step foot outside is the earth. Every breath you take in and out is the air, one with the winds that circle the globe. Over your head or your roof is the sun or the moon reflecting the sun's light. Maybe there's a fire in a woodstove or heat from another source. All heat comes from the sun, whether stored in trees or fossil fuels or solar panels, and all light. If you are still enough, you can feel your heartbeat, the rhythm of your own inner sea. Pause, take a drink of water. All the waters of the world are connected, and every bite of food you eat is made of all the elements.

> I had an intense awareness that I ate not only the bread, vegetables, olives, and grapes, but also the sun, the rain, the soil, the very mystery that called them forth from the earth. I took into my body the underwater life of the fish in the warm shallows, the cold currents and springs, the filtered light of sun and moon.

> —from *The Passion of Mary Magdalen*

HONORING THE ELEMENTS

In many traditions, elements correspond with a direction, east, south, west, north. The correspondences differ from one culture and group to another. At High Valley we honored the elements without assigning them a quarter. I don't know the origin of one of my favorite elemental chants. It has been passed from circle to circle, the tune changing slightly, but the rhythm echoing a heartbeat. Though I no longer attend many ritual gatherings, I still sing that song in my backyard.

> Earth my body
> Water my blood
> Air my breath
> And fire my spirit

Elemental honoring is nothing new. Likely it goes back to the dawn of our time here when we knew our lives depended on the elements, their interplay, their balance, as they still do. Nor is it exclusive to any one culture or religion. In *Carmina Gadelica: Hymns and Incantations Collected in the Highlands and Islands of Scotland* by Alexander Carmichael, there are prayers to the new moon, to the sun; prayers for smooring (banking) the fire before bed; prayers for healing cattle; prayers for every aspect of fishing and farming. Christ is hailed as King of the Elements. In his "Canticle to the Sun," St. Francis of Assisi praises God for the elements but also invokes their power and beauty.

> *Be praised, my Lord, through all your creatures, especially through my lord Brother Sun, who brings the day; and you give light through him. And he is beautiful and radiant in all his splendor! Of you, Most High, he bears the likeness.*
> *Be praised, my Lord, through Sister Moon and the stars; in the heavens you have made them, precious and beautiful.*

Be praised, my Lord, through Brothers Wind and Air,
and clouds and storms, and all the weather, through which
you give your creatures sustenance.

Be praised, My Lord, through Sister Water; she is very
useful, and humble, and precious, and pure.

Be praised, my Lord, through Brother Fire, through
whom you brighten the night. He is beautiful and cheerful,
and powerful and strong.

Be praised, my Lord, through our sister Mother Earth,
who feeds us and rules us, and produces various fruits with
colored flowers and herbs.

ELEMENTAL LIFE AND DEATH AND LIFE

My fairytale novel-in-progress, the one with the Beauty Singers, features four grannies, each one the embodiment of an element in the form of an old woman. Granny Sweep, Granny Spark, Granny Dirt, and Granny Brine. The trouble is, the grannies don't remember who, or what, they are. Sometimes they have nightmares of elemental devastation, done to them, done by them—nightmares they struggle to remember and equally try to forget. Opposed to the grannies, with intent to control and obliterate them, is the secret creator of Dome World. His ultimate ambition is to defeat death for himself and the few he shall select for literal immortality.

There is a tendency in some varieties of Christianity to view the earth as a vale of tears, a place where we are only sojourners. Our responsibility to be good stewards of God's Creation gets lost along the way. We are only passing through. Our real and eternal home is Heaven. My father was very scornful of what he saw as self-centered preoccupation with individual salvation. Many, including me, feel concerned for the ecological consequences of what sometimes seems like disregard for the earth.

As I get older, I have more sympathy with the human longing

for things to be set right in another world where the wicked will cease to trouble and the tears of the broken-hearted will be wiped away by a loving God. That arc, bending towards earthly justice, is so ephemeral sometimes, dissolving into a mist like a rainbow. If we can't have resolution in this life, what about the next? No wonder people wonder. Heaven and hell on earth are what we know, the latter often what we inflict on each other.

In our brief mortal lives, we are surrounded by elemental seasons and cycles, life, death, life. Birds and animals, trees and plants, life seen and unseen, companions on the way. Heartbeat, breath. St. Francis greets Bodily Death as Sister. Sister Death, Sister Life. Both so terrifying and tender, both elemental.

*

I recently spoke with a friend who has stage four cancer. Having explored all options, she has reached the conclusion that aggressive and invasive treatments are unlikely to cure the cancer or prolong her life. She has decided just to live as well and as long as she can. In the course of our conversation, she asked me what I think happens after death.

We spoke for a long time about our speculations, our possible experiences with people after they had died, our intimations of death in dreams and what lies beyond it. At last I said,

"I have lots of beliefs, and maybe they will turn out to be true. But there is one thing we know for sure. Our bodies will return to the elements—earth, air, fire, and water—like everyone and everything before us. That thought comforts me."

It comforted her, too.

"The hardest thing," she said, "is leaving this earth. I love the earth so much."

"You will be the earth. You are the earth."

"Yes," she said, "yes."

Broken Home

Everything is here to stay
one with the place we forgot to call home.
Shake the dust from your feet
and it remains the ground beneath them
there is only change, river becoming rain
becoming river, fallen leaves
feeding the roots of trees feeding leaves,
the slow redemption of rot.
It's the indestructible that destroys,
the things that won't break down
that may break us—unless
we break first, as an egg shatters
to release the bird
or a seed splits open and
takes hold in the earth

—from my collection of poems, *Small Bird*

CHAPTER EIGHTEEN

MY WILL, THY WILL

WHOSE WILL?

*"Father, if thou be willing, remove this cup from me: never-
theless not my will, but thine, be done."*

—The Gospel of Luke 22:42

These are Jesus's famous words in the Garden of Gethsemane just
before he is arrested for treason against Rome and subsequently
tried and executed. Which is presumably the Father's will for his
son. What was Jesus's will for himself? To stay alive? To go on healing and preaching? To break bread and drink wine with friends and
strangers? We don't know. We only know it was presumably *not* his
will to be crucified.

It was God's will.

It is God's will. People sometimes offer these words as comfort, usually when something atrocious has happened. God's will is
inscrutable and infallible. We are supposed to submit to it. Really,
what choice do we have?

Well, we had a choice. Allegedly. In the Garden of Eden. As
the story goes, we were given free will, as in the freedom to obey or
disobey God. And the first time we exercised that free will (eating
the apple or pomegranate or maybe a fig, given the fig-leaf aprons
that immediately came into fashion) we were kicked out of paradise,

assigned hierarchal (and for women, oppressive) gender roles, and sentenced to sweated labor and pain in childbirth. Plus women, in particular, were to have enmity towards snakes (a symbol of the goddess).

Free will is no free ride. It seems a bit of a setup. Submit to God's will or suffer the consequences of willfulness, a word synonymous with sinfulness. Willfulness has been something to be beaten out of a child—or a wife? Will has been something to be broken in a horse or other animals or in a subordinate (woman, child, slave). Will seems not free but costly. Unless you are (the one God put) in charge.

MY WILL BE DONE, UM, I MEAN GOD'S...

If willfulness was traditionally sinful, punished in people—as noted, especially women, children, serfs and slaves, and animals—how did will become a virtue, as in "where there's a will, there's a way" and "God helps those who helps themselves"?

Being neither a historian nor a theologian, I am going to go in for some undocumented, unfootnoted speculation. I suspect attitudes towards will—individual will, especially—changed with the Protestant Reformation, which was really more of a rebellion or revolution. Protestants did not reform the Roman Catholic Church. They broke away from it and its authority. No more ecclesiastical hierarchy standing between man and God or between people and the Bible (or at least not for those who could read). The break with Rome caused a splintering which is ongoing. There are an estimated 40,000 protestant denominations in the world today, from mainstream to extreme in their theologies. Everyone gets to interpret God's highly confusing, often contradictory, Word for himself (I use the masculine pronoun deliberately). In the Bible there is something for everyone and something to justify everything (for example, slavery, subjugation of women, eradication of indigenous peoples).

This challenge to ecclesiastical and social hierarchy contributed to the rise of the bourgeoisie, capitalism, the industrial revolution, the conquest and colonization by Europeans of the rest of the world. Skimming right along, in feudal Roman Catholic Europe there was the Pope; the divine right of kings, dependent on the Pope; and a land-holding aristocracy who owed fealty to the king, etc. When that established order fell apart, it became possible for individuals (mostly of the merchant class) to pursue their own gain.

The Calvinist doctrine of predestination, (as far as I can understand it, which may not be very far) states that God chooses (or has already chosen?) who will be saved and who will be damned (so much for free will). Since there is no ecclesiastical authority, no priest or pope, to tell you who is saved or what you have to do to ensure salvation (it's not up to you, anyway), an unofficial extension of this doctrine was to look for signs of God's favor, like prosperity. If people are poor, it's a sign God doesn't favor them and/or it's their own damned fault.

(Dear Lord and Savior Jesus Christ, who warned that it is easier for a camel to pass through the Needle's Eye's than for a rich man to enter into the Kingdom of Heaven, what the hell!?)

There were fortunes to be made in the New (to Europeans) World. For the early British settlers, Puritans especially, it wasn't enough to be out for what you could get. There was a Biblically based and reinforced narrative. The New World was the New Jerusalem, and it was God's will that his people inhabit it and subdue or slaughter the heathen savages. (There is a grizzly, little-known history of Thanksgiving as a holiday decreed by Governor William Bradford after the settlers torched a Wampanoag village in retaliation for an alleged murder of one man.) And that was just the beginning of a story played out over hundreds of years, from sea to shining sea, glorified as Manifest Destiny, justified as God's will.

*

Deeply ingrained in (especially white) American culture is the belief that anyone can achieve anything. That's the American Dream. (We don't like to talk about the American Nightmare.) Any child can be president; anyone can be affluent. Rags to riches is a perennial storyline. It just takes hard work and a determined will. People from all over the world have fled life-threatening scarcity and oppression for the chance at social and economic mobility in the United States, and some have found it, often after running the gauntlet of prejudice and exploitation. If they had white skin, no matter where they came from, it was easier to assimilate.

But we are not simply a nation of can-do immigrants, flush with success by the second or third generation. Some people's ancestors were brought here in the holds of slave ships. Some people's ancestors were driven from their lands and forced onto reservations, which were, for a long time, prisons, the models for concentration camps. Despite Lady Liberty's message, refugees from wars and famines (caused in large part by US policies) are still being deported or turned back from our borders. What about wage slaves who don't make enough to live on? Migrant workers and other workers who are exposed to toxins? The list could go on and on.

Not everyone can or will be rich. Not everyone even has enough to eat or water that's safe to drink or bathe in. Yet to the burden of poverty is added shame. If you do not succeed, if you can't get by, if you need help, if you are beyond help, it must be your own fault. You have free will. You made bad choices. It's hard for many Americans to admit, the source of much suffering is not individual will—or God help us—divine will, but collective human will. How do we get a handle on that? How do we change it? Maybe first we have to acknowledge the complexities and limitations of human will.

MY WILL: TRUE CONFESSIONS

I have never suffered economically or socially thanks to what I could call an accident of birth, something mainstream culture has been reluctant to acknowledge plays a part in success. But I have had a stubborn (willful) ambition or, to dress it up, a sense of vocation as in a sacred calling. "For this I was born...."

When I finished writing my first novel at the age of twenty-five, I assumed publication—and success—would follow. Thirteen years and three more completed novels later, it had not. Somewhere during that time I did have a chance at publication. My then-agent's best friend was an editor at the fiction division of Playboy Books. She offered me a contract (the most lucrative one I ever had) and I signed it, shaking in my (hopelessly compromised) feminist shoes. *The Wild Mother* with the iconic Playboy Bunny on the spine? Had I sold my soul to the devil? Punishment, if that's what it was, came swiftly. The imprint was sold to Berkely books, and both *The Wild Mother* and my next (never published) novel were rejected.

Years went by. I kept writing books. Rejections from all the major and many minor houses piled up. The rejections boiled down to "this novel fits no genre; no market category." Later it became acceptable to mix fantasy and reality, retell fairytales, have characters who were children in books for adult readers. But not then. I was also told that my subjects were not literary enough for literary fiction and my writing was too literary for commercial fiction.

One of the shocking things to me, when I first encountered Wicca in my quest for the Goddess, was the idea that will, and working my will, was acceptable. Nor did I have to think the right thoughts; I just had to know what I wanted. Desire was not wrong; it was inherent in the life force, a refreshing, and, to me, disconcerting, point of view. There were spells and rituals for finding love, success etc. You could follow them like recipes or invent your own. "And it harm none," your will was just fine. Harming none is an admirable and stringent ethic, right up there with loving your neighbor as yourself. I did not see how it could harm anyone for me to find a publisher.

(Although later, when *The Passion of Mary Magdalen* was published, extreme Christians, who had not and would not read the book, claimed that I was causing harm by writing fiction about holy people.)

Yes, I confess, I tried spells. I willed. I willed with all my might.

You better believe I prayed, too.

ASK

Tsk, tsk. Spells *and* prayers? No wonder nothing worked! What a desperate, willful, hopelessly confused person you were and are, Elizabeth!

Yes, I am confused. And why not? The Lord's Prayer, the one Jesus taught his disciples, the first prayer I learned, contains this appeal to God (of the hallowed name): "*Thy kingdom come, thy will be done, on earth as it is in heaven.*" Heaven being a different location from earth and yet, as Jesus also teaches, heaven is "in your midst" or in one translation "within you."

Jesus also admonishes us to "*ask and it shall be given to you, seek and ye shall find, knock and it shall be opened to you.*" And "*which of you if his child asks for bread will give him a stone?*"

Then there is the seemingly contradictory saying of Jesus's that Billie Holiday made into a song, "Them that's got shall get, them that's not, shall lose." Which seems a precursor to predestination wherein God's will trumps everything, though one recent translation/interpretation suggests that Jesus is talking about knowledge and understanding, not material wealth.

I have heard people say that when you ask, and it is not given to you, it doesn't mean God isn't listening or doesn't exist, it means the answer is no. I suppose if people can say yes or no, then whatever

God is can also say yes or no. But this justification for why we don't get what we want supposes that God is outside of creation, omnipotent, dispensing or withholding favor, willfully allowing the wicked to prosper, the war and holocausts to go on unimpeded, the widows and orphans to starve.

If this is how God operates, then I had good reason for my plan to roll a boulder off a cliff and squash him.

If whatever God is said no to me about finding a publisher and topping the *New York Times* bestseller list, I never stopped asking, even though sometimes I can see that the way my life has worked out has its own beauty and meaning that I might have missed if things had gone according to my plan. I would not have become a minister and a counselor. I would not have learned how to sit with people in their own rage, grief, and despair.

And at last Maeve and I did find our long, winding way to our current publisher. (Thank you, Monkfish!) At the time of the following memory, we had been a long time wandering.

"You *called* me to write this story," I prompted the Recipient of my anguished prayer.

Translation: it is your will, your divine will that I am doing what I am doing, suffering what I am suffering, drinking whatever is in this dang cup, not my will but thine....

Nope. The answer, if that's what it was, came back clearly, shockingly. *We're not playing that game with you. If you say 'Enough already!' and stop writing, you will not be judged, you will not be condemned. So. What do you want to do?*

For a moment it was quiet inside me, still. I felt myself going down through layers and fathoms of my being to some cool, dark, underground spring. What do I want? What do I want if no one is making me do anything? What do I want if no one is calling me, if no one is rewarding me in heaven or on earth?

I want to write this story.

I long to tell this story, I hunger and thirst for it.

I want to tell this story.
No matter what.
And so I did.

WAR, PEACE AND WILL

I was born eight years after the end of the Second World War just as the Korean War was ending while McCarthy still held sway. I spent my childhood in the atmosphere of the Cold War and came of age during the Vietnam War. During my life there has scarcely been a time when my country was not involved in a war, directly or by proxy, overtly or covertly; or in making policies that resulted in violence and poverty. For most of this millennium, until very recently, our military has been at war in Afghanistan and Iraq.

While I have been working on this book, Russia invaded Ukraine, and as of this writing, the war is ongoing. One more war among more than two dozen wars in the world today. A war between two European nations, who supply much of the world's wheat. Failure of this harvest or its distribution will mean famine far beyond their borders, among other global repercussions.

Whenever I want to throw up my hands or sit in judgment on my kind's propensity for war, I remember our personal failure to make peace on a small piece of land with people who were our neighbors and friends. We had the option to sell and move, locally, with everything we needed to go on with our lives. What happens when a whole planet is in various stages of war or catastrophe? Where do we go?

WHO WILLS WAR?

If most people want peace, going about the business of living, raising young, dying in due season just like other creatures, whose will makes war? Is it inherent in our nature? There seems to be no consensus on that, but some agreement that wars began when we evolved (?!) from hunter gatherers into more complex settled societies sometime around the end of the last ice age almost 12,000 years ago.

In modern times leaders invoke defending democracy, national security, or toppling dictators as the rationale for war. It is less than 1,000 years since European Christians waged the holy wars known as the Crusades. (Of course in most cases, ancient and modern, the official justification dresses up other motivations: control of trade routes, ports, resources, wealth…)

The Biblical King Saul lived some 3,000 years ago. According to Samuel 15, the Lord Almighty commands King Saul (via his mouthpiece Samuel) *"to attack the Amalekites and totally destroy everything that belongs to them. Do not spare them; put to death men and women, children and infants, cattle and sheep, camels and donkeys."* There has never been a war without atrocities. There has never been a war that has not devastated civilian life. Although it is not mentioned in this account, there has never been a war without widespread rape, and that is as true today as it ever was.

When King Saul spares the King of the Amalekites and *"the best of the sheep and cattle, the fat calves and lambs—everything that was good,"* the Lord Almighty is grieved because Saul disobeyed orders. Oh, well, protests Saul (perhaps somewhat disingenuously), I was going to sacrifice them to *you.* But the Lord prizes obedience above sacrificial offerings. Samuel demands the execution of the Amalekite king, presumably on the Lord's behalf. But Saul's failure to kill everything and everyone has permanently ruptured his relationship with the Lord and Samuel.

Because Saul disobeyed God.

Same reason Adam and Eve got kicked out of Eden.

Surely there are choices other than obedience or disobedience?

As bombs level cities and military forces overrun them, what choices are there? Run for your life, leaving everything behind? Stay and risk torture and death? Resist, surrender?

If free will is a divine gift to humans (God help us), who will save us from ourselves?

What I believe today

That I don't need to believe, not consistently,
god can move in and out of me like breath,
inside or beyond, I don't have to choose,
and it is all right to blame God even if such
a blameworthy being does not exist if it means
an end to hatred of myself and my own kind.

I feel sorry for us all sometimes, the wicked,
the brilliant, the cruel, the kind. Who gave us
such tricky minds and thumbs, such a need
to say no or yes? We murder and make beauty
helplessly, deliberately. Someone please love us,
hold us at the end of time and tell us it's all right.

—from my collection of poems,
So Ecstasy Can Find You

BACK TO THE GARDEN

Once, between sleeping and waking, I heard these words:

People misunderstand God's will. It is not imposed. It is not opposed. It is more like a seed that grows. Not my will or thy will. It is tending a garden.

I remember entering into relationship with my mother-in-law's long-untended garden, how patient and tenacious its life, how willing it was to teach me if I was willing to pay attention. That's what tending is, paying attention: to light, shade, soil, water, what conditions does this or that plant need to thrive.

Maybe all relationships are or could be such cocreations. Friendships, marriages, the ever-changing balance between parents and children, communities, nations. What if, before we willed anything, we asked, what is thriving here, what is needed here, what is or isn't my part to play?

It would take patience, we would make mistakes, but maybe something would grow. It always seems like a miracle when a seed breaks open, puts down roots, reaches for light, becomes what it is.

CHAPTER NINETEEN

BETWEEN WAKING AND DREAMING

NIGHT SCHOOL

It usually happens, when it does, between 3:00 and 4:30 a.m. the small hours of the morning when it is still dark. Though it is not midnight, it often feels like the proverbial midnight hour to me. It's when my soul cries out like a baby. When I quiet, I sometimes ask questions; sometimes answers come between waking and dreaming. And sometimes I am left with more questions and take them with me into my dreams.

Many, though not all, of my conversations are with Jesus, as I know him. I am not asking any reader—or even myself—to decide whether these conversations are wholly imagined or not. It doesn't matter. What I do know is that this interchange shifts me out of my habitual (anxious) patterns of thinking into another kind of consciousness. Also much of the content is about prayer. At times it has almost felt like prayer school.

To recreate these conversations, I will put in italics voices that seem like more or other than mine.

Here is a sample of my standard opening gambit.

"I don't know why you are with me when there are so many people suffering and I have enough to eat, shelter, etc...so much privilege, no real problems...."

This preamble is repetitive and tedious and serves little purpose, unless there is some purpose to self-conscious self-abnegation. It irritates my Listener.

Tell me when you're done became *Skip it!* followed by *I've already explained how it works.…*

Here is what Jesus has said, more than once; I am supposed to remember it and trust it:

> *I can be with you and with everyone, anyone who needs me, whatever name they call me, however they know or don't know me, because I live in the heart. Your heart, every heart. That is who and what I am. The heart of the heart. Sometimes I am locked up so deep in a heart, it's like a dungeon; sometimes I am locked out. But the heart is where I live. You can always call me without fear that you are taking me from someone else. This is the fruit of what our friend Maeve calls the god-making death.*

And yes, I talk to Maeve, too. Our conversations are mostly about some immediate personal problem. She has limited patience for moral quandaries, and when I venture into that territory, she will often say, *Go talk to him!*

I don't always talk to Jesus or Maeve. Or talk at all. There is something I have learned to call the Presence. Here's an attempt at a description:

I can see and feel, in my half-dreaming state, a Presence strong and golden, not human yet knowing of the human, compassionate, not form yet not void. It feels (this is an approximation) like a waterfall of fire (but not cold or hot) flowing through my body.

Below are selections of what I have heard, seen, or felt between waking and dreaming, recorded the next day in my journal. An asterisk separates the entries.

*

Grace is always flowing. Prayer opens channels for that flow.

Why doesn't everything work out all the time?

If channels can be opened, they can also be blocked, deliberately or through neglect or oblivion. Like a spring that gets covered over with dirt and leaves and eventually stops welling in that spot.

What about the state of the world, all the harm, deliberate or unintentional, all the suffering?

The answer is an image:

So many layers and dimensions interweaving in time and space. The thread and flow of grace is hard for one person to trace.

*

my questions:

is there a god?

what if god is like parents

they appear as gods, for better and worse

then we grow up and find out

they are just like us

we are just like them

they die

we are on our own.

is it like that with god?

do we have to grow up?

does god die?

do we grow into being god

for better, for worse

till we die?

is our longing for god

like a child's longing

for someone bigger and stronger
someone who knows what to do
who feeds, comforts, chastises, rewards?
do we ever get over longing
for the seemingly limitless
omnipotent, even awful love?

where is god, what is god?
is there one?
are we all (each one of us) alone?

I hear: *it is and isn't like that.*
god is and isn't like that.

*

me: I know you love everyone, but how do you do it? (I name several people who are, to me, particularly repugnant and unlovable public figures.)

Jesus: *I see the person as a baby. Actually we* (the deities?) *see all of you as babies.*

me: Shall I pray for people that way when I need to?

Yes.

*

You are a salmon swimming up the stream of grace.

*

How to pray for people?
Bring them into the Presence.
Aren't they already there?

237

Of course. Bring them into the Presence.

I also hear when I wake feeling desperate and tense:

It is all right to pray for yourself.
Bring yourself into the Presence.
Prayer is necessary
We need you to be a prayer.

I wonder: if there is a Presence, is there also an Absence? Are both Divine?

I do not quite ask the question. I do not quite receive an answer.

*

After the preamble, I begin to pester him with questions. Why am I (still) here?

him: *I came into this world to bear witness to the truth. How about you? Write about it.*

me: Seriously? You're giving me a writing exercise? And by the way, what is truth? Pilate's question always struck me as a fair response to your declaration.

him: *Write about it.*

The next morning, I do both assignments.

I came into this world….

I came into this world, but it wasn't my idea
I came into this world, and it was my idea. What was I thinking?

I came into this world to be my parents' child
to heal their unhappiness and fail

I came into this world to climb trees and fall out of them
to fall in love with them and mourn their falling

I came into this world to have children
to love them, miss them, misunderstand and be misunderstood

I came into this world to have my say
even if no one listens

I came into this world to fall in love
until I didn't know what it means anymore

I came into this world to witness endings
so many painful endings

I came into this world to resist and succumb to
the powerful pull of ruin

I came into this world to witness flowers
live and die, so I could learn how

what is truth?

who tells it
who hears it
who hides it
who denies it
who believes it?

what is truth?

who owns it

is there more than one
does it change
how do we know it
what will happen if we tell it?

what is truth?

it is ugly
it is beautiful
it hurts
it heals
it will kill me
I can't live without it.

*

I died young. Old age is like crucifixion. You are vulnerable, exposed, you lose everything, you suffer, you die.

*

Last night I say to the heart of my heart, I do not know directly what it is like to be part of an oppressed people. But you do know. In your life on earth, your country was occupied by the Romans. You were tried on trumped-up charges and executed, like so many people, before and since. And then I say (although of course he knows): your church became the oppressor. Among so many other crimes, your church ran the residential schools, abducted, persecuted, sexually abused, and murdered indigenous children....

I don't understand. How could this happen? How could you let it?

No answer but this dream:

after disaster
my house becomes a refuge
crowded with people
food half prepared, half cleaned up
I hold strangers in my arms

*

Dream: I'm working with a rabbi's liturgy or liturgies that speak to primary emotions. Grief, fear. I am working on fear. I say something to someone about how Christianity lost sight of compassion. At one point I am railing at God, how could you leave us helpless with these emotions? And then I see it, something like a cloud shot through with light. Whoever, whatever it is feels everything more intensely than we do, has infinite, incomprehensible compassion. I hear:

You are not more compassionate than God.

*

This is resurrection. Life coming back out of suffering and ruin over and over.

It is hard to put into words what was more felt and seen than heard. Everything happens at once, not juxtaposed, but simultaneous, the way a river is always rising and always meeting the sea.

*

Prayer rhymes with aware.

You pray to your deep self, which is part of all that is, and so you pray to that all.

When you pray to Jesus (who is who he says he is) it is like having a lens to focus your awareness. That is a good way for you to pray, not the only way.

When I pray for someone, for their healing, what am I praying for?

You are praying for restoration of connection. The ones you are praying for might recover from an illness; they might not. What you hope for them might happen; it might not. You are praying that they become connected and aware that they are connected.

Prayer is awareness.

What is evil? Why do people do such terrible things?

Evil is the things you have asked to heal in yourself—jealousy, resentment, rage, hurt, fear of rejection, sense of inadequacy—writ large, acted out because of the absence of awareness. These individual wounds can become part of a collective body, a people, a nation, a world....

*

Consciousness is crucifixion.

We know not what we do. To each other, to the earth. Unconsciousness crucifies.

*

The Presence is always there, oceanic grace, prayer is a conduit. The words, intention, mental activity, is not the prayer itself but infrastructure for the prayer. The prayer is more than the pray-er but the pray-er makes the more of the prayer possible.

Don't worry about screwing up your prayer, your words, your thoughts; just pray. The prayer knows what to do.

*

Prayer changes the one who prays. The prayer hears. Pray for mercy, become merciful, Pray for courage, become courageous. Pray for change, be changed. For love, love.

*

I ask Jesus how to pray for people in Ukraine, not comprehending the role of prayer, which does not seem to stop horrors from happening. I think of Mary, who is, for Godsake, a Goddess, praying for us. That seems to be one of her tasks, to pray for us, to intercede for us: with God? With her Son?

me: Do you pray for us?
him: *Yes. There is a prayer I taught that anyone can pray.*
me: Our Father? I can't even begin.
him: *Translate.*

> O singing radiance
> hallowed be thy names
> sing to us, sing in us
> let us see, let us hear
> as you do....

I am asleep before I finish.

*

Prayer is like/makes a humanitarian corridor.
Clearly not a literal one, but something? Maybe for the collective human spirit?

*

A question is put to me:
What if prayer had/has no effect? Would you continue to pray?

I am still answering.

CHAPTER TWENTY

DAILY PRAYER

PRACTICING THE PRESENCE

I have a not-very-definitive memory of Miss Sang reading aloud the Office for Daily Morning Prayer. Or perhaps she read from the Daily Devotions for Individuals and Families. If I remember, I must have read the prayers with her, at least on occasion. Whether my memory is accurate or not, Miss Sang's fictional counterpart from my novel *Murder at the Rummage Sale*, mystic and sleuth Lucy Way, reads aloud the Daily Office. Writing from Lucy's point of view, more than twenty years after Miss Sang's death, gave me a new way to connect with her, to the beauty she created around her and carried within her.

My evolving, eclectic daily practice would be unfamiliar to Miss Sang, except for phrases from The Book of Common Prayer that find their way into what is otherwise invented or improvised. I pray for "*all those in trouble, sorrow,* danger, *need, sickness, or any other adversity.*" When I look up the original, I see that I have added the word danger. I keep adding to the list, war, poverty, hunger, thirst, terror. All who have lost home or habitat, all who remember and care for them....

For almost twenty years, I studied Tai Chi and Qigong with a brilliant teacher who is now reluctantly retired because of memory loss and dementia of unknown origin. We are still friends, and I continue to practice all the forms I learned from him. My daily office takes place outside during my standing meditation practice. Most often I speak aloud, sometimes I sing. A friend who is a shaman impressed on me the power of voice meeting and mingling with air.

"This is Elizabeth," I say (my name for now, in this life, in this body). "I am praying to, with, and for the spirit that lives in and through all things."

That all-pervasive spirit is what my Tai Chi teacher always invoked. The "to, with, and for" is something that came to me one day. A different sort of trinity, or maybe not so different. It is a way to locate whatever, whoever it is I pray to.

A TISKET, A TASKET

Years ago, I asked my late artist friend Jo for help creating a prayer basket. I wanted to find a way to remember everyone in my prayers. I had tried drawing a map but it was too one-dimensional. We wove a basket of willow wands and copper wire, lined it with cutout paper leaves, softened and stained with tea (a process she'd been working on). I still have the basket, its wands rising, the woven copper strands bright when the sun touches them. Things are tucked into the basket—feathers, talismanic bundles. But after a time I stopped using it as a receptacle for written names and prayers. The basket tended to fill up very fast. Another friend suggested I needed to empty the basket ritually and burn the prayers. It all became too complicated, high church, and high maintenance. But I love looking at the basket, which surely still holds prayers, even if not on scraps of paper. It will always hold the memory of Jo, her artistry, our friendship.

Now I pray without any sacred objects, doing my best to remember everyone. Interesting that another way to say memorize is "learn by heart." You could say that I pray "by heart." My prayers follow a pattern but vary daily. I do see something like a map in my mind's eye, or maybe it is more like a web, woven and rewoven, caught in different lights, a spoken prayer basket.

Sometimes I begin by praying for someone I know is in crisis, or for a world crisis, for the "all" mentioned above. I pray for people by name—babies, children, their parents and grandparents, clients, friends, communities I am or have been part of, readers, everyone who has supported my work. I pray for my family, human and otherwise. I pray for the life in my yard, my region, prayers spinning out and out into a prayer for all our relations, all life, supported and connected by air, earth, water, light. I say thank you for my life, the chance to walk on the earth. I pray not to miss my part. I often conclude by praying for my kind to see, love, and care for this earth as the garden, wilderness, paradise, sanctuary it is, was, and can be.

Is it all right to pray for people without their permission? I am not sure I know the answer. Many of the people I pray for do know that I have this practice. I've confessed it, with some embarrassment, often enough. One friend said, "I don't have any belief about prayer or God, but it makes me happy that you remember me in this way."

Prayer as remembering

I remember
we are as connected as tree roots, all fed by the same earth
but we forget

I remember
just a little when I pray each day
what I forget

I remember
all the names I can remember
pray twice for the ones I forget

I remember
so many horrors overheard, heard over and over
I wish I could forget

I remember
I pray in litanies of lists
I pray not to forget

—from my *journal*

Whatever prayer for others is or isn't, it is remembering. When I
search the nooks and crannies of my memory, I feel a kind of awe for
whoever, whatever God might be. The one who lives in the heart of
every heart, the one who watches sparrows fall and fly, numbers the
hairs on heads. That everything might be held in some vast memory, some timeless attention span puts in perspective my attempts to
remember. However limited and incomplete my memory, maybe in
prayer I am participating in some greater mystery.

I also need to remember not to take too much on myself, not to
become inflated with an exaggerated sense of responsibility.

HAIBUN: TEACH ME ANOTHER WAY TO PRAY

I confess: I have been praying more as if I were a god, an ineffectual
one, than to whatever divine mercy or mystery I want to believe
exists. I know I know nothing, but I forget. I pray for what I think
would be best for the people, the planet. I pile cares on my back and
shoulder the world. How can I fail to stagger under the weight, and,

more than likely, fall on my face, fall down on the earth I love so much. I want to pray like leaves falling when it's time, flying on the wind. I want to entrust all the ones I love to love. I want to believe they, we, all of us will find our way. The earth knows how to circle and spin. All green life knows how to die and rise, responsible for everything or for nothing.

> do I turn to prayer
> because I can't bear to see
> so much suffering
> what if I prayed for new eyes
> prayed with curiosity

—from my *journal*

BUT WHAT DOES PRAYER DO?

Is anyone rising up and walking? Have the wicked ceased to trouble? Have the bombs stopped falling? And so forth. The first time I remember asking that question I was a continent away from a child in crisis. If you want to know what it means to pray without ceasing, ask any mother. I was sitting on a beach, adding a little saltwater to the Pacific Ocean when this answer came.

Prayer is like a fair wind. You can send it to the one who is suffering, help create favorable conditions.

No guarantee of an outcome, but an image I could hold onto, or rather release. My prayers flying across the country enfolding my child. Decades later, praying in the backyard and on walks in the Shawangunks, such images still come to me.

> prayer as tree roots whispering
> across vast distances through mycelia

prayer as water falling
into a deep clear pool

prayer as soft soaking rain
prayer as fragrance

—from my *journal*

I have experienced being enveloped in inexplicable comfort in the midst of disaster. Who knows? Maybe someone was praying for me then.

SILENCE AS PRAYER

It is hard for someone as verbal as I am to give words the slip. So maybe what I mean by silence is listening. Intently with intent. Attentively with attention. Solitary, silent walks are for me part of writing. When I am writing fiction, new scenes begin playing. Writing this book, I get information about what I need and don't need to include. Yesterday on a walk, I became aware that I need to write about silence.

At some point on almost every walk I stop, find a place to sit, look, listen, detect scents, feel each shift of air. When I am beside a river or stream, I try to hear each note, overtones, undertones. From watching the tumble of water over stone and rock, I have come to see that the fall and flow varies even over the same rocks on the same day in the same conditions. Water has a scent and rocks drying in the sun have a scent. Yesterday, even though it was still chilly after a cold spell, there were gnats circling over the water and river swallows darting and circling over them. Two hawks swooped down and joined in the spiraling. Icicles clung to the cliff above brush that was just beginning to green.

Silence is not the absence of sound or any other sense perception; it is spaciousness, release from habitual preoccupations. Is this
state a kind of prayer?

> be still and know that I am god
> be still and know that I am
> be still and know
> be still
> be

What is the word beyond be, the one you can't hear or
see. How to write it? How to turn into it?

—from my *journal*

WHEN TWO OR THREE ARE GATHERED

My other experience of intentional silence is as a counselor. It is not
that I never speak to respond or ask questions; it is that my focus is
wholly on the other person. All other thoughts and preoccupations
are gone for that time. So maybe it is a state of heightened awareness. When a client seems at a loss, or there is a tangle of thought, a
repetitive loop, I will suggest that we sit silently, eyes closed, and see
what wants surface. (A spring bubbling from underground, something shy emerging from hiding.) Almost always something new
and/or ancient emerges, something that changes the course of the
session and maybe (who knows?) a life.

As noted, when I work with couples or families, and the talk
becomes rapid-fire with people speaking over each other, I call for
silence and ask people to speak from the silence leaving silences
between each speaker. Silence slows the pace, people start breathing
and listening, gaining confidence that they, in turn, will be heard.

When I ponder this kind of silence, the image comes of that

network of roots in the forest. Above ground, each tree is separate, underground they are connected and communicating.

I don't speak of prayer or God unless that is a client's language and request. What happens in many sessions is that we come into or create what I know as Presence. There we have access to a knowing beyond our small, individual knowing. We have ears to hear and eyes to see.

CATECHISM: KINDS OF PRAYER

In the Catechism near the end of The Book of Common Prayer, seven kinds of prayer are listed: adoration, praise, thanksgiving, penitence, oblation, intercession, and petition. It strikes me that my daily morning prayer practice is weighted heavily toward intercession (all those names) with a bit of petition on the side, and a dash of thanksgiving sprinkled over everything at the end.

A summary might look like this:

Help, help, help, help, help, help, help...........help (me!)........help, help, help, help!

And by the way, thank you, thank you, and thank you...

Help!

I wonder about the other kinds of prayer and if they are or could be part of my life as a prayer.

ADORATION

I don't know if I adore the Creator except through the Creation. If that is heretical, so be it, or so, in any case, it is. I confess to adoration at the sight of every flower, wild or cultivated, from the first snowdrops to the last asters. Why do I call that adoration? What distinguishes flowers from other forms of beauty? I don't know that I can explain it. It is a heart-bursting. I don't always fall down on my knees, but the impulse is there.

I know I have adored my children. Being in love can also be a state of adoration. In strict Christian theology, I am describing idolatry. Some Christian mystics might more gently remind me that the flowers, and the children, and the beloved are pointing the way toward the divine mystery. I have no quarrel with that.

I suppose there is danger when adoration of Creation becomes a desire to acquire and control, maybe a uniquely human temptation. One form of evil that we witness over and over is the drive to destroy what you cannot control (or cannot admit you cannot control).

I believe more often adoration leads to a desire to tend and protect. So back to the flowers, the source of pollen and nectar for honey bees and other pollinators, the fruit that follows blossom, the living sign of a regenerating planet. Back to unabashed adoration.

PRAISE

See adoration above, add poetry and song, libation poured out on the earth, circle dancing, sharing the feast, welcoming the stranger as friend.

THANKSGIVING

"It is meet, right, and our bounden duty to give God thanks and praise." The phrase from the Eucharistic prayer comes back to me.

I have a memory of overhearing a conversation between a mother and a child in church. The child said something to the effect of "we're lucky." The mother said, "No, we're not lucky, we're blessed. Jesus blesses."

It is no doubt meet and right to give thanks. But it leads me to a thorny thicket where I often find myself gathering wool. I can't countenance the idea that I am blessed with so much while other people are shivering in refugee camps and giving birth in bomb shelters.

No, as far as I know, I am just lucky, damned lucky.

W. S. Merwin's poem "Thanks" is a way of thanksgiving I aspire to. Giving thanks for everything, without judgment. Every day I say, "Thank you for this chance to walk on this earth." Maybe that is what I mean. As Maeve notes, "in the Country of Life the stones are hard; they can cut your feet." And still she chooses that country, where the other worlds hover at the edge of her vision.

Thank you for everything, for all of it, thank you.

PENITENCE

One day when I was on hermitage retreat, I sat by the river and prayed for help doing a life review. To the best of my ability I remembered every occasion when I had hurt someone or caused harm. I revisited every regret. Many of the people I had hurt were not part of my life any longer, so admitting wrong and asking forgiveness had to be done soul to soul, in the Presence. I can't know what, if any, effect this penitence had. I am not even sure of its effect on me. All I know is that it seemed—maybe seems—necessary. It had nothing to do with the vague sense of guilt and floating anxiety that often pervades my life like a noxious gas. It was direct and purposeful.

There is also the harm of which I am unaware, harm to other peoples and forms of life that I cause just by participating in unjust systems, including carbon-costly ones. I don't know if I included that kind of harm in the riverside penitential prayer. Maybe becoming more aware is a form of penitence.

Did I/do I have any sense of being absolved or forgiven? I'm not sure. It makes sense to me now that we confessed every week in church. Maybe penitence needs to be reintroduced into my daily prayer practice along with another petition: show me, show us, how to make amends.

OBLATION

My first pass at oblation was quick, almost flip. I was at the end of a writing session, and I thought, sure, oblation. Got that one down. The prayer of oblation is an offering of ourselves, our lives, our labors, the catechism says, in union with Christ, for the purposes of God. I thought of all the years and years of writing novels without any assurance of publication. In Emily Dickinson's word, "my letter to the world that never wrote to me." I remember trying to wheedle the divine into confirming writing as my sacred calling. Oblation may be the counterpart of calling. An unasked for offering without even the assurance that it will be accepted. Though the catechism implies that if the oblation is in union with Christ, for the purposes of God it will be accepted or at least acceptable. How do you—or maybe I mean I—how do I know if it is for divine purposes? What if the offering is heretical and for my own purposes? Is it still a prayer of oblation?

As I pondered the nature of oblation, I remembered getting ready to board a flight while on a book tour—much of that time remains a blur, the flights and the appearances. Only a few memories stand out. This is one. The woman who processed our boarding passes took care to look at each one of us and to wish us well by name. And there was nothing rote about it. When it came my turn, I felt seen by this woman and blessed. I remember her kind attention more than a decade later. She transformed what could have been a tedious job into a prayer of oblation, whether she offered that gift to God or just to us.

The prayer of oblation may be what I mean by life as a prayer. It may be what in Judaism is called a mitzvah or Buddhists mean by mindfulness. Or what Brother Lawrence called practicing the Presence of God while sweeping the floor, or scrubbing pots. The attention and devotion Miss Sang gave to setting the table. What if we made all tasks, each small act, an oblation? Nothing to do with success or failure, obscurity or recognition. Just an offering. I believe that the Dalai Lama once said that his religion is kindness, and religion is only useful in so far as it helps him to be kind. If it helps to make an offering to a deity, then good. An offering is an offering even if we never know to whom it is made or who receives it.

THE LITURGY OF THE HOURS

In this time of climate crisis, I find comfort in marking the path of sunrise and sunset from solstice to solstice, the changing light during the course of the day, the moon's waxing and waning, dimming or sharpening the appearance of the stars at night. As someone who is ready for bed not long after dinner, I don't know much about the constellations. But I am a devotee of the planet Venus (yes, I adore her) her appearances as morning and evening star, at dawn and dusk.

Monastics and priests in many Christian traditions pray the Liturgy of the Hours. I never have, but I find I take comfort in their very names: Lauds (dawn), Prime (sunrise), Terce (mid-morning), Sext (midday), None (midafternoon), Vespers (sunset), Compline (retiring). And an eighth called Night Watch. I don't think I am going to adopt a practice of formal Liturgy of the Hours, reading aloud Psalms or other passages from Christian scripture, although who knows what I will do as an older and older woman? But I wonder if I might find a way to pause at these times, to ponder the rotating and circling of this small planet as sacred. To wonder at the sky's great lights, burning and reflected, the vast, unknown expanse of bright darkness that holds all that is, seen and unseen.

summer solstice tree villanelle

the great old oak tree will gather me in
when earth shifts its tilt to gathering night
and three hundred spiraling circles spin

I call to the woman and child I've been
the child at play, the mother full of might
the great old oak tree will gather us in

the deep noon silence stills the human din
all that I am floats to the tree's great height
and three hundred spiraling circles spin

drawn to the core by the deep-rooted yin
I yield my eyes to arboreal sight
the great old oak tree has gathered me in

see the acorn, the whole tree held within
falling to earth through ancient autumn light
till three hundred spiraling circles spin

when waxing light ends, waning must begin
fathoms underground the first root holds tight
to my core I've gathered my old selves in
and numberless spiraling circles spin

—from my *journal*

CHAPTER TWENTY-ONE

A WAY
OUT OF NO WAY

BEING A PRAYER

I would like to write a comforting, conclusive last chapter. Lately I have been waking in sorrow—my own, more than my own? I don't know; maybe I don't need to know. Recently I asked a friend I hadn't seen in some time how she was, and instead of saying, "good" or "fine," or even a tentative, "all right," she actually told me. Her condition seemed akin to mine. The next day, when someone asked me how I was, I told the truth. And this friend expressed his relief to know he was not alone in his own hard-to-fathom sorrow.

> "…speak what we feel, not what we ought to say."
> —William Shakespeare, *King Lear*

As I write, I am remembering a ravine I recently discovered on a walk in the Shawangunks. Many tiny streams flowed down steep slopes to join the stream at the heart of the ravine. The ridge with its ancient rock made a way for the water and the water in turn shaped the ravine. When I watch water flow, I always think: it knows where it's going, it will find its way down and down to the sea. Water makes a way. Maybe the tears I can't explain know where they are going. I can just let them fall.

THE WORLD IS ALWAYS ENDING—AND BEGINNING

I wonder if it is common for older people to feel that the world is coming to an end, because our own end is in sight, though death can come at any moment for anyone. In truth, many peoples, not just individuals, in many times and places have faced the end of the world as they know it. It is one of the oldest stories in the world and as new as the latest headlines.

I wrote two more volumes of Maeve's story after Jesus exits the stage. People kept asking me why. What is the story without him? Resurrected or not, he was in his early thirties when he split the scene. I wanted an incarnate deity or BIFF (Best Imaginary Friend Forever) to walk the whole way with me, through child-raising, caring for aging parents, my own old age. Of course, Maeve's life is far more adventurous and eventful than mine—exile, seafaring, hermitage in a cave, and finally, war. But the trajectory bears similarities. Youthful Maeve struts onto her own stage declaring herself the "hero of a story with a plot." In her old age she becomes a witness of others' stories, a shapeshifter. At one point she retells a story from her late, estranged father's point of view, something I also felt compelled to do for my own father and mother.

In *Red-Robed Priestess*, Maeve can pass (and protect herself) as the Grey Hag. She travels from the east to west of the Holy Isles and back again, from Romans to Celts, warriors and druids, trying to prevent the destruction of the druid college at Mona as well as the devasting battle she has repeatedly foreseen in waking nightmare.

"It doesn't have to happen," she keeps saying. "It doesn't have to be this way."

But despite Maeve's best efforts, the groves of Mona burn, and the Insular Celts suffer a devastating defeat, the end of the world as they know it and the beginning of several hundred years of Roman rule. Even as she witnesses what she tried so hard to prevent, Maeve leaves room for beginnings she cannot foresee, for the story to go on without her.

As a witness to increasingly hard times (that sometimes feel, to me, like the end of the world) I aspire to do the same. Babies keep being born in the midst of wars and climate catastrophes. Green life is amazingly persistent, resourceful, and regenerative. Perhaps, in our own kind, there is something kindred to that vital spirit. As it sometimes boggles my mind to note: we, too, are the earth, rising from and returning to the same elements as all life.

WAY WILL OPEN

I am standing again in the thicket by the stream, brambles and mud everywhere. I wait. A way opens, just a few clear steps. Then I wait again for the way to open.

Way will open.

Maybe my life as a prayer is nothing more or less than that, a way out of no way, a prayer for myself, a prayer for my kind, a prayer for the earth.

Spirit that lives in and through all that is, seen and unseen—whoever, whatever you are, within us, beyond us, between us—I am praying to, with, and for you; praying for way to open, a way out of no way.

Thank you.

Amen and Blessed Bees.

ACKNOWLEDGMENTS

"Child," said the Lion, "I am telling you your story, not
hers. No one is told any story but their own."
        —C. S. Lewis, *The Horse and His Boy*

That admonition from Aslan has always resounded in my mind. My
intention has been to tell only my own story, even though my life,
like everyone's, is interwoven with many others. I have included portraits of people, living and dead, who have had a formative influence
on my life as a prayer. The living have generously given their permission for including them. I am grateful to those who have died for
their ongoing presence in my memory.

There are many people to thank. Robert Wexelblatt has been my
teacher, mentor, and friend for more than fifty years. I want to thank
all the readers of my early and later drafts: Cait Johnson, Rebecca
Singer, Ruth Cunningham, Tom Cowan, Jack Maguire, and Tim
Dillinger-Curenton. Debbie Stone has read all the drafts of all my
books from the beginning. My husband Douglas Smyth has listened
to me read aloud each word. All of you have given me immense
comfort and encouragement in my work and in my life.

I would also like to thank all the communities remembered in
this book: Grace Episcopal Church, Bullshead-Oswego Monthly
Friends Meeting, the New Seminary, and the Center at High Valley.
It has been an honor to be in your midst.

Almost twenty years ago my agent Deirdre Mullane and my publisher Paul Cohen took a leap of faith with me and Maeve. Thank you both for your ongoing support.

And thank you to everyone at Monkfish. Thanks to Paul Cohen for editorial wisdom. Thanks to Susan Piperato for helping to connect the first and second parts of the book. Thanks to Colin Rolfe for the book's gorgeous design and for answering questions with promptness and patience. Thanks to Anne McGrath for her care, enthusiasm and kindness. Thanks to Jon M. Sweeney guiding the book into the world.

ABOUT THE AUTHOR

Novelist and poet Elizabeth Cunningham is best known for The Maeve Chronicles, a series of award-winning novels featuring a Celtic Magdalen. As the descendant of generations of Episcopal priests, Cunningham grew up in a small-town church next door to an overgrown, enchanted wood. Equally influenced by scripture and fairytale, she has spent her life writing stories that traverse the worlds. After resisting the temptation to follow in her forefathers' footsteps to become the first woman in a line of priests, Cunningham became an ordained interfaith minister and counselor at midlife. *My Life as a Prayer* is her debut work of nonfiction. She lives in the valley of the Mahicantuck (aka the Hudson, the river that flows both ways) on unceded land that was home to the Esopus Tribe of the Lenape.

Printed in the USA
CPSIA information can be obtained
at www.ICGtesting.com
JSHW080738141023
50189JS00002B/2

9 781958 972106